羅馬哲學家皇帝省思經典
歷久彌新・傳世不朽的生命反思語錄

—— 中英對照全譯本 ——

Meditations

沉 思 錄

 附中文朗讀
MP3線上音檔

Marcus Aurelius

馬可・奧理略————著

盛世教育————譯

笛藤出版

前　言

PREFACE

「我年輕時就嘗試過寫對話錄，嚮往哲學家們薄衣硬枕、粗茶淡飯的生活，並對與希臘哲學有關的一切都倍感興趣。」

——馬可・奧理略

「沉思錄」一書為古羅馬哲學家皇帝馬可・奧理略（Marcus Aurelius）在兩千多年前利用出征空檔時，用希臘文在羊皮紙寫下與自己對話的十二篇省思語錄。傳世不朽的心靈智慧，至今仍洗滌無數人的心靈，許多領導者如邱吉爾、柯林頓、溫家寶…等，更將此書作為焠鍊自己人生智慧的必讀枕邊書。

蘇格拉底曾說：「未經檢視的人生，是不值得活的。」身處現今煩擾動盪的環境、網路媒體的虛實言論此起彼落讓人無所適從…，面對世間種種不幸、亂象時，常讓人無所依歸、迷失自我，此時閱讀「沉思錄」能讓人遠離喧囂燥鬱、追尋清明智慧，回歸自己的心靈，獲得平靜自在的力量重新出發。就如馬可・奧理略在沉思錄中曾說：

「對待一切事物都要剝去表面的外殼，沉思行為的目的，冥想什麼是痛苦，什麼是快樂，什麼是死亡，什麼是榮耀和名聲。對一個人來說，他本身即是真正適合自己的安寧休憩地，沒有人會被其它人干擾阻礙，一切都取決於你的觀點。」

　　「沉思錄」作為一本作者自我的靈性修行筆記，之所以能傳世不朽，皆因深刻睿智的哲學思想蘊含在文字深處，值得您反覆細品慢讀領略精要。本書收錄「沉思錄」全文共十二卷，並採中英對照全譯註解方式，讓讀者能將此書做更透徹的理解閱讀。另外，英文閱讀中常會遇到很多生字、難句以及不熟悉的文化歷史背景和典故，本書皆在註解上做了非常詳盡的解釋。盼能幫助讀者從兩種不同的語言中鍛鍊自己的閱讀力並獲得深度啟發與靈性上的提升。

導　讀

INTRODUCTION

羅馬人綜合了雅典人和斯巴達人的性格特徵，延續著希臘文明。羅馬人有雅典人文雅、喜好哲學的一面，又有斯巴達人果敢、務實的一面。因而，羅馬人不僅在哲學方面成就斐然，在政治方面也功績卓著。

　　本書的作者，馬可‧奧理略，是羅馬帝國五賢帝時代最後一個皇帝，他身上深深烙印著羅馬人的典型性格特徵。

　　馬可‧奧理略‧安東尼‧奧古斯都（Marcus Aurelius Antoninus Augustus）於公元121年4月26日生於羅馬，他本來的姓名是Marcus Aurelius Verus ，後被安東尼皇帝收養為義子，改名為Marcus Aurelius Antoninus。140年，擢升為執政官。145年與養父安東尼皇帝之女Faustina結婚，兩年後，育有一女。162年，即帝位。即位後，頻繁遭遇戰事，馬可‧奧理略指揮有方，戰果輝煌。其中，最令人稱道的是174年與奎地族(Quadi)作戰，當時幾乎成敗局，幸賴雷雨大作使敵人驚散，才轉敗為勝，因而其軍隊得名 "Thundering Legion" 。175年，東部諸省總督Avidius Cassius自恃戰功，誤信奧理略病死之訊而自立為帝，後被人刺殺，將其頭顱獻給馬可。馬可‧奧理略不予接受，並赦免Cassius的遺族，彰顯其寬厚仁慈的一面。176年，赴日耳曼作戰體力已不支，180年3月17日卒，享年59歲。

馬可‧奧理略身兼皇帝與哲學家的雙重身分。作為皇帝，盡其心血維護羅馬帝國的穩定繁榮；作為哲學家，他一心嚮往清淨內省的生活。「沉思錄」是作者寫給自己的書，書中十二卷對話大部分是在外出征戰的旅途中寫成。

「沉思」本來是一種宗教靈修的方式，即透過內省自己的生活經歷和狀態，讓心靈達到平和的境地。由本書的主題，我們可以有這樣的期待：了解馬可‧奧理略的心靈狀態，及其待人處事之道，從而在個人心智層次上有所提升。但「沉思」這種文體，也有其限制，因為對自身心靈狀態的專注，對其自身經歷往往會輕描淡寫，因此，儘管本書是作者寫給自己的書，但卻不可視為自傳，兩者有著顯著區別。

「沉思錄」全書有著濃厚的斯多噶派哲學背景，很多哲學主張現在看來著實令人費解，在這裡，有必要把斯多噶派的主要觀點解釋一下，方便讀者閱讀理解。

斯多噶派崇尚宇宙理性，認為宇宙是一個統一的整體，存在著一種支配萬物的普遍法則，即「自然法」，有時又稱為「邏各斯」、「世界理性」、「上帝」或「命運」。這種普遍法則，最為自然的必然性滲透瀰漫於宇宙萬物之中，它是宇宙秩序的創造者和主宰者。人是宇宙的一部分，同樣要受到這種普遍法則的支配，它也是人類行為的最高準則。馬可‧奧理略在書中反覆詳述了斯多噶派的這個觀點，以不同的言辭強調了個人順從宇宙理性的重要性和必要性。

在倫理方面，斯多噶派主張不論外在環境怎樣變換遷移，內心都應該保持平和，有所節制。只要內心對外在的憂患禍福無所感，人就能長久保持幸福的狀態。因而，其倫理學專注對內心激情的克制，而不對外在環境有所強求。斯多噶派的觀點深受羅馬當權者的賞識，在羅馬統治者支持下盛極一時。為了保持內心的平和，斯多噶派認為，如果外在環境過於惡劣，在生而無所眷戀的情況下，可以放棄自己的生命，斯多噶派許多代表人物都踐行了這個理念，馬可‧奧理略在書中也多次論及此理念。

馬可‧奧理略的思想不是短短一篇導讀所能道盡，這裡只是提供一些背景知識，方便大家閱讀。欲透徹深入了解，還需大家沉浸其中，一覽其貌。相信大家在不同的心境、不同的時機下會有不同的收獲。如同品茶，只有自己一口口慢酌細品，方聞茶香，別人的頌揚之詞只不過能勾起我們品茗的慾望，好茶的滋味豈是這些溢美之詞所能代替？

目　錄

CONTENTS

【配樂朗讀MP3音檔請至連結下載】

https://bit.ly/THEMEDITATIONS

※請注意英數字母大小寫區別

■MP3中文發聲│常青

「風從樹頂掠過，樹葉飄零落地，

人也是如此。」

"Leaves, some the wind scatters on the ground –

So is the race of men."

第一卷

從我的祖父維勒斯身上，我學到了高尚的品格，以及如何控制情緒。

　　從別人對父親的稱讚和自己對他的追憶中，我不僅懂得了謙遜，還學到了男子應有的果敢。

　　從我母親那裏，我濡染了虔誠、仁愛、節制的品格；不僅戒除惡行，還摒除惡念；並且滿足於粗茶淡飯，遠離富貴之家常見的奢侈。

　　從我的曾祖父那裏，我懂得了不必經常去公立學校，要在家裏聘請良師；懂得了在求學方面要不吝錢財。

　　從教導我的老師那裏，我明白了不要加入競技場中的綠派或藍派，也不要加入角鬥場中的輕盾武士或重盾武士。他還教導我做人應該吃苦耐勞、清心寡慾、親力親為，不干涉他人事務，不輕信流言

---

1. Marcus Annius Verus，作者祖父，羅馬著名政治家，哈德良皇帝（羅馬帝國五賢帝之一，117年～138年在位）的親戚。作者孩時父親去世，祖父收養了他。
2. 作者親生父親，名字是Marcus Annius Verus，約於124年去世。
3. 作者母親，名字是Domitilla Lucilla，一位富有、受過教育的女性，在作者父親過世後把作者撫養成人。

BOOK 1

From my grandfather **Verus**[1] I learned good morals and the government of my temper.

From the reputation and remembrance of **my father**[2], modesty and a manly character.

From **my mother**[3], **piety**[4] and beneficence, and abstinence, not only from evil deeds, but even from evil thoughts; and further, simplicity in my way of living, far removed from the habits of the rich.

From my great-grandfather, not to have frequented public schools, and to have had good teachers at home, and to know that on such things a man should spend **liberally**[5].

From **my governor**[6], to be neither of the green nor of the blue party at the games **in the Circus**[7], nor a partizan either of the Parmularius or the Scutarius at the gladiators' fights; from him too I learned endurance

---

4. piety [ˈpaɪətɪ] n. 虔誠，虔敬　　5. liberally [ˈlɪbərəlɪ] adv. 慷慨地
6. 姓名不詳，可能是一個奴隸，而不是下面提到的著名學者。
7. "circus"在拉丁文中為「圓圈」的意思，意指圓形競技場。公元前500年的古希臘，在最早的奧林匹克競賽上，每個比賽項目間的娛樂性節目為：人們在競技場上發出嘶吼並各以單腳騎乘在2匹沒有上馬鞍的馬上來娛樂觀眾。古羅馬人繼

蜚語。

從戴奧吉納圖斯那裏，我學會了不讓自己陷於瑣事之中，不輕信術士、巫師經常說的他們能夠驅除鬼怪精靈之類的話；學會了不沉溺於鬥鵪鶉的遊戲，不對此類事情太過狂熱；學會了不為別人的忠言直諫而氣惱；學會了勤修哲學。我先後聽了巴克斯、坦德西斯和馬爾塞勒斯的言論；我年輕時就嘗試過寫對話錄，嚮往哲學家們薄衣硬枕、粗茶淡飯的生活，並對與希臘哲學有關的一切都倍感興趣。

從拉斯蒂克斯那裏，我意識到我的性格需要改進和砥礪，知道了不應熱衷於詭辯，不寫陳腔濫調的文字，不進行繁瑣的勸誡，不賣弄自己的學問，不炫耀自己的修養，或者以仁慈的行為圖慕虛榮；學會了不追求辭藻華麗、以辭害意的寫作；不穿著出門的衣服在室內行走及諸如此類之事；學會了以樸素的風格寫信，就像拉斯蒂克斯從錫紐埃瑟給我的母親寫的信那樣；對於那些冒犯我的人，一旦他們表現出和解的意願，就樂意與他們和解而不耿耿於懷。從他那裏，我還學會了認真仔細地閱讀，不滿足於表面的一知半解，不隨便附和那些誇誇其談之輩；我對拉斯蒂克斯深表感激，正是由於他把埃比克提圖的

承了古希臘傳統，在競技場中進行兩輪戰車競技、馬術展覽、鬥劍者與獵獸的比賽，不管人或是野獸，最終都被迫相互決鬥一求生死。競技和角鬥的派系鬥爭在當時引起了公眾巨大的熱情，斯多噶派對這種熱情予以批評。
1.meddle [`mɛdl] vi. 干涉　2.Diognetus，據說是作者的啟蒙老師，主要教授作者繪畫和哲學。　3.daemon ['dimən] n. 守護神，古希臘神話中半神半人的精靈。

of labour, and to want little, and to work with my own hands, and not to **meddle**[1] with other people's affairs, and not to be ready to listen to slander.

From **Diognetus**[2], not to busy myself about trifling things, and not to give credit to what was said by miracle-workers and jugglers about incantations and the driving away of **daemons**[3] and such things; and not to breed quails for fighting, nor to give myself up passionately to such things; and to endure freedom of speech; and to have become intimate with philosophy; and to have been a hearer, first of **Bacchius**[4], then of Tandasis and Marcianus; and to have written dialogues in my youth; and to have desired a plank bed and skin, and whatever else of the kind belongs to the Grecian discipline.

From **Rusticus**[5] I received the impression that my character required improvement and discipline; and from him I learned not to be led **astray**[6] to sophistic **emulation**[7], nor to writing on speculative matters, nor to delivering little **hortatory**[8] orations, nor to showing myself off as a man who practises much discipline, or does **benevolent**[9] acts in order to make a display; and to abstain from **rhetoric**[10], and poetry, and fine writing; and not to walk about in the house in my outdoor dress, nor to do other things of the kind; and to write my letters with simplicity, like the letter which Rusticus wrote from Sinuessa to my mother; and with respect to

---

4.Bacchius，柏拉圖派哲學家。　5.Quintus Junius Rusticus（約100年～170年），古羅馬傑出政治家，當時最著名的斯多噶派代表人物，對奧理略轉向斯多噶學派有重要影響。　6.astray [ə'stre] adv. 歧途　7.emulation [ˌɛmjə`leʃən] n. 競爭，仿效　8.hortatory [`hɔrtəˌtori] adj. 勸告的　9.benevolent [bə`nɛvələnt] adj. 仁慈的　10.rhetoric [`rɛtərɪk] n. 修辭學

《回憶錄》借給我，我才會對這本書有點認識。

　　從阿珀洛尼厄斯那裏，我懂得了何謂意志的自由和目標的堅定不移；懂得了在任何時候都要依賴理性，而不能理所當然；懂得了不論是遭受極度的痛苦，還是遭遇喪子之痛或久病折磨，都要鎮定如常。在他身上我清楚地看到了一個既堅定又靈活，在教導人時親切溫和、諄諄善誘的榜樣；清楚地看到了他在我的面前闡述哲學原理，既有經驗，又有技巧。這還只是他品德中的冰山一角，從他那裏，我也學會了如何從值得尊敬的朋友那裏博得好感而又絲毫不會使自己顯得卑微和喪失尊嚴，同時也不會對這些視為理所當然。

　　從塞克斯都那裏，我看到了一種仁愛的氣質，一個以父愛管理家庭的榜樣；他恪守合乎自然的生活觀念，莊嚴而不做作，對朋友的利

---

1. Apollonius，西元1世紀到2世紀，古羅馬演說家，斯多噶派學者，奧理略的知己、帝師和智囊，曾兩次被奧理略任命為執政官。在這本書裏他的形象是很正面的，但是在其他材料裏被刻劃為自命不凡的人。
2. M. Anniuss於169年夭折，長子於147年出生後死亡。

those who have offended me by words, or done me wrong, to be easily disposed to be pacified and reconciled, as soon as they have shown a readiness to be reconciled; and to read carefully, and not to be satisfied with a superficial understanding of a book; nor hastily to give my assent to those who talk overmuch; and I am indebted to him for being acquainted with the discourses of Epictetus, which he communicated to me out of his own collection.

From **Apollonius**[1] I learned freedom of will and undeviating steadiness of purpose; and to look to nothing else, not even for a moment, except to reason; and to be always the same, in sharp pains, on the occasion of **the loss of a child**[2], and in long illness; and to see clearly in a living example that the same man can be both most resolute and yielding, and not **peevish**[3] in giving his instruction; and to have had before my eyes a man who clearly considered his experience and his skill in **expounding**[4] philosophical principles as the smallest of his merits; and from him I learned how to receive from friends what are **esteemed**[5] favours, without being either humbled by them or letting them pass unnoticed.

From **Sextus**[6], a benevolent disposition, and the example of a family governed in a fatherly manner, and the idea of living conformably to nature;

3.peevish [`pivɪʃ] adj. 易怒的
4.expound [ɪk`spaʊnd] vt. 闡述　　5.esteem [ɪs`tim] vt. 尊重，尊敬
6.Sextus，柏拉圖學派哲學家，普魯塔（Plutarch）之孫，一說是普魯塔之外甥。
普魯塔是很有名的學者和傳記作家。

益考慮得細心周到，對無知者和粗俗者亦能包容。他有一種能使自己和所有人愉悅相處的能力，以致和他交往比聽任何奉承都更為愉快；同時，他也受到那些與其交往者的高度尊敬。他理性而有條理，具有一種把握生活原則的能力並對這些原則加以整理，試圖發現它們對人們生活的影響。他從不表現出一點憤怒或別的激情，他對身邊的人總是溫柔寬厚，他對別人表示嘉許卻不會顯得過分，他擁有淵博的知識卻從不賣弄。

　　從文法家亞歷山大那裏，我學會了不求全責備，不去苛責那些在表達上有粗俗、欠文理、冷僻和發音錯誤等毛病的人們，而是針對同一件事巧妙地透過回答、證實或探討事物本身的方式來發現正確的答案，或者用其他恰當的方式去啟發他們做出正確的表達。

　　從弗朗特那裏，我知道了什麼是暴君作為。他專制霸道、善於忌妒、偽善和口是心非，也知道了我們中間那些被稱為上等人的人一般總是缺乏仁愛之情。

1.tolerate ['tɑləˌret] vt. 容忍，包容　　2.intercourse [`ɪntɚˌkors] n. 交際
3.venerate [`vɛnəˌret] vt. 尊敬　　4.ostentation [ˌɑstɛn`teʃən] n. 炫耀
5.Alexander，145年在羅馬，曾下榻宮中，精通荷馬，也教授Aelius Aristides的修辭學。Aelius Aristides 是西元2世紀活躍在羅馬的修辭學家。
6.utter [`ʌtɚ] vt. 表達

and gravity without affectation, and to look carefully after the interests of friends, and to **tolerate**[1] ignorant persons, and those who form opinions without consideration: he had the power of readily accommodating himself to all, so that **intercourse**[2] with him was more agreeable than any flattery; and at the same time he was most highly **venerated**[3] by those who associated with him: and he had the faculty both of discovering and ordering, in an intelligent and methodical way, the principles necessary for life; and he never showed anger or any other passion, but was entirely free from passion, and also most affectionate; and he could express approbation without noisy display, and he possessed much knowledge without **ostentation**[4].

From **Alexander**[5] the grammarian, to refrain from fault-finding, and not in a reproachful way to chide those who **uttered**[6] any **barbarous**[7] or **solecistic**[8] or strange-sounding expression; but **dexterously**[9] to introduce the very expression which ought to have been used, and in the way of answer or giving confirmation, or joining in an inquiry about the thing itself, not about the word, or by some other fit suggestion.

From **Fronto**[10] I learned to observe what envy, and duplicity, and **hypocrisy**[11] are in a **tyrant**[12], and that generally those among us who are called Patricians are rather deficient in paternal affection.

7.barbarous [`bɑrbərəs] adj. 野蠻的    8.solecistic [ˌsɑlɪ`sɪstɪk] adj. 失禮的
9.dexterously [`dɛkstərəslɪ] adv. 巧妙地
10.Fronto（約95年～166年），古羅馬修辭學家，同時也是辯論家，教導作者修辭。
11.hypocrisy [hɪ`pɑkrəsɪ] n. 偽善    12.tyrant [`taɪrənt] n. 暴君

從柏拉圖派學者亞歷山大那裏，我懂得了除非確有必要，否則不應該常常對人說或在信中寫『我沒有空』，更不能以此為藉口，假裝有緊急的事務，來拖延我們對朋友和熟人應盡的義務。

從卡特勒斯那裏，我懂得了不能對一個朋友的抱怨不理不睬，即使是無理的抱怨，也要試圖幫助他，使他恢復平常的冷靜；懂得對師長要心懷敬意、慷慨讚美，正像人們所說的多米蒂厄斯和雅特洛多圖斯一樣。從他那裏，我還懂得了要由衷地疼愛孩子們。

從我的兄弟西維勒斯那裏，我懂得了愛我的親人、愛真理、愛正義；從他那裏，我知道了關於思雷西亞、黑爾維蒂厄斯、加圖、戴昂，和布魯特斯的知識；從他那裏我接受了法律面前要眾生平等，世人享有平等權利和言論自由的政治觀念，也接受了君主政體應尊重大多數被統治者自由的統治觀念；從他那裏，我也獲得一種對哲學始終如一、堅定不移的尊重，一種行善的品質，一種對生活達觀的態度和相信自己為朋友所愛的自信；我也看到他從不隱瞞他對他所不滿意的那些人的意見，所以他的朋友根本無需猜測他的意願，這些意願都是相當透明的，他是一個光明磊落的人。

1.Alexander，柏拉圖派哲學家和修辭學家，作者的希臘語秘書。　2.Catulus，可能是斯多噶派學者。　3.Domitius，是雅特洛多圖斯的老師。　4.Athenodotus，斯多噶派學者，弗朗特的老師。　5.Severus，146年任執政官，其兒子娶了作者的長女，和作者同為皇帝安東尼的養子，與作者共享帝位達8年（161年～169年）。　6.Thrasea，斯多噶派學者，於66年被尼祿（Nero）逼迫自殺。

From **Alexander**[1] the Platonic, not frequently nor without necessity to say to any one, or to write in a letter, that I have no leisure; nor continually to excuse the neglect of duties required by our relation to those with whom we live, by alleging urgent occupations.

From **Catulus**[2], not to be indifferent when a friend finds fault, even if he should find fault without reason, but to try to restore him to his usual disposition; and to be ready to speak well of teachers, as it is reported of **Domitius**[3] and **Athenodotus**[4]; and to love my children truly.

From my brother **Severus**[5], to love my kin, and to love truth, and to love justice; and through him I learned to know **Thrasea**[6], **Helvidius**[7], **Cato**[8], **Dion**[9], **Brutus**[10]; and from him I received the idea of a polity in which there is the same law for all, a polity administered with regard to equal rights and equal freedom of speech, and the idea of a kingly government which respects most of all the freedom of the governed; I learned from him also consistency and **undeviating**[11] steadiness in my regard for philosophy; and a disposition to do good, and to give to others readily, and to cherish good hopes, and to believe that I am loved by my friends; and in him I observed no **concealment**[12] of his opinions with respect to those whom he condemned, and that his friends had no need to conjecture what he wished

---

7.Helvidius，有兩個同名的人分別於74年被Vespasian和於93年被Domitian處死。 8.Cato，公元前46年，不屈服於凱撒，自殺身亡。 9.Dion，受柏拉圖學說影響，西元前4世紀中葉，試圖推翻暴君狄奧尼修斯二世統治，但未成功。 10.Brutus，是Cato的表兄，西元前44年刺殺凱撒未果，最後自殺。 11.undeviating [ʌnˋdivɪˌetɪŋ] adj. 不迷失的 12.concealment [kənˋsilmənt] n. 隱瞞

　　從克勞狄烏斯·馬克西默斯那裏，我學會了自制，不為任何事情或任何人所左右，在任何困難環境裏及類似疾病的災難中都保持積極樂觀的心態，養成一種既親切和藹又莊重威嚴的道德品質；我學會了面對自己面前的任何事情都毫無怨言。我注意到他從不口是心非，所有人都相信他是表裏如一的人，他的任何行為都不存惡意；他從未表現過奇怪和驚駭；他從不匆忙，從不拖延，從不困惑或沮喪；他從沒有不得體的言行舉止，也不狂熱或多疑；他為人正直並習慣於對人仁慈，寬宏大量；他給人的印象與其說是不斷地完善自我而使自己正直，不如說是他一貫正直。我也注意到：任何人都不會認為自己受到了他的蔑視，或者自以為是地認為自己是比他更好的人。另外，他還具有一種令人愉快的幽默感。

　　從我的養父那裏，我感覺到一種親切和善，但是他對自己經過深思熟慮之後所決定的事情，又有不可更改的堅決。他能把自己從所謂的榮耀和名利中抽離；他熱愛勞作，能持之以恆；他樂意傾聽一

1.Maximus，斯多噶派哲學家，在Apuleius的辯護中被描寫為有學識和聰慧的哲學家。

2.指養父安東尼·派厄斯（Antoninus Pius）羅馬皇帝，138年～161年在位。作者認為安東尼是支持真哲學的人，是一個按照傳統羅馬倫理而不是按照哲學原理

or did not wish, but it was quite plain.

From **Maximus**[1] I learned self-government, and not to be led aside by anything; and cheerfulness in all circumstances, as well as in illness; and a just admixture in the moral character of sweetness and dignity, and to do what was set before me without complaining. I observed that everybody believed that he thought as he spoke, and that in all that he did he never had any bad intention; and he never showed amazement and surprise, and was never in a hurry, and never put off doing a thing, nor was perplexed nor dejected, nor did he ever laugh to disguise his vexation, nor, on the other hand, was he ever passionate or suspicious. He was accustomed to do acts of beneficence, and was ready to forgive, and was free from all falsehood; and he presented the appearance of a man who could not be diverted from right rather than of a man who had been improved. I observed, too, that no man could ever think that he was despised by Maximus, or ever venture to think himself a better man. He had also the art of being humorous in an agreeable way.

In **my father**[2] I observed mildness of temper, and unchangeable resolution in the things which he had determined after due deliberation; and no **vainglory**[3] in those things which men call honours; and a love of labour

---

行動的人。作者認為安東尼透過這種方式取得的成就可與透過哲學方式所取得的
成就媲美。
3.vainglory [ˌvenˈɡlorɪ] n. 虛榮

切有利於公共福利的建議；他在論功行賞方面公正無私、不偏不倚；他擁有足夠的智慧和技巧知道什麼時候該堅持、什麼時候該放棄。我注意到他克服了對男孩的喜好；他把自己視為和別人一樣的普通人；他既不強求他的朋友與他吃飯喝茶，也不要求他們在自己外出時相伴左右，那些由於緊急事務而沒有陪伴他的人，總是發現他對自己一如既往。我也發現他有仔細探討所有需要考慮的事情的習慣；他堅持不懈，絕不滿足於初步了解就停止他的探究；他重視朋友間的情誼，不會很快厭倦朋友，同時又不放縱自己的柔情；他對所有環境都感到滿足和快樂；他見微知著並富有遠見但卻從不因此自誇；他不允許別人在公開場合對他歌功頌德，也對一切諂媚深惡痛絕；他對帝國事務的管理兢兢業業並保持警醒，善於量入為出，精打細算，耐心地忍受由此而來的責難；他尊敬神靈但不迷信；他關愛臣民但不以賞賜、娛樂或奉承大眾等獻殷勤的方式去討好他們；他在所有事情上都顯得頭腦清醒、意志堅定，不表現任何卑賤的思想或行為，擁有不好新驚奇的優秀品德。對於幸運之神恩賜，可以豐富生命和享受生活的東西，他會欣然接受而不去炫耀。所以，當他擁有這些東西時，他毫不做作地享受它們；而當他沒有這些東西時，他也不渴求它們。沒有人會說他是一個詭辯家、一個能言善道的奴才，或者是個賣弄學問的人，而都會承認他是個思想成熟、性格完善的人。他不會受那些阿諛奉承之輩和奸邪之人的讒言影響，能夠妥善安排自己和別人的事務。除此之外，他十分尊重那些真正的哲學家，但他也不譴責那些自稱是哲學家

1.weal [wil] n. 福利
2.古羅馬有供養孌童的風氣。
3.extravagant [ɪk`strævəɡənt] adj. 無節制的；過度的

and perseverance; and a readiness to listen to those who had anything to propose for the common **weal**[1]; and undeviating firmness in giving to every man according to his deserts; and a knowledge derived from experience of the occasions for vigorous action and for remission. And I observed that he had overcome all **passion for boys**[2]; and he considered himself no more than any other citizen; and he released his friends from all obligation to sup with him or to attend him of necessity when he went abroad, and those who had failed to accompany him, by reason of any urgent circumstances, always found him the same. I observed too his habit of careful inquiry in all matters of deliberation, and his persistency, and that he never stopped his investigation through being satisfied with appearances which first present themselves; and that his disposition was to keep his friends, and not to be soon tired of them, nor yet to be **extravagant**[3] in his affection; and to be satisfied on all occasions, and cheerful; and to foresee things a long way off, and to provide for the smallest without display; and to check immediately popular applause and all flattery; and to be ever watchful over the things which were necessary for the administration of the empire, and to be a good manager of the expenditure, and patiently to endure the blame which he got for such conduct; and he was neither superstitious with respect to the gods, nor did he court men by gifts or by trying to please them, or by flattering the populace; but he showed sobriety in all things and firmness, and never

的人，只不過他從不受他們的影響罷了。他在社交方面也是左右逢源、遊刃有餘。他的平易近人使人感到愜意且他性格隨和，分寸適度。他懂得適度地保持身體健康，而不是過分依戀生命、貪生怕死；他雖然對個人形象不大關心，但也不是不修邊幅（雖然還是有點漫不經心）；他透過自身的適當保養，很少需要看醫生，吃藥或進補品。他最值得稱道的一點就是他很樂意並毫無嫉妒心地給擁有任何特殊才能的人開路，對那些具有雄辯才能或擁有法律、道德等知識的人，他幫助他們，使每個人都能各得其所各展所長。使他們能夠透過自我才能的自由發揮而享有名聲。儘管他總是按照他的祖先留下的方式來治理國家，但他並不讓人覺得墨守成規、不知變通。他不喜歡變動，而是喜歡住在同一個地方、專注於同一件事情。在他的頭痛病發作過後，他又馬上恢復如初，精力充沛地去做他的日常工作。他的秘密不多，而且即使是他少數的秘密也都是有關公事。他對修建公共娛樂設施和公共建築十分謹慎，不想拿人民的錢來鋪張浪費，處處表現出謹慎和節約。在這些事情上，他關心的是是否應當做這些事，而不是想從這些事情上獲取名聲。他不在不合時宜的時刻洗澡、不喜歡大興土木、營建金碧輝煌的皇家宮殿，也不關注他的飲食是否精美、他衣服的質料和色彩是否華麗，以及他的奴隸是否美貌。他的衣服來自洛裏姆的海濱別墅以及拉努維姆，我們知道在圖斯庫盧姆時，收費員請他原諒自己對他的無禮。他一貫如此行事，在他身上，找不到任何粗暴、專橫，和無情的影子，他也不是人們所說的那種一貫對人花言巧

1.arrogance [`ærəgəns] n. 傲慢
2.flippant [`flɪpənt] adj. 輕率的

any mean thoughts or action, nor love of novelty. And the things which conduce in any way to the commodity of life, and of which fortune gives an abundant supply, he used without **arrogance**[1] and without excusing himself; so that when he had them, he enjoyed them without affectation, and when he had them not, he did not want them. No one could ever say of him that he was either a sophist or a home-bred **flippant**[2] slave or a **pedant**[3]; but every one acknowledged him to be a man ripe, perfect, above flattery, able to manage his own and other men's affairs. Besides this, he honoured those who were true philosophers, and he did not reproach those who pretended to be philosophers, nor yet was he easily led by them. He was also easy in conversation, and he made himself agreeable without any offensive affectation. He took a reasonable care of his body's health, not as one who was greatly attached to life, nor out of regard to personal appearance, nor yet in a careless way, but so that, through his own attention, he very seldom stood in need of the physician's art or of medicine or external applications. He was most ready to give way without envy to those who possessed any particular faculty, such as that of **eloquence**[4] or knowledge of the law or of morals, or of anything else; and he gave them his help, that each might enjoy reputation according to his deserts; and he always acted conformably to the institutions of his country, without showing any affectation of doing so. Further, he was not fond of change nor unsteady, but he loved to stay

---

3.pedant [`pɛdnt] n. 賣弄學問的人
4.eloquence [`ɛləkwəns] n. 雄辯

語的人。他逐一考察所有的事情，彷彿有充分的時間；他毫不混淆、有條有理、精力充沛、始終一貫。那些描述蘇格拉底的文字也可以用在他身上，他能夠享受那些東西——那些是許多人由於太軟弱以致既不能夠放棄又不能夠有節制地享受的東西，但又不會沉溺於他們。這種一方面能足夠強健地承受，另一方面又能保持清醒的品格，正是一個擁有完善且不可戰勝的靈魂的人的標誌，馬克西默斯在疾病中的表現就是這樣。

1.paroxysms [`pærəksˌɪzəm] n. 發作

2.Lorium，位於羅馬西面的古村。

3.Lanuvium，位於羅馬東南的一座古城。

in the same places, and to employ himself about the same things; and after his **paroxysms**[1] of headache he came immediately fresh and vigorous to his usual occupations. His secrets were not but very few and very rare, and these only about public matters; and he showed prudence and economy in the exhibition of the public spectacles and the construction of public buildings, his donations to the people, and in such things, for he was a man who looked to what ought to be done, not to the reputation which is got by a man's acts. He did not take the bath at unseasonable hours; he was not fond of building houses, nor curious about what he ate, nor about the texture and colour of his clothes, nor about the beauty of his slaves. His dress came from **Lorium**[2], his villa on the coast, and from **Lanuvium**[3] generally. We know how he behaved to the toll-collector at **Tusculum**[4] who asked his pardon; and such was all his behaviour. There was in him nothing harsh, nor implacable, nor violent, nor, as one may say, anything carried to the sweating point; but he examined all things severally, as if he had abundance of time, and without confusion, in an orderly way, vigorously and consistently. And that might be applied to him which is recorded of Socrates, that he was able both to abstain from, and to enjoy, those things which many are too weak to abstain from, and cannot enjoy without excess. But to be strong enough both to bear the one and to be sober in the other is the mark of a man who has a perfect and invincible soul, such as he showed in the illness of Maximus.

4.Tusculum，義大利拉丁姆古城，在後來的共和國和帝國時期（西元前1世紀～西元前4世紀）是富裕的羅馬人喜愛的度假勝地，也是西塞羅的故鄉。

諸神讓我有好的祖輩、好的父母、好的姐妹、好的老師、好的同伴、好的親友，幾乎我所有的一切都是諸神賜予的。我為此而感謝神明，所以我從沒有因為一時衝動而冒犯任何一位神明——雖然我的天性讓我有可能做出這樣的事情。如果有機會，我想自己是有可能做出這種事情，但是，由於他們的保佑，還沒有這種機緣巧合使我鑄成這種大錯。

另外，我還要感謝神明：小時候便不由我祖父的愛妾撫養，如此守護了我的青春花朵，使它不致過早受到傷害。使我直到恰當的時機甚至比這個恰當的時機還要晚的時刻才接近女色。感謝神讓我有一個作為統治者的父親來管教我，他能夠讓我去掉身上所有的虛浮驕傲並帶給我這樣的知識，即懂得一個王子是可以生活在一個沒有衛兵守衛，沒有華衣美食，沒有火把照明，沒有雕像裝飾等類似物品的宮殿裏，而且身為一個統治者的兒子過普通人的生活不會降低自己的身份地位，也不會因此而忽視他作為一個統治者為了公眾的利益所必須做的事情。

1.祖輩指Mannlus Verus及P. C alvisius Tullus.
2.torch [tɔrtʃ] n. 火炬

To the gods I am indebted for having good **grandfathers**[1], good parents, a good sister, good teachers, good associates, good kinsmen and friends, nearly everything good. Further, I owe it to the gods that I was not hurried into any offence against any of them, though I had a disposition which, if opportunity had offered, might have led me to do something of this kind; but, through their favour, there never was such a concurrence of circumstances as put me to the trial.

Further, I am thankful to the gods that I was not longer brought up with my grandfather's concubine, and that I preserved the flower of my youth, and that I did not make proof of my virility before the proper season, but even deferred the time; that I was subjected to a ruler and a father who was able to take away all pride from me, and to bring me to the knowledge that it is possible for a man to live in a palace without wanting either guards or embroidered dresses, or **torches**[2] and statues, and such-like show; but that it is in such a man's power to bring himself very near to the fashion of a private person, without being for this reason either meaner in thought, or more remiss in action, with respect to the things which must be done for the public interest in a manner that befits a ruler.

我感謝神明給了我這樣一個兄弟，他能以他的道德品格使我警醒，讓我不斷地以他為榜樣來提高自身修養，同時他的尊重和影響又使我感到愉悅。感謝神明讓我擁有聰明的孩子，他們既沒有天生畸形也沒有任何天生的缺陷。感謝神使我並不諳修辭、詩歌和其它學問。假如我看到自己在這些方面取得進展的話，就有可能完全沉醉於其中。我感謝神明使我能夠及時地給予那些培養過我的人，在他們看來願意擁有的榮譽，而沒有延遲他們曾對我的未來寄予的厚望（因為他們那時還年輕，能夠看到我日後實現他們的願望）。我感謝神明使我認識了阿珀洛尼厄斯、拉斯蒂克斯、馬克西默斯。因為他們，我經常有機會有效地進行自我思考，思考什麼是按照自然的方式生活，以及這種生活的方式和性質，對那種依賴神靈及他們的恩賜、幫助和靈感而過的生活，有了清晰而鞏固的印象。事實上，沒有什麼事情能阻止我立刻按照自然方式來生活，就算現在我還沒有按照那種方式生活，那也完全是因為我個人因素（因為我沒有注意到神靈的勸告，甚至是神靈的直接指示）。感謝上天使我的身體置於這樣一種生活環境之中還能活到如此之久。我也從未像本尼迪克特或希歐多爾圖斯那樣，雖然被情慾所苦，但我很快就痊癒了。雖然我常常與拉斯蒂克斯鬧得不愉快，但我還沒有對他做出令我悔恨的事情。雖然我的母親紅顏薄命，但我很欣慰自己能陪伴她度過人生最後的旅程。感謝神讓我能夠幫助那些需要幫助的人們，他們或深陷貧困或有其他的困難。在任何

1.Benedicta，安東尼的愛妾。
2.Theodotus，安東尼的男僕。
3.amatory [`æməˌtərɪ] adj. 愛情的

I thank the gods for giving me such a brother, who was able by his moral character to rouse me to vigilance over myself, and who, at the same time, pleased me by his respect and affection; that my children have not been stupid nor deformed in body; that I did not make more proficiency in rhetoric, poetry, and the other studies, in which I should perhaps have been completely engaged, if I had seen that I was making progress in them; that I made haste to place those who brought me up in the station of honour, which they seemed to desire, without putting them off with hope of my doing it some time after, because they were then still young; that I knew Apollonius, Rusticus, Maximus; that I received clear and frequent impressions about living according to nature, and what kind of a life that is, so that, so far as depended on the gods, and their gifts, and help, and inspirations, nothing hindered me from forthwith living according to nature, though I still fall short of it through my own fault, and through not observing the admonitions of the gods, and, I may almost say, their direct instructions; that my body has held out so long in such a kind of life; that I never touched either **Benedicta**[1] or **Theodotus**[2], and that, after having fallen into **amatory**[3] passions, I was cured; and, though I was often out of humour with Rusticus, I never did anything of which I had occasion to repent; that, though it was my mother's fate to die young, she spent the last years of her life with me;

場合，我都不曾感到自己缺乏這樣做的能力。對我自己來說卻不會有這樣的需要，即需要從別人那裏得到類似的幫助。感謝神讓我有一個十分溫順、深情和樸實的妻子，還讓我擁有許多有能力的教師來教育我的孩子。感謝神托夢給我，幫助我，以及諸如此類，尤其是讓我知道了該如何止血以及治療我的眩暈症。還要感謝神明，當我開始學習哲學時，沒有讓我屈服在任何詭辯家的腳下、沒有浪費時間在史書的作者上、也沒有浪費時間在三段論推理上，或者天上的現象上。所有這些事情如果沒有神靈和命運之神的幫助是不可能實現的。

寫於格拉努瓦與奎第人征戰之際。

1.指Faustina，羅馬皇帝安東尼的女兒，145年～175年為作者的妻子。謠傳她與Avidius Crassus調情，但是作者在提及自己的妻子時，仍然很尊重。
2.syllogism [ˋsɪləˏdʒɪzəm] n. 三段論

that, whenever I wished to help any man in his need, or on any other occasion, I was never told that I had not the means of doing it; and that to myself the same necessity never happened, to receive anything from another; that I have such **a wife**[1], so obedient, and so affectionate, and so simple; that I had abundance of good masters for my children; and that remedies have been shown to me by dreams, both others, and against bloodspitting and giddiness...; and that, when I had an inclination to philosophy, I did not fall into the hands of any sophist, and that I did not waste my time on writers of histories, or in the resolution of **syllogisms**[2], or occupy myself about the investigation of appearances in the heavens; for all these things require the help of the gods and fortune.

Among the **Quadi**[3] at the **Granua**[4].

3.Quadi，奎地族，指作者在日耳曼戰爭（171年～173年）時征戰的部落之一。
4.Granua，多瑙河的一條北部支流，即今天的River Hron。

第二卷

每天清晨之際，我就對自己說：我將遇見好管閒事的人、忘恩負義的人、野蠻無禮的人、陰險狡詐的人、易生忌妒的人或是孤僻無情的人。他們染有這些惡習，是因為他們無法分辨善惡。但是我是能夠明辨善惡的，知道前者是好的，而後者則是醜陋的、令人羞愧的；我還知道染上這些惡習的人們的本性和我相似，不僅因為我們擁有同樣的血統和淵源，而且因為我們分享著同樣的理智和擁有同樣部分的神性。所以我絕不可能被他們之中的任何一個人傷害，因為任何人都不可能把惡強加於我，我也不可能遷怒於這些與我同類的人，或者憎恨他們。我們命中註定是要互相合作的，就像我們的雙手、雙腳、上下眼皮和上下兩排牙齒相互合作。如果我們不是相互合作而是相互對抗的話，就是違反自然，就是自尋煩惱。相互仇恨和遷怒對方無疑是相互作對。

我之所以是我，只不過是一團肉、一絲氣息和主宰的部分。丟開你的書本吧，不要再讓你自己分心，因為人生轉瞬即逝，你隨時都可能瀕臨死亡。不要太執著於肉體，那不過是一攤血、幾根骨頭和皮膚，被神經、靜脈和動脈巧妙地連接在一起，不過如此而已。至於

1.thyself 為古英語中 yourself 的拼法。

2.vexed [vɛkst] adj. 煩惱的

3.奧裡略似乎樂於順應命運安排，但也忠於責任。140年，他被擢升為執政官，147年，任護民官，以後許多國家榮譽不斷向他走來。

BOOK 2

Begin the morning by saying to **thyself**[1], I shall meet with the busy-body, the ungrateful, arrogant, deceitful, envious, unsocial. All these things happen to them by reason of their ignorance of what is good and evil. But I who have seen the nature of the good that it is beautiful, and of the bad that it is ugly, and the nature of him who does wrong, that it is akin to me, not only of the same blood or seed, but that it participates in the same intelligence and the same portion of the divinity, I can neither be injured by any of them, for no one can fix on me what is ugly, nor can I be angry with my kinsman, nor hate him, For we are made for co-operation, like feet, like hands, like eyelids, like the rows of the upper and lower teeth. To act against one another then is contrary to nature; and it is acting against one another to be **vexed**[2] and to **turn away**[3].

Whatever this is that I am, it is a little flesh and breath, and the ruling part. Throw away thy books; no longer distract thyself: it is not allowed; but as if **thou**[4] **wast**[5] now dying, despise the flesh; it is blood and bones and a network, a contexture of nerves, veins, and **arteries**[6]. See the breath also,

---

4.thou [ðaʊ] pron. [古]你
5.wast為古英語中is，第二人稱單數（主語為thou時使用）時使用。
6.artery [`ɑrtərɪ] n. 動脈

你的氣息，想想看它是什麼吧，不過是一縷空氣而已。它不斷變化，時時刻刻都在排出和吸入。第三就是主宰你的那一部分了。我們這樣來想想吧：假如你是一個老人，不要再讓自己成為一個奴隸，任人擺佈，不要再像線拉木偶一樣被人操縱，不要再不滿意你現在的處境，或者因為擔心未來而憂心忡忡，因為命運已經都幫你安排好了。

所有神直接賜予的東西都充滿神意。即使那些我們稱為命運的東西也並非與自然或最初的廣泛聯繫毫無關聯，相反，它們顯然是受到神意的指點才發生的，所以萬物都因此而產生。此外，還有必然性，這種必然性有利於宇宙整體，而我們是這個整體中的一部分。但整體本性所帶來的，對本性的每一部分都是好的，有助於保持這一本性。現在，宇宙得以保存，是透過元素，以及元素化合物的變化。懂得這些道理就足夠了，把它作為自己的行為準則吧！丟開你對書本的渴望，這樣在你死去的時候才不會充滿抱怨，而是內心充滿了真正的歡樂和對神明衷心的感激。

記住，你已經把這些事情延宕過久，你從神靈那裏得到的機會已經夠多了，但你沒有好好把握。現在是必須去思索領悟那個你只是其中一部分的宇宙的時候了，領悟你的存在只是其中一個極小份子的宇

1.puppet [`pʌpɪt] n. 玩偶
2.mayest 為古英語中may，第二人稱單數（現在陳述語氣，主語為thou）時使用）。

what kind of a thing it is, air, and not always the same, but every moment sent out and again sucked in. The third then is the ruling part: consider thus: Thou art an old man; no longer let this be a slave, no longer be pulled by the strings like a **puppet**[1] to unsocial movements, no longer either be dissatisfied with thy present lot, or shrink from the future.

All that is from the gods is full of Providence. That which is from fortune is not separated from nature or without an interweaving and involution with the things which are ordered by Providence. From thence all things flow; and there is besides necessity, and that which is for the advantage of the whole universe, of which thou art a part. But that is good for every part of nature which the nature of the whole brings, and what serves to maintain this nature. Now the universe is preserved, as by the changes of the elements so by the changes of things compounded of the elements. Let these principles be enough for thee; let them always be fixed opinions. But cast away the thirst after books, that thou **mayest**[2] not die murmuring, but cheerfully, truly, and from thy heart thankful to the gods.

Remember how long thou hast been putting off these things, and how often thou hast received an opportunity from the gods, and yet dost not use it. Thou must now at last perceive of what universe thou art a part,

宙到底是怎樣的。思索你從這個宇宙中消失時它又是如何。你的時間有限，因為生命是有限的，如果你不用這段時間來消除你思想上的困惑，那麼你以後就再也不會有這樣的機會了。你將逝去，永遠從世上消失，再也不會回來。

時時刻刻都要堅定地思考，就像一個羅馬人，像一個男子漢一樣，完整、認真、保持尊嚴地去完成應該做的事情。要始終懷著友愛、自由和正義之情去做事情。專注於你所做的事，心裏不要有其他的雜念。你應該把生活中的每一件事情都當做是你生命中的最後一件事情來完成，這樣你就會更加果斷地抉擇，更加客觀公正，也不會磨磨蹭蹭、猶豫不決。你再也不會自私虛偽、牢騷滿腹，因為你讓自己徹底地解脫了。你瞭解到一個人只要做得很少、擁有很少的東西就能過著一種寧靜、樸實的生活。就神靈來說，他們不會向這種追求簡單生活方式的人們要求更多的東西。

做不道德的事，做不道德的事，哦，我的靈魂啊，你將不再有機會來榮耀自身。每個人的生命都是短暫的，你的生命甚至已近尾聲而你卻仍未獲得榮耀，但你還不考慮自身，而是把自己幸福寄予別的靈魂之上。

1.efflux [`ɛflʌks] n. 流逝
2.thee [ði] pron. [古]（thou的賓格）你
3.seest為古英語中 see的第二人稱單數（現在陳述語氣，主語為thou時使用）。

and of what administrator of the universe thy existence is an **efflux**[1], and that a limit of time is fixed for thee, which if thou dost not use for clearing away the clouds from thy mind, it will go and thou wilt go, and it will never return.

Every moment think steadily as a Roman and a man to do what thou hast in hand with perfect and simple dignity, and feeling of affection, and freedom, and justice; and to give thyself relief from all other thoughts. And thou wilt give thyself relief, if thou doest every act of thy life as if it were the last, laying aside all carelessness and passionate aversion from the commands of reason, and all hypocrisy, and self-love, and discontent with the portion which has been given to **thee**[2]. Thou **seest**[3] how few the things are, the which if a man lays hold of, he is able to live a life which flows in quiet, and is like the existence of the gods; for the gods on their part will require nothing more from him who observes these things.

Do wrong to thyself, do wrong to thyself, my soul; but thou wilt no longer have the opportunity of honouring thyself. Every man's life is sufficient. But thine is nearly finished, though **thy**[4] soul reverences not itself but places thy **felicity**[5] in the souls of others.

4.thy [ðaɪ] pron. [古]你的
5.felicity [fə`lɪsətɪ] n. 幸福

為什麼周圍發生的這些事會使你如此分心呢？給自己時間來學習嶄新的、良善的東西吧，不要再彷徨不定、來回搖擺了。你也要注意不要像另一種彷徨的人一般，雖然他們這輩子做牛做馬，但卻沒有目標來引導他們的行為，所以他們的辛苦都成了徒勞無功。

很少聽說有人因為不注意別人心裏在想些什麼而不快樂，但是不觀察自己心靈活動的人必然不快樂。

這些事情你要時刻謹記在心：宇宙的本質，尤其是我的本質是什麼？兩者之間有何關聯？我作為整體的一部分的性質怎麼樣？另外還要明白沒有人能阻止你說或者做那些符合自然的事情，因為你原本就是其中的一部分。

西奧菲拉斯圖斯在比較各種惡行時是按照人類的普遍觀念進行的，他像一個真正的哲學家那樣說：因慾望而犯的罪比那些因憤怒而所犯的罪更嚴重。因為一個憤怒的人似乎是因痛苦、內心矛盾的掙扎而失去了理智，但那些為了滿足私慾而犯罪的人卻是因為忍不住快樂

1.Theophrastus（西元前371年～西元前287年），古希臘哲學家，亞里斯多德的弟子。繼亞里斯多德後於西元前322年主持呂克昂學園。他的相關著作已經遺

Do the things external which fall upon thee distract thee? Give thyself time to learn something new and good, and cease to be whirled around. But then thou must also avoid being carried about the other way. For those too are triflers who have wearied themselves in life by their activity, and yet have no object to which to direct every movement, and, in a word, all their thoughts.

Through not observing what is in the mind of another a man has seldom been seen to be unhappy; but those who do not observe the movements of their own minds must of necessity be unhappy.

This thou must always bear in mind, what is the nature of the whole, and what is my nature, and how this is related to that, and what kind of a part it is of what kind of a whole; and that there is no one who hinders thee from always doing and saying the things which are according to the nature of which thou art a part.

Theophrastus[1], in his comparison of bad acts – such a comparison as one would make in accordance with the common notions of mankind – says, like a true philosopher, that the offences which are committed through desire are more blameable than those which are committed through anger.

失，但是他在亞里斯多德倫理學中對於慾望（appetite）和憤怒（anger）的比較是極為重要的。

的誘惑，他的罪惡表明他更缺乏自制力，性格更軟弱。於是，他用堪稱哲學的方式說：因貪圖快樂而犯下的罪行，比因受到痛苦折磨而犯的罪更應該受到譴責。因為後者是先受到了不公正的對待，才因為痛苦怒髮衝冠；而為了滿足自己的慾望作惡的人則是咎由自取。

　　既然我們很有可能此刻離開人世，那麼就相應調整每一個行為和想法吧。談到死亡，如果有神靈存在，那離開人世也不是一件令人恐懼的事情，因為你可以放心，神靈不會讓你捲入邪惡；如果沒有神靈，或者神靈不在乎人間的事務，那我為什麼還要活在一個沒有神或神意的世界呢？不過，神靈當然是存在的，他們關心世人。至於那些真正邪惡的東西，神靈已經賜予我們能力，如果我們願意的話，就能避免染上惡習和邪惡。除了這些真正的邪惡之外，如果還有別的惡行，神靈也會注意不使人陷入其中。如果這些事情不會使人本身變得更壞，我們為什麼要覺得這對人世的生活不利呢？我們絕不能認為是由於宇宙的本性無知而讓這些事情發生，或者是雖然知道這些事情但卻沒有辦法防止或糾正它們。它絕不可能是因為沒有力量或技巧以致

For he who is excited by anger seems to turn away from reason with a certain pain and unconscious contraction; but he who offends through desire, being overpowered by pleasure, seems to be in a manner more intemperate and more womanish in his offences. Rightly then, and in a way worthy of philosophy, he said that the offence which is committed with pleasure is more blameable than that which is committed with pain; and on the whole the one is more like a person who has been first wronged and through pain is compelled to be angry; but the other is moved by his own impulse to do wrong, being carried towards doing something by desire.

Since it is possible that thou mayest depart from life this very moment, regulate every act and thought accordingly. But to go away from among men, if there are gods, is not a thing to be afraid of, for the gods will not involve thee in evil; but if indeed they do not exist, or if they have no concern about human affairs, what is it to me to live in a universe devoid of gods or devoid of Providence? But in truth they do exist, and they do care for human things, and they have put all the means in man's power to enable him not to fall into real evils. And as to the rest, if there was anything evil, they would have provided for this also, that it should be altogether in a man's power not to fall into it. Now that which does not make a man worse, how can it make a man's life worse? But neither through ignorance, nor having

犯下大錯，使好事和壞事竟然不加區別地降臨於善人和惡人身上。生死、榮辱、苦樂、貧富，所有這些事情確實都會同樣地發生在善人和惡人的身上，但是這些東西既不能使我們變得更好，也不能使我們變得更壞，因而它們既不善也不惡。

　　萬事萬物都轉瞬即逝！不論是宇宙之中的物質形體，還是在時間中對它們的記憶。可感事物的本質是什麼，特別是那些伴有快樂的誘惑或駭人的痛苦的事物，或者是那些有著耀眼的光環的事物，它們的本質都是無價值的、值得蔑視的、骯髒、腐朽的，所有這些事物都需要用我們的理性來辨別。我們要用我們的理性來分析那些以見解和言論獲得名聲的人究竟是怎樣的人，用我們的理性來分析什麼是死亡。如果一個人透過考察死亡本身，透過抽象的反思把所有有關死亡的觀點在想像中加以分解，他就將理解死亡只不過是自然的一種運轉。如果有什麼人害怕自然的運轉，那他就像小孩一樣無知。實際上，死亡不僅是自然的一種運轉，也是一件有利於自然本身的事情。你還要這樣想：人是透過身體的哪一部分與神進行交流的，當這一部分像人們說的那樣『散播』的時候，它是如何做到的。

1.sordid [`sɔrdɪd] adj. 污穢的；骯髒的

the knowledge, but not the power to guard against or correct these things, is it possible that the nature of the universe has overlooked them; nor is it possible that it has made so great a mistake, either through want of power or want of skill, that good and evil should happen indiscriminately to the good and the bad. But death certainly, and life, honour and dishonour, pain and pleasure, all these things equally happen to good men and bad, being things which make us neither better nor worse. Therefore they are neither good nor evil.

How quickly all things disappear, in the universe the bodies themselves, but in time the remembrance of them; what is the nature of all sensible things, and particularly those which attract with the bait of pleasure or terrify by pain, or are noised abroad by vapoury fame; how worthless, and contemptible, and **sordid**[1], and perishable, and dead they are, – all this it is the part of the intellectual faculty to observe. To observe too who these are whose opinions and voices give reputation; what death is, and the fact that, if a man looks at it in itself, and by the abstractive power of reflection resolves into their parts all the things which present themselves to the imagination in it, he will then consider it to be nothing else than an operation of nature; and if any one is afraid of an operation of nature, he is a child. This, however, is not only an operation of nature, but it is also a thing which conduces to

　　世上沒有比這種人更不幸的了：他們對身邊的任何事情都要探究竟，就像詩人所說的那樣連地下的事情都要追根究底。他們還喜歡察言觀色，猜測別人心裏的想法，卻不知道只要專注於他心中的神靈並真誠地尊奉就足夠了。對心中神的尊奉在於避免所有強烈的激情和邪惡的影響，避免表現出對神或是世人心懷不滿的行為。因為來自神靈的東西是有價值的、不凡的，值得我們尊敬。而別人的言行，因他們是我們的兄弟，所以我們也應該永遠用愛來感受。有時，對他們不辨善惡（這種無知正如我們是非不分一樣）的言行舉止，我們要抱有同情和憐憫之心。

　　就算你可以活上三千年，甚至上萬年，你還是要記住這一點：人只會失去他現在過的生活，他每時每分都在失去他所過的生活。因此，就此意義上來說生命的長短和本質沒有什麼差別。儘管過去的生命對於每個人來說都不盡相同，但是現在的這一刻對於所有人都具有同樣的意義。在我們死亡的那一刻，我們就能明白，我們失去的不過是短暫的片刻，因為一個人不可能喪失過去和未來。一個人怎麼能

1.wretched [`rɛtʃɪd] adj. 不幸的
2.指Pindar（品達），西元前5世紀希臘著名的抒情詩人。
3.shouldst =should（主語為thou時用）。

the purposes of nature. To observe too how man comes near to the deity, and by what part of him, and when this part of man is so disposed.

Nothing is more **wretched**[1] than a man who traverses everything in a round, and pries into the things beneath the earth, as **the poet**[2] says, and seeks by conjecture what is in the minds of his neighbours, without perceiving that it is sufficient to attend to the daemon within him, and to reverence it sincerely. And reverence of the daemon consists in keeping it pure from passion and thoughtlessness, and dissatisfaction with what comes from gods and men. For the things from the gods merit veneration for their excellence; and the things from men should be dear to us by reason of kinship; and sometimes even, in a manner, they move our pity by reason of men's ignorance of good and bad; this defect being not less than that which deprives us of the power of distinguishing things that are white and black.

Though thou **shouldst**[3] be going to live three thousand years, and as many times ten thousand years, still remember that no man loses any other life than this which he now lives, nor lives any other than this which he now loses. The longest and shortest are thus brought to the same. For the present is the same to all, though that which perishes is not the same; and so that which is lost appears to be a mere moment. For a man cannot lose either the

失去他所沒有的東西呢？因此，你必須記住這兩件事：一是在這個永恆的、生死輪迴、循環往復的世界上，所有的事物在本質上都是一致的。不管是在一兩百年，還是無限長的時間裏，人所看到的東西都是一樣的，沒有哪個時期特別偉大。另外是長壽者和短命者是相同的，因為他們只有現在，他們能失去的也只有現在，一個人不可能失去他所沒有的東西。

要記住所有的一切只不過是我們的意見，犬儒派的摩尼穆斯所說的那些事情是顯而易見的。而且如果我們能樂於接受這些事情當中的真理，那這些事情的作用也是顯而易見的。

人的靈魂在某些情況下會做錯事，自我褻瀆。首先，尤其是在靈魂變成了宇宙的一個腫塊，或者說就其而言變成一個整體的累贅時，為了世上發生的事情而煩惱使我們脫離了宇宙的本性，因為一切個體都是宇宙整體的一部分。第二，在它仇恨別人或是懷著惡意攻擊別人的時候，那些憤怒的靈魂就是這樣。第三，在它沉溺於快樂或深陷痛苦的時候。第四，在它企圖掩飾某事而言行不真誠的時候。第五，在它讓行動漫無目的、匆忙、不加考慮和不顧後果地做事的時候。如果沒有考慮到這件事情的後果，哪怕是最微不足道的事我們也不該去

1.Monimus，西元前4世紀犬儒學派的哲學家。

2.manifest [`mænəˌfɛst] adj. 清楚的

3.tumour [`tjuməˈ] n. 腫瘤

past or the future: for what a man has not, how can any one take this from him? These two things then thou must bear in mind; the one, that all things from eternity are of like forms and come round in a circle, and that it makes no difference whether a man shall see the same things during a hundred years or two hundred, or an infinite time; and the second, that the longest liver and he who will die soonest lose just the same. For the present is the only thing of which a man can be deprived, if it is true that this is the only thing which he has, and that a man cannot lose a thing if he has it not.

Remember that all is opinion. For what was said by the Cynic **Monimus**[1] is **manifest**[2]: and manifest too is the use of what was said, if a man receives what may be got out of it as far as it is true.

The soul of man does violence to itself, first of all, when it becomes an abscess and, as it were, a **tumour**[3] on the universe, so far as it can. For to be vexed at anything which happens is a separation of ourselves from nature, in some part of which the natures of all other things are contained. In the next place, the soul does violence to itself when it turns away from any man, or even moves towards him with the intention of injuring, such as are the souls of those who are angry. In the third place, the soul does violence to itself when it is overpowered by pleasure or by pain. Fourthly, when it plays

做。而對所有理性的動物而言，他們的目標就是要遵循理性和這個最
古老城邦的法律。

　　人的一生只不過是稍縱即逝的一個點而已。我們的本質在不斷
變動，感覺模糊不清；我們身體的整個結構很容易分解；我們的靈魂
不得安寧；我們的命運未卜；我們的名聲值得懷疑。總之，屬於身
體的一切只是一道激流，而屬於靈魂的一切則如夢似煙。人生是一場
戰爭，不過是段旅途。在死後，名聲會被人忘卻，什麼能夠存留下來
呢？唯有哲學。哲學的功用就在於能使一個人保持內心的靈魂遠離摧
殘和傷害，超越一切苦樂；能讓我們不衝動地做事，或是弄虛作假，
完全受自己和自己行為的支配；能讓我們從容接受所有發生的事情，
這一切對我們來說就像命中註定，不管它們是什麼，似乎都是自有道
理、理所當然。最終我們能以一種順從和平靜的歡樂心情等待死亡，
把死亡看作是對那些一切生物的組成元素的分解。

a part, and does or says anything insincerely and untruly. Fifthly, when it allows any act of its own and any movement to be without an aim, and does anything thoughtlessly and without considering what it is, it being right that even the smallest things be done with reference to an end; and the end of rational animals is to follow the reason and the law of the most ancient city and polity.

Of human life the time is a point, and the substance is in a flux, and the perception dull, and the composition of the whole body subject to putrefaction, and the soul a whirl, and fortune hard to divine, and fame a thing devoid of judgment. And, to say all in a word, everything which belongs to the body is a stream, and what belongs to the soul is a dream and vapour, and life is a warfare and a stranger's sojourn, and after-fame is oblivion. What then is that which is able to conduct a man? One thing and only one, philosophy. But this consists in keeping the daemon within a man free from violence and unharmed, superior to pains and pleasures, doing nothing without purpose, nor yet falsely and with hypocrisy, not feeling the need of another man's doing or not doing anything; and besides, accepting all that happens, and all that is allotted, as coming from thence, wherever it is, from whence he himself came; and, finally, waiting for death with a cheerful mind, as being nothing else than a dissolution of the elements of

這些元素在這過程中並沒有什麼損失，它們處在不斷的相互轉化中。我們為什麼要害怕這種人人都會發生的分解和轉化呢？這難道不是合乎自然的嗎？只有不合乎自然的東西才是邪惡的。

　　寫於卡農圖姆。

1.Carnuntum，奧勒留在日耳曼戰爭（171年～173年）中的駐地，古羅馬的一個重要軍營，現為奧地利境內。

which every living being is compounded.

But if there is no harm to the elements themselves in each continually changing into another, why should a man have any apprehension about the change and dissolution of all the elements? For it is according to nature, and nothing is evil which is according to nature.

This in **Carnuntum**[1].

第三卷

一　個人不應該只想到我們的生命每日都在消逝，剩下的時日越來越少，還應該想到，如果我們能活得久些，我們無法確定我們的理解力仍會堅定如初，足以使我們謹慎地考慮事物，或是進行自省，以獲得有關神和人的真正知識。如果一個人齒牙動搖，雖然他的呼吸、消化、想像力、胃口和諸如此類的功能也許都還一樣，但是，發揮自我、恪盡職責、清楚區分所有現象，考慮何時離開塵世諸如此類的能力，絕對需要一個訓練有素的理性，但是這些能力都已經消失了。所以你必須抓緊時間，這不僅是因為你在一天天地接近死亡，而且你對事物的感知和理解會先行消失。

二　你也應當注意到這一點：按照自然產生的事物，其附帶物也是頗為美好而富有誘惑力的。例如，當我們烘烤一塊大麵包時，它的一部

1.divine [də`vaɪn] adj. 神的

2.dotage [`dotɪdʒ] n. 衰老；老迷糊

3.指自殺，這是斯多噶派的信條之一，斯多噶派認為生命長久未必是一件好事，

BOOK 3

We ought to consider not only that our life is daily wasting away and a smaller part of it is left, but another thing also must be taken into the account, that if a man should live longer, it is quite uncertain whether the understanding will still continue sufficient for the comprehension of things, and retain the power of contemplation which strives to acquire the knowledge of the **divine**[1] and the human. For if he shall begin to fall into **dotage**[2], perspiration and nutrition and imagination and appetite, and whatever else there is of the kind, will not fail; but the power of making use of ourselves, and filling up the measure of our duty, and clearly separating all appearances, and **considering whether a man should now depart from life**[3], and whatever else of the kind absolutely requires a disciplined reason, all this is already extinguished. We must make haste then, not only because we are daily nearer to death, but also because the conception of things and the understanding of them cease first.

We ought to observe also that even the things which follow after the things which are produced according to nature contain something pleasing

---

認為如果為了朋友或國家，避免毀滅或不可治癒的疾病而自殺是合乎理性的。斯多噶派的芝諾（Zeno）與克萊安西斯（Cleanthes）都是自殺而死的。

分會裂開，有一部分會裂成碎片，讓麵包皮變得凹凸不平。這些裂開的部分不是我們烘烤的時候想要的，但是它們在某種意義上是美的，能夠以一種奇特的方式引起我們的食慾。無花果也是如此，它們熟透之時會裂開；橄欖也是如此，它們爛熟之際自有一種特殊的美。那低垂的葡萄、獅子緊鎖的眉頭、從野豬嘴裏流出的白沫，以及很多其它類似的例子，雖然單獨地來看，它們一點也不美，但由於它們是自然而然的，所以是美麗的、令人愉快的。**如果人能用感覺和深刻的認知來洞察這個宇宙所產生的一切事物，那麼，就連這些事物的細節和附加物都是他的快樂之源。**當他看到野獸真的張開血盆大口時，和他看到技藝高超的畫家和雕刻家所模仿的作品時一樣快樂；不論是老嫗還是老翁，他都能看到他們的成熟之美；他總是能很快地不偏不倚地發現任何事物美和迷人的地方。他所發現的這些和很多其他的事物，**並不見得所有的人都喜歡，只有真正深諳自然之理及其造化的人，才能深刻地領悟這些事物的迷人之處。**

1.sculptor [`skʌlptə] n. 雕刻家

and attractive. For instance, when bread is baked some parts are split at the surface, and these parts which thus open, and have a certain fashion contrary to the purpose of the baker's art, are beautiful in a manner, and in a peculiar way excite a desire for eating. And again, figs, when they are quite ripe, gape open; and in the ripe olives the very circumstance of their being near to rottenness adds a peculiar beauty to the fruit. And the ears of corn bending down, and the lion's eyebrows, and the foam which flows from the mouth of wild boars, and many other things, – though they are far from being beautiful, if a man should examine them severally, – still, because they are consequent upon the things which are formed by nature, help to adorn them, and they please the mind; so that if a man should have a feeling and deeper insight with respect to the things which are produced in the universe, there is hardly one of those which follow by way of consequence which will not seem to him to be in a manner disposed so as to give pleasure. And so he will see even the real gaping jaws of wild beasts with no less pleasure than those which painters and **sculptors**[1] show by imitation; and in an old woman and an old man he will be able to see a certain maturity and comeliness; and the attractive loveliness of young persons he will be able to look on with chaste eyes; and many such things will present themselves, not pleasing to every man, but to him only who has become truly familiar with nature and her works.

雖然希波克拉底治癒了許多的病人，但是自己卻因病而亡。雖然占星家們預告了許多人的死亡，最後卻沒有預言出自己的命運。雖然亞歷山大、龐培、凱撒摧毀了這麼多城池，在戰場上屠殺了數十萬的騎兵和步兵，但最後也與世長辭。雖然赫拉克利特多次預言了世界將毀於大火，最後自己死的時候卻全身水腫、渾身積水、沾滿牛糞。蝨子殺死了德謨克利特，而蘇格拉底則死在另一隻蝨子手裏。這意味著什麼呢？就如同你上了條船，開始航行，然後靠岸下來。如果你到了另一個世界，那裏不再需要神了。如果航向一個無知無覺之鄉，你將不會感受到痛苦或是快樂，也不會再是身體的奴隸；身體多麼下賤，它所服務的物件就有多優越，因為後者是理智和神性，前者是泥土和腐朽。

不要把你剩下的生命浪費在思考別人的事情上，除非你能把這些想法聯繫到共同的利益上去，因為你已經失去做其他事情的機會了。當你在琢磨這個人在做什麼，目的是什麼，他說了什麼，想了什麼，爭論什麼等諸如此類的事情，你已經偏離對自己主宰力量的觀察。我們應該暫停思想序列中無目的和無用的部分，尤其是那些過於好奇的和邪惡的想法。你必須讓自己只想到這些事情：當有人突然問你"你

1.Hippocrates（西元前460年～西元前377年），古希臘名醫，西方醫學鼻祖。
2.Alexander（西元前356年～西元前323年），馬其頓國王，領軍馳騁歐亞非大陸，使古希臘文明廣泛傳播。 3.Pompeius（西元前106年～西元前48年），古羅馬統帥和政治家。 4.Caesar（西元前100年～西元前44年），古羅馬統帥和政治家。 5.cavalry [`kæv!rɪ] n. 騎兵部隊 6.Heraclitus（約西元前540年～西元前480年），前蘇格拉底時期哲學家。 7.smeared [smɪrd] adj. 污跡斑斑的
8.Democritus（約西元前460年～西元前370年），前蘇格拉底時期哲學家，原子

Hippocrates[1] after curing many diseases himself fell sick and died. The Chaldaei foretold the deaths of many, and then fate caught them too. **Alexander**[2], and **Pompeius**[3], and **Caiu Caesar**[4], after so often completely destroying whole cities, and in battle cutting to pieces many ten thousands of **cavalry**[5] and infantry, themselves too at last departed from life. **Heraclitus**[6], after so many speculations on the conflagration of the universe, was filled with water internally and died **smeared**[7] all over with mud. And lice destroyed **Democritus**[8]; and other lice killed **Socrates**[9]. What means all this? Thou hast embarked, thou hast made the voyage, thou art come to shore; **get out**[10]. If indeed **to another life**[11], there is no want of gods, not even there. But if to a state without sensation, thou wilt cease to be held by pains and pleasures, and to be a slave to the vessel, which is as much inferior as that which serves it is superior: for the one is intelligence and deity; the other is earth and corruption.

Do not waste the remainder of thy life in thoughts about others, when thou dost not refer thy thoughts to some object of common utility. For thou **losest**[12] the opportunity of doing something else when thou hast such thoughts as these, What is such a person doing, and why, and what is he saying, and what is he thinking of, and what is he contriving, and whatever else of the kind makes us wander away from the observation of

---

論代表人。死於蝨說法未見其他文獻，作者可能把德謨克利特與另一前蘇格拉底時期哲學家Pherecydes混淆，有文獻說Pherecydes是被蝨子咬死的。　9. Socrates（西元前470年～西元前399年），與柏拉圖、亞里斯多德並稱希臘三賢，文中指的是西元前399年，蘇格拉底以不敬神和腐蝕雅典青年這兩條罪名判處死刑，但蘇格拉底一生摯愛雅典城邦。按照《申辯篇》的解釋，蘇格拉底並不認可這兩條罪名，但卻維護當時雅典不公正的法律。　10.指死亡，古埃及的婉曲語。11.亦指死亡。 12.losest為古英語中lose的第二人稱單數（主語為thou時使用）。

現在在想什麼』的時候，你能自在坦白回答，表明你的內心是淳樸和仁厚的，這恰恰適合一個社會性動物，不追求享樂或沉溺於感官愉悅中，也沒有敵意、嫉妒和疑心，或者任何別的令你羞於承認的念頭。這樣的人會毫不猶豫地抓住最好的東西，就像神的牧師和使者，聽從內心的神性行事，這種神性使他們不沾染追求享樂的惡習，不受痛苦的傷害，不犯錯或是驕傲自大，也不會去傷害別人。他是最崇高戰爭中的鬥士，不被內心的激情所打倒，內心始終堅守正義，坦然接受自己的命運。除了出於必然和公眾利益的考慮之外，他並不會總是想別人說什麼，做什麼，目的又是什麼，因為他只能控制自己做什麼，目的是什麼，這些才是他自己的。他總是在思考在整個宇宙中，上天賦予了他什麼樣的使命。這些東西是屬於他的，也是他有能力掌握的。他服從於上天的安排，因為這種安排是好的；至於那些發生在他身上的事情，他也相信它們是好的。上天分配給各人的命運是天生註定的，無法改變的，但每個人總能從命運的安排中得到好處。他也牢記每個有理性的動物都是他的同胞，關心所有人符合人的本性，但是一個人不應該聽取所有人的意見，而只聽取那些堅定不移地按照自然生活者的意見。對於那些不如此生活的人，他也記得很清楚：他們在家和在外面是什麼樣的人；白天是什麼樣的人，晚上是什麼樣的人；他們做什麼工作，和什麼人一起消磨時光。自然地，他就不看重來自這些人的稱讚，因為他們甚至對自己都無法滿意。

1.malignant [mə`lɪgnənt] adj. 邪惡的
2.hadst為古英語中have的單數，第二人稱過去式（主語為 thou 時使用）。

our own ruling power. We ought then to check in the series of our thoughts everything that is without a purpose and useless, but most of all the over-curious feeling and the **malignant**[1]; and a man should use himself to think of those things only about which if one should suddenly ask, What hast thou now in thy thoughts? With perfect openness thou mightest, immediately answer, This or That; so that from thy words it should be plain that everything in thee is simple and benevolent, and such as befits a social animal, and one that cares not for thoughts about pleasure or sensual enjoyments at all, nor has any rivalry or envy and suspicion, or anything else for which thou wouldst blush if thou shouldst say that thou **hadst**[2] it in thy mind. For the man who is such and no longer delays being among the number of the best, is like a priest and minister of the gods, using too the deity which is planted within him, which makes the man uncontaminated by pleasure, unharmed by any pain, untouched by any insult, feeling no wrong, a fighter in the noblest fight, one who cannot be overpowered by any passion, **dyed**[3] deep with justice, accepting with all his soul everything which happens and is assigned to him as his portion; and not often, nor yet without great necessity and for the general interest, imagining what another says, or does, or thinks. For it is only what belongs to himself that he makes the matter for his activity; and he constantly thinks of that which is **allotted** [4] to himself out of the sum total of things, and he makes his own acts fair, and

---

3.dye [daɪ] vi. 被染色
4.allot [ə`lɑt] vt. 分配

　　不要做違背良心的事，不要違背公共利益，要三思而後行，不要猶豫不決，不要用漂亮的言詞來掩飾空洞的思想，既不要喋喋不休也不要變成好管閒事的人。讓你心中的神監督你，做一個有男子氣概的、成熟的、從事政治的人，成為一個羅馬人，成為一個統治者，堅守崗位像一個等待生命召喚信號的人，既無需誓約的約束，也無需別人的證言。

　　要保持愉悅的心情，不要指望別人來幫助你或照顧你，或是從

1.ornament [`ɔrnəmənt] n. 增添光彩的人或物；裝飾品
2.testimony [`tɛstə,monɪ] n. 證言
3.tranquility [træŋ`kwɪlətɪ] n. 安寧

he is persuaded that his own portion is good. For the lot which is assigned to each man is carried along with him and carries him along with it. And he remembers also that every rational animal is his kinsman, and that to care for all men is according to man's nature; and a man should hold on to the opinion not of all, but of those only who confessedly live according to nature. But as to those who live not so, he always bears in mind what kind of men they are both at home and from home, both by night and by day, and what they are, and with what men they live an impure life. Accordingly, he does not value at all the praise which comes from such men, since they are not even satisfied with themselves.

Labour not unwillingly, nor without regard to the common interest, nor without due consideration, nor with distraction; nor let studied **ornament**[1] set off thy thoughts, and be not either a man of many words, or busy about too many things. And further, let the deity which is in thee be the guardian of a living being, manly and of ripe age, and engaged in matter political, and a Roman, and a ruler, who has taken his post like a man waiting for the signal which summons him from life, and ready to go, having need neither of oath nor of any man's **testimony**[2].

Be cheerful also, and seek not external help nor the **tranquility**[3] which

別人那裏獲得休憩和平靜。寧願做一個憑自己的力量就能筆直站立的人，無需他人扶持。

　　假如你在生活中發現有比正義、真理、節制和堅忍更好的東西，或是發現有什麼東西比心靈自我滿足感更好（這個自我滿足感能夠讓你按照正確的理性，在未經你選擇而是聽從分配的情況下去做事情）我的意思是說，假如你找到了比這更好的東西，那就全身心地投入吧，不管你發現的最好的東西是什麼，都盡情享受吧。不過，如果你發現沒有什麼東西比你心中培育的神性更好，這種神性能夠讓所有的慾望屈服，仔細審視所有印象，而且正如蘇格拉底所說，這種神性能使你遠離感官的誘惑，不僅如此，這種神性也能使你潛心敬奉神靈並博愛濟世。如果你發現所有別的一切與之相比都不值一提，轉瞬即逝，那不要容忍其他的想法。一旦你有了這些別的想法就再也無法專注地追求你所應當追求的善了，而這才是真正適合和屬於你的善良美德。如果讓任何別的、低下的東西——不管是眾人的稱讚、權力、財富還是享樂——來和這種理智上的、政治上的、實踐上的好的東西相抗衡是錯誤的。所有這些東西，一旦它們開始滿足我們，雖然只是那麼一會兒，很快就會控制我們，並把我們引上歧途。所以我說，你要直接選擇那更好的並且要始終不變地堅持它。有人會說，有用的東西才是更好的——那麼，如果他們說有用是對理性的人有用，那你就接受它，堅持它吧；但如果他們說的只是對於一個缺乏理性的像動物一樣的人

1.findest 為古英語中 find 的第二人稱單數（主語為 thou 時使用）。

others give. A man then must stand erect, not be kept erect by others.

If thou **findest**[1] in human life anything better than justice, truth, temperance, fortitude, and, in a word, anything better than thy own mind's self-satisfaction in the things which it enables thee to do according to right reason, and in the condition that is assigned to thee without thy own choice; if, I say, thou seest anything better than this, turn to it with all thy soul, and enjoy that which thou hast found to be the best. But if nothing appears to be better than the deity which is planted in thee, which has subjected to itself all thy appetites, and carefully examines all the impressions, and, as Socrates said, has detached itself from the persuasions of sense, and has submitted itself to the gods, and cares for mankind; if thou findest everything else smaller and of less value than this, give place to nothing else, for if thou dost once diverge and incline to it, thou wilt no longer without distraction be able to give the preference to that good thing which is thy proper possession and thy own; for it is not right that anything of any other kind, such as praise from the many, or power, or enjoyment of pleasure, should come into competition with that which is rationally and politically or practically good. All these things, even though they may seem to adapt themselves to the better things in a small degree, obtain the superiority all at once, and carry

有用，那你就要拒絕它，並且維持你的判斷，但是不能驕傲自大，要留意你是否使用了適當的探討方法。

　　不要認為以下的任何事情會對你有利：那些使你不守諾言，失去自尊，讓你憎恨別人、多疑、詛咒、虛偽、有貪念，令你不能光明正大或令你懷有不可告人秘密的事情。那些重視自己的理性和神性，以及由此而生的神聖美德的人，從不抱怨、無病呻吟、亂發牢騷。他們既不刻意獨處，也不一定要和眾人打成一片。最重要的是，他既不追求死亡，也不害怕死亡。至於生命，不管他的靈魂究竟能在這身體中寄寓多久，他並不害怕。即便他馬上就要離開人世，他也將像做別的事情一樣，從容不迫地準備好迎接死亡。在他的生命中，他只關心一點，他的思想從不背離屬於一個理性動物和社會公民所有的東西。

　　在那些曾經真正被訓練過和淨化過的人的心裏，你不會發現任何

1.makest 為古英語中 make 的第二人稱單數（主語為 thou 時使用）。
2.groan [gron] n. 呻吟聲
3.wilt 為古英語中 will 的第二人稱單數（主語為 thou 時使用）。

us away. But do thou, I say, simply and freely choose the better, and hold to it. – But that which is useful is the better. – Well then, if it is useful to thee as a rational being, keep to it; but if it is only useful to thee as an animal, say so, and maintain thy judgment without arrogance: only take care that thou **makest**[1] the inquiry by a sure method.

Never value anything as profitable to thyself which shall compel thee to break thy promise, to lose thy self-respect, to hate any man, to suspect, to curse, to act the hypocrite, to desire anything which needs walls and curtains: for he who has preferred to everything intelligence and daemon and the worship of its excellence, acts no tragic part, does not **groan**[2], will not need either solitude or much company; and, what is chief of all, he will live without either pursuing or flying from death; but whether for a longer or a shorter time he shall have the soul inclosed in the body, he cares not at all: for even if he must depart immediately, he will go as readily as if he were going to do anything else which can be done with decency and order; taking care of this only all through life, that his thoughts turn not away from anything which belongs to an intelligent animal and a member of a civil community.

In the mind of one who is chastened and purified thou **wilt**[3] find no

腐朽的、污穢的、不純潔的東西，或是像潰爛發膿的東西。當命運來
襲時，跟人們常說的戲未演完就離開舞臺的演員不同，你的生命不會
不完整。此外，他身上沒有奴性、不矯揉、不過分依賴他物、也不遠
離他物、無可指摘，也無需隱瞞。

要尊重產生意見的能力，因為有了這種能力，你的主宰的部分才
沒有出現有悖於自然和理性動物本性的意見。這種能力讓你不盲目衝
動行事，對人友善，對神順從。

拋開所有別的一切，遵循這幾項真理吧！此外還要記住：每個人
都只能活在現在，而現在也是不可分割的點。生命的其他部分不是已
經過去了就是不可預知的。每個人的生命都是短暫的，每個人生活的
地方都只是地球上的一個小小角落罷了，就連那死後獲得的最久的英
名也是短暫的，即使這名聲被那些可憐的後人所傳頌，但他們同樣也
將很快死去，而且他們活著的時候都不知道自己在做些什麼，他們又
怎麼能知道那些早已死去的人做的事呢！

1.posthumous [`pɑstjuməs] adj. 死後獲得的；死後的

corrupt matter, nor impurity, nor any sore skinned over. Nor is his life incomplete when fate overtakes him, as one may say of an actor who leaves the stage before ending and finishing the play. Besides, there is in him nothing servile, nor affected, nor too closely bound to other things, nor yet detached from other things, nothing worthy of blame, nothing which seeks a hiding-place.

Reverence the faculty which produces opinion. On this faculty it entirely depends whether there shall exist in thy ruling part any opinion inconsistent with nature and the constitution of the rational animal. And this faculty promises freedom from hasty judgment, and friendship towards men, and obedience to the gods.

Throwing away then all things, hold to these only which are few; and besides bear in mind that every man lives only this present time, which is an indivisible point, and that all the rest of his life is either past or it is uncertain. Short then is the time which every man lives, and small the nook of the earth where he lives; and short too the longest **posthumous**[1] fame, and even this only continued by a succession of poor human beings, who will very soon die, and who know not even themselves, much less him who died long ago.

　　承上所言，我再補充一段：你對呈現給你的事物要特別下一個定義或做一個描述，以便透過其實體、裸露及其整體性辨別出它為何物，給它們取恰當的名字，替組成和分解它的部分取名。沒有什麼比系統、真實地觀察和思考呈現在你生活中的所有事物更能有效地提升思想的事情了。探索事物的同時我們也會想到：宇宙為何物？宇宙中每個事物的效用？相對於整個宇宙，宇宙中事物的價值是什麼？宇宙中的事物對人又有什麼價值？人乃是最高組織的公民，與此相比，其他的組織就類似於家庭。目前給我印象的東西是什麼？由什麼東西組成？它能持續多久？考慮到它，我現在需要什麼美德？是溫順、堅毅、誠實、忠誠、真誠、滿足，還是別的什麼。在每種情況下，你都應該說，這是神的安排，是透過命運的連結，或是透過類似的機緣巧合來實現的。這個想法來自我的同族、我的兄弟和我的夥伴，雖然他並不知道什麼是合乎本性的，但我知道，因此我要以同胞之義來公正、善良地對待他們。同時，對於非善非惡的事物，我要嘗試確定這種事物的價值。

1.斯多噶派哲學家認為這個宇宙為一個國家，所有人皆為公民，尊奉一個宇宙理性。

2.fellowship [`fɛloˌʃɪp] n. 友誼

To the aids which have been mentioned let this one still be added: Make for thyself a definition or description of the thing which is presented to thee, so as to see distinctly what kind of a thing it is in its substance, in its nudity, in its complete entirety, and tell thyself its proper name, and the names of the things of which it has been compounded, and into which it will be resolved. For nothing is so productive of elevation of mind as to be able to examine methodically and truly every object which is presented to thee in life, and always to look at things so as to see at the same time what kind of universe this is, and what kind of use everything performs in it, and what value everything has with reference to the whole, and what with reference to **man**[1], who is a citizen of the highest city, of which all other cities are like families; what each thing is, and of what it is composed, and how long it is the nature of this thing to endure which now makes an impression on me, and what virtue I have need of with respect to it, such as gentleness, manliness, truth, fidelity, simplicity, contentment, and the rest. Wherefore, on every occasion a man should say: this comes from God; and this is according to the apportionment and spinning of the thread of destiny, and such-like coincidence and chance; and this is from one of the same stock, and a kinsman and partner, one who knows not however what is according to his nature. But I know; for this reason I behave towards him according to the natural law of **fellowship**[2] with benevolence and justice. At the same

當你做擺在你面前的工作時，如果能遵循正確理性的指引，一心一意、堅持不懈、不急不躁，不分心於任何別的事情，保持內心的純淨，就好像你馬上要把它歸還給造物主一樣；如果你對別人都無所奢求亦無所畏懼，滿足符合自然的活動，滿足於你所發出來的每個詞和音節中所蘊含的大膽的真實，那麼你就會生活得很幸福，也沒有任何人能阻止你過得幸福。

就像醫生總是隨身攜帶他們的工具以搶救突如其來的的病患一樣，你也要準備隨時學習有關人和神的知識。不管你做什麼，哪怕是最細枝末節之處，你也必須記住神界和人世事物的相互聯繫。如果沒有神的指引，你無法完成人世間的事情，反之亦然。

不要再信步漫遊，因為你無法活著讀到有關自己的著作，或是古羅馬人和古希臘人的豐功偉績，或是你為自己準備的在晚年時所閱讀的讀書摘錄。趕緊朝著一個目標前行吧，丟開虛無的希望，如果你還

1.workest 為古英語中 work 的第二人稱單數（主語為 thou 時使用）。
2.holdest 為古英語中 hold 的第二人稱單數（主語為 thou 時使用）。

time however in things indifferent I attempt to ascertain the value of each.

If thou **workest**[1] at that which is before thee, following right reason seriously, vigorously, calmly, without allowing anything else to distract thee, but keeping thy divine part pure, as if thou shouldst be bound to give it back immediately; if thou **holdest**[2] to this, expecting nothing, fearing nothing, but satisfied with thy present activity according to nature, and with heroic truth in every word and sound which thou **utterest**[3], thou wilt live happy. And there is no man who is able to prevent this.

As physicians have always their instruments and knives ready for cases which suddenly require their skill, so do thou have principles ready for the understanding of things divine and human, and for doing everything, even the smallest, with a recollection of the bond which unites the divine and human to one another. For neither wilt thou do anything well which pertains to man without at the same time having a reference to things divine; nor the contrary.

No longer wander at hazard; for neither wilt thou read thy own **memoirs**[4], nor the acts of the ancient Romans and Hellenes, and the selections from books which thou wast reserving for thy old age. Hasten

3.utterest 為古英語中 utter 的第二人稱單數（主語為 thou 時使用）。

4.這裏提到的著作已經不可考，可能就是指這本書本身。

關心你自己的話，就應該及時自助。

　　他們不瞭解有多少事情是透過語言的偷竊、播種、和購買來進行的，保持安靜、看看應該做什麼，因為這不是靠眼睛能夠看到的，而是需要另一種視覺。

　　身體、靈魂、理智：感官屬於身體；慾望屬於靈魂；而真理則屬於理智。透過表相獲得關於形式的印象，甚至連動物也可做到；被慾望所牽引的，屬於野獸和女人化的男人，法勒裏斯和尼祿就屬於這類；把理智引向貌似合理的事物，也屬於那些不信神的、背叛國家的、關上門做骯髒勾當的人。如果所有其他的東西也同樣為上述我所提到的人共有，那麼，只有如下這些是好人所獨有的，即對所有發生在他身上的事情、對命中註定的事情都能欣然接受，不會用虛無的幻想來玷污和攪亂他心中的神性，而是使它保持寧靜，對它敬若神明，絕不說任何違背真理的話，也不做違背正義的事。

1.carest 為古英語中 care 的第二人稱單數（主語為 thou 時使用）。

2.這裏身體、靈魂、理智的三重區分同印象（impression）、衝動（impulse）、判斷（judgment）功能的三重區分是聯繫在一起的，這種觀點可以追溯到柏拉圖時代。

then to the end which thou hast before thee, and throwing away idle hopes, come to thy own aid, if thou **carest**[1] at all for thyself, while it is in thy power.

They know not how many things are signified by the words stealing, sowing, buying, keeping quiet, seeing what ought to be done; for this is not effected by the eyes, but by another kind of vision.

Body, soul, intelligence[2]: to the body belong sensations, to the soul appetites, to the intelligence principles. To receive the impressions of forms by means of appearances belongs even to animals; to be pulled by the strings of desire belongs both to wild beasts and to men who have made themselves into women, and to a **Phalaris**[3] and a **Nero**[4]: and to have the intelligence that guides to the things which appear suitable belongs also to those who do not believe in the gods, and who betray their country, and do their impure deeds when they have shut the doors. If then everything else is common to all that I have mentioned, there remains that which is peculiar to the good man, to be pleased and content with what happens, and with the thread which is spun for him; and not to defile the divinity which is planted in his breast, nor disturb it by a crowd of images, but to preserve it tranquil, following it obediently as a god, neither saying anything contrary to the truth, nor doing anything contrary to justice.

3.Phalaris（西元前570年～西元前554年），西西里的著名暴君，以殘虐聞名，曾活燒俘虜。

4.Nero（37年～68年），古羅馬帝國的有名暴君。

　　這樣一個人，即使別人都不相信他過得簡樸、節制和滿足，他既不會對他們中的任何一個人感到憤怒，也不會偏離通往人生目標的道路。人應當過得純粹，隨時準備離去，安心於命運的安排，而不覺有任何壓迫。

And if all men refuse to believe that he lives a simple, modest, and contented life, he is neither angry with any of them, nor does he deviate from the way which leads to the end of life, to which a man ought to come pure, tranquil, ready to depart, and without any compulsion perfectly reconciled to his lot.

第四卷

我們心中的主宰力量，當其合乎本性時，如此強烈地受所發生事物的影響，以致於總是能輕而易舉地調整自身適應可能發生的以及呈現給它的東西。因為它不需要特質，而是在某種條件下朝著它的目標前進，把阻礙它的東西轉化為自身的材質，就像火焰吞沒落入它裏面的東西一樣：若是小小的火苗，可能會被這些東西撲滅，但當火勢強大時，它很快就能將這些東西佔有和吞噬，並且燃燒殆盡，讓火苗越燒越旺。

做事不要漫無目的，而要遵循盡善盡美的藝術法則。

人們總是在尋找隱居之所，比如鄉村茅屋、海邊或是山野。你自己也渴望到這些地方隱居，但這些都是庸俗的體現。因為不論任何時候你都有能力選擇回歸心靈。沒有任何地方比退隱到自己的靈魂中更為寧靜、自在，尤其當他明白關注自身便能立刻獲得全然的寧靜

1.shalt 為古英語中 shall 的第二人稱單數（陳述語氣現在時，主語為 thou 時使用）。

BOOK 4

That which rules within, when it is according to nature, is so affected with respect to the events which happen, that it always easily adapts itself to that which is and is presented to it. For it requires no definite material, but it moves towards its purpose, under certain conditions however; and it makes a material for itself out of that which opposes it, as fire lays hold of what falls into it, by which a small light would have been extinguished: but when the fire is strong, it soon appropriates to itself the matter which is heaped on it, and consumes it, and rises higher by means of this very material.

Let no act be done without a purpose, nor otherwise than according to the perfect principles of art.

Men seek retreats for themselves, houses in the country, sea-shores, and mountains; and thou too art wont to desire such things very much. But this is altogether a mark of the most common sort of men, for it is in thy power whenever thou **shalt**[1] choose to **retire into thyself**[2]. For nowhere either

---

2. 『回歸心靈』這樣一種理念再現了古代哲學的主題，這本來是斯多噶派的 Seneca, Eposties等的主張。

時。我所理解的寧靜是指井然有序的心靈，擺脫了一切困頓和喧嘩。那麼，不斷地像這樣回歸內心吧！這樣就能使自己煥然一新，重獲新生。讓這些訓誡簡潔有力地指導你的行為，一旦你想起它們，它們就足以完全淨化你的心靈。在這短暫的回歸內心之後，當你再重新回到之前的生活時，你對什麼都會感到很滿意。你是對什麼感到不滿呢？是對人們的邪惡不滿嗎？想想這個結論吧：所有有理性的動物都是互相依存的，相互忍耐亦是正義的一部分，人們內心並不想行惡；想想自古以來有多少人曾經像這樣打擊仇敵、心懷疑慮和仇恨，然後激烈地競爭，但是現在他們早就已經撒手人寰，化為灰燼了。是該停止這些思緒之際。也許你對從宇宙中分配給你的那一份感到不滿，想想你該怎麼選吧：要不是存在神，就是存在偶然聚集起的原子，或者是想想那些證明了世界是一個政治共同體的證據，最終你會安靜下來。也許你還被肉體所糾纏，進一步想想當心靈將自身抽離出來，發現自己的力量時，就不會與氣息相混，不論這種氣息是平緩的，抑或是急促的。想想你聽到並認可的關於快樂和痛苦的道理，最終平靜下來吧！也許你被聲望之欲所折磨，想想所有這些東西被遺忘得有多麼迅速，而在它們之前或之後都是永恆無邊的混沌。再想想那些讚美之詞有多麼浮誇，人們的想法和意見有多麼善變和不一致，而我們所居住的地方又是多麼狹小和侷促，最終平靜下來吧！整個地球只是一個點，我們居住的地方又只是地球上的一個小小部分，而在這一部分裏又能有多少人，什麼樣的人會讚揚你呢？

1.returnest 為古英語中 return 的第二人稱單數（主語為 thou 時使用）。
2.當人作惡時，無人有意作惡，這是一個蘇格拉底的悖論。這個悖論被斯多噶派在探討愚蠢和聰明的觀念時所繼承和發展。

with more quiet or more freedom from trouble does a man retire than into his own soul, particularly when he has within him such thoughts that by looking into them he is immediately in perfect tranquility; and I affirm that tranquility is nothing else than the good ordering of the mind. Constantly then give to thyself this retreat, and renew thyself; and let thy principles be brief and fundamental, which, as soon as thou shalt recur to them, will be sufficient to cleanse the soul completely, and to send thee back free from all discontent with the things to which thou **returnest**[1]. For with what art thou discontented? With the badness of men? Recall to thy mind this conclusion, that rational animals exist for one another, and that to endure is a part of justice, and that **men do wrong involuntarily**[2]; and consider how many already, after mutual enmity, suspicion, hatred, and fighting, have been stretched dead, reduced to ashes; and be quiet at last. – But perhaps thou art dissatisfied with that which is assigned to thee out of the universe. – Recall to thy recollection this alternative; either there is providence or atoms, fortuitous concurrence of things; or remember the arguments by which it has been proved that the world is a kind of political community, and be quiet at last. – But perhaps corporeal things will still fasten upon thee. – Consider then further that the mind mingles not with the breath, whether moving gently or violently, when it has once drawn itself apart and discovered its own power, and think also of all that thou hast heard and

　　那麼剩下的就是：要經常像這樣回歸到自己的內心，回歸到自身的小天地裏去，最重要的是不要分心，不要太過熱情，而要保持心靈從容自在，要像個男人，像個人，像個公民，像個凡人一樣去考慮所有的事物。你手中最便於參照的有兩條原則：一是外在事物與目標並不觸及靈魂，它們只是靜靜地存在於靈魂之外，我們靈魂的意見才是所有喧嘩和煩惱的來源；二是你眼前所見的一切事物，很快就會改變和消失。你要始終牢記你一生中已經目擊過許多這樣的變化。世界在不停地變化，生活只是見解。

　　如果理智是我們共有的，那麼使我們成為理性動物的理性也是我

1.perturbation [ˌpɝtɚˋbeʃən] n. 煩惱；不安
2.在古希臘，真理（truth）和見解（opinion）是一對相對的範疇，古希臘哲學家認為真理作為是者，是不變的、永恆的『一』；而意見則是變動不拘的

assented to about pain and pleasure, and be quiet at last. – But perhaps the desire of the thing called fame will torment thee. – See how soon everything is forgotten, and look at the chaos of infinite time on each side of the present, and the emptiness of applause, and the changeableness and want of judgment in those who pretend to give praise, and the narrowness of the space within which it is circumscribed, and be quiet at last. For the whole earth is a point, and how small a nook in it is this thy dwelling, and how few are there in it, and what kind of people are they who will praise thee.

This then remains: Remember to retire into this little territory of thy own, and above all do not distract or strain thyself, but be free, and look at things as a man, as a human being, as a citizen, as a mortal. But among the things readiest to thy hand to which thou shalt turn, let there be these, which are two. One is that things do not touch the soul, for they are external and remain immovable; but our **perturbations**[1] come only from the opinion which is within. The other is that all these things, which thou seest, change immediately and will no longer be; and constantly bear in mind how many of these changes thou hast already witnessed. The universe is transformation: **life is opinion**[2].

If our intellectual part is common, the reason also, in respect of which

『多』。這裏作者把世界理解為不停變化的，所以才有後面的「生活只是意見」，這裏強調的是作為凡人的我們在俗世是不可能得到真理的，我們唯一能固守的就是心靈的平靜。

們共有的；告訴我們要做什麼和不做什麼的理性也是我們共有的。如果這樣的話，那我們所奉行的法律也是如此；我們就是同一類公民，是某個政治共同體的夥伴；如果是這樣的話，在某種意義上，世界就是一個國家。除了說它是一個國家，整個人類的這個組織還能是什麼呢？正因如此，從這個國家中我們獲得了理智、理性和法律。否則，它們是從哪裏來的呢？正如我身上的土是來自土元素，水是來自另外一種元素，熱的部分有某種奇異的源頭（因為無中不能生有，有不能復歸於無），所以我們的理智也有某種源頭。

　　出生和死亡一樣都是自然的奧秘：某些元素混合在一起然後又分解，這沒有什麼好羞愧的。它既不違反一個理性動物的本性，與人自身生命活動的規律也不衝突。

　　一個人做這樣的事，是自然而且必然的。如果一個人覺得這樣

1.「無中不能生有，有不能復歸於無」乃是古希臘、古羅馬時期對於事物變化的一種基本看法。

we are rational beings, is common: if this is so, common also is the reason which commands us what to do, and what not to do; if this is so, there is a common law also; if this is so, we are fellow-citizens; if this is so, we are members of some political community; if this is so, the world is in a manner a state. For of what other common political community will any one say that the whole human race are members? And from thence, from this common political community comes also our very intellectual faculty and reasoning faculty and our capacity for law; or whence do they come? For as my earthly part is a portion given to me from certain earth, and that which is watery from another element, and that which is hot and fiery from some peculiar source (**for nothing comes out of that which is nothing, as nothing also returns to non-existence**[1]), so also the intellectual part comes from some source.

Death is such as generation is, a mystery of nature; a composition out of the same elements, and a decomposition into the same; and altogether not a thing of which any man should be ashamed, for it is not contrary to the nature of a reasonable animal, and not contrary to the reason of our constitution.

It is natural that these things should be done by such persons, it is a

有什麼不對，就等於覺得無花果樹有汁液有什麼不對一樣。總之，要記住這點：你和別人都將很快死去，而你們的名字也將很快被後人忘記。

拋開自己的主觀想法，這樣就會拋開『我受到傷害』的抱怨；拋開『我受到傷害』的抱怨，這樣就等於拋開了傷害。

不能讓人變得比過去更糟，不會讓人的生活變得更糟，也不會對人的內在或外在造成傷害。

普遍有用的東西的本性不得不如此。

如果你仔細留心觀察的話，你將發現這世界上萬物皆有理。我說的不僅是一系列事物的連續性，還有正義，彷彿事物的一切價值都自有安排，各得其所。像你已經開始了的那樣繼續留心觀察吧，無論你做什麼，都要記住這個條件，像一個好人（褒義的『好』）那樣參照著善去做，不管做什麼都要遵循這一點。

1.observest 為古英語中 observe 的第二人稱單數（主語為 thou 時使用）。

matter of necessity; and if a man will not have it so, he will not allow the fig-tree to have juice. But by all means bear this in mind, that within a very short time both thou and he will be dead; and soon not even your names will be left behind.

Take away thy opinion, and then there is taken away the complaint, "I have been harmed." Take away the complaint, "I have been harmed," and the harm is taken away.

That which does not make a man worse than he was, also does not make his life worse, nor does it harm him either from without or from within.

The nature of that which is universally useful has been compelled to do this.

Consider that everything which happens, happens justly, and if thou **observest**[1] carefully, thou wilt find it to be so. I do not say only with respect to the continuity of the series of things, but with respect to what is just, and as if it were done by one who assigns to each thing its value. Observe then as thou hast begun; and whatever thou doest, do it in conjunction with this, the being good, and in the sense in which a man is properly understood to

不要被傷害你的人引入歧途，或是被他牽著鼻子走，而是要對事物本身進行研究，發現其真相。

你一定要時刻牢記這兩項規則：一是你所做的一切事情都應該以合乎理性法則和眾人的利益為唯一宗旨；另一個是如果有人能夠改正你的錯誤或是使你不被錯誤的勸導迷惑，你要隨時準備改變你的意見。但這種改變只能出自對正義、公眾利益及諸如此類的考量，而不應是為了貪圖享樂或沽名釣譽。

你有理性嗎？我有。那為什麼你不運用它呢？如果你的理性發揮其應有的作用，你還會要求額外的東西嗎？

你作為一部分而存在。你終將消失於產生你的事物中，更正確地說，你透過變形復歸於它的生殖原則中。

在同一個祭壇上會有許多小塊的乳香，有一滴先落了下來，滲進

be good. Keep to this in every action.

Do not have such an opinion of things as he has who does thee wrong, or such as he wishes thee to have, but look at them as they are in truth.

A man should always have these two rules in readiness; the one, to do only whatever the reason of the ruling and legislating faculty may suggest for the use of men; the other, to change thy opinion, if there is any one at hand who sets thee right and moves thee from any opinion. But this change of opinion must proceed only from a certain persuasion, as of what is just or of common advantage, and the like, not because it appears pleasant or brings reputation.

Hast thou reason? I have. – Why then dost not thou use it? For if this does its own work, what else dost thou wish?

Thou hast existed as a part. Thou shalt disappear in that which produced thee; but rather thou shalt be received back into its seminal principle by transmutation.

Many grains of frankincense on the same altar: one falls before, another

地裏，然後又有一滴落下。它們之間並沒有什麼區別。

只要你重新遵循原則和理性的指引，那麼十天之內，那些現在視你如野獸、猿猴的人就會敬你如神明。

不要以為自己還能活上幾千年，死亡已經在你的頭頂窺視著你。趁你現在還活著，趁你還能有所作為，好好做人、及時行善吧。

如果一個人不去探究他的鄰人說什麼、做什麼或想什麼，而只關注他自己的行為是否公正和神聖，那他就會省掉很多麻煩！或者用俄伽松的話說，不要為別人的道德墮落而生氣，而是要沿著正途一路前進！

那些貪圖死後英名的人沒有想到，那些懷念他的人很快也要死去，他們的後代同樣要死去。世世代代的人先是崇拜然後死去，最後，所有的記憶都會湮滅。即便那些懷念你的人和他們對你的記憶都是不朽的，那對你又有什麼意義呢？這對死者沒什麼意義，可是對生者又能有什麼意義呢？除了它有某種實際的功用，此外還有什麼呢？你現在不合宜地拒絕了自然賦予你的天性，卻追逐其他的東西，這是極不明智的行為。

1.livest 為古英語中 live 的第二人稱單數（主語為 thou 時使用）。

2.Agathon（約西元前448年～西元前400年），古希臘悲劇詩人，曾出現在柏拉圖《會飲篇》中。

3.vehement [`viəmənt] adj. 感情強烈的

falls after; but it makes no difference.

Within ten days thou wilt seem a god to those to whom thou art now a beast and an ape, if thou wilt return to thy principles and the worship of reason.

Do not act as if thou wert going to live ten thousand years. Death hangs over thee. While thou **livest**[1], while it is in thy power, be good.

How much trouble he avoids who does not look to see what his neighbour says or does or thinks, but only to what he does himself, that it may be just and pure; or as **Agathon**[2] says, look not round at the depraved morals of others, but run straight along the line without deviating from it.

He who has a **vehement**[3] desire for posthumous fame does not consider that every one of those who remember him will himself also die very soon; then again also they who have succeeded them, until the whole remembrance shall have been extinguished as it is transmitted through men who foolishly admire and perish. But suppose that those who will remember are even immortal, and that the remembrance will be immortal, what then is this to thee? And I say not what is it to the dead, but what is it to the

　　任何事物如果有其美妙之處，其本身便是美的，無需旁求，讚美算不上其中的部分。受到讚揚並不會使一個事物變好或變壞。我認為即使是那些通常被認為美的事物也是如此，例如有形的事物或藝術品。至於那些真正好的東西，除了正義和真理，或者是善良和謙虛，它還需要什麼呢？所有這些東西哪一個會因為受到讚揚而變得漂亮，或者因為受到譴責而變醜呢？難道翡翠會因為沒有受到讚美而變糟或是變醜嗎？黃金、象牙、王位、七弦豎琴呢？更遑論平凡無奇的刀、鮮花和樹呢？

　　如果人死後有靈魂，在永恆的時間裏，大氣怎麼能容納得下這些靈魂呢？大地又怎麼能容納得下那些古往今來被埋葬之人的屍體呢？屍體存在一段時間後會變化、溶解，為別的屍體騰出空間。人死後移到空中的靈魂也是如此，它們在那裏停留一段時間之後，不是變形就是被溶解，或是被焚毀，再次融入那作為萬物之源原始的理性物質，為新的靈魂騰出了空間。這些靈魂之前與軀體連在一起，現在開始單獨存在。這是我們對假定靈魂存在所能給出的答案。但在此，除了那些掩埋在地底下的軀體，我們要進一步考慮被人和其他生物吃掉的

1.rejectest 為古英語中 reject 的第二人稱單數（主語為 thou 時使用）。
2.shrub [ʃrʌb] n. 灌木
3.transmute [træns`mjut] vt. 使變化

living? What is praise except indeed so far as it has a certain utility? For thou now **rejectest**[1] unseasonably the gift of nature, clinging to something else...

Everything which is in any way beautiful is beautiful in itself, and terminates in itself, not having praise as part of itself. Neither worse then nor better is a thing made by being praised. I affirm this also of the things which are called beautiful by the vulgar, for example, material things and works of art. That which is really beautiful has no need of anything; not more than law, not more than truth, not more than benevolence or modesty. Which of these things is beautiful because it is praised, or spoiled by being blamed? Is such a thing as an emerald made worse than it was, if it is not praised? Or gold, ivory, purple, a lyre, a little knife, a flower, a **shrub**[2]?

If souls continue to exist, how does the air contain them from eternity? – But how does the earth contain the bodies of those who have been buried from time so remote? For as here the mutation of these bodies after a certain continuance, whatever it may be, and their dissolution make room for other dead bodies; so the souls which are removed into the air after subsisting for some time are **transmuted**[3] and diffused, and assume a fiery nature by being received into the seminal intelligence of the universe, and in this way make room for the fresh souls which come to dwell there. And this is the

各種動物的數目。儘管每天都有這麼多的動物被吞入腹中，但是同樣的這個地方和這副軀體卻能夠容得下它們，因為它們一部分轉化成了血，一部分轉化成了如空氣或火焰一般的元素。

在這些事上怎樣探究真理呢？要把它們分成質料因和形式因。

不要游移不定，每一舉動都要合乎正義，每個印象都要保持領悟和理解力。

啊，宇宙！一切與你和諧的東西也與我和諧。那適於你的一切事物，對我來說絕不會不合時宜或過時。你的季節交替所帶來的一切於我都是幸福的果實。啊，自然！你是萬物之始，萬物之載體，也是萬物之終點。如果詩人用『你這親愛的西克洛普之城』來形容雅典，難道你不能用『你這親愛的宙斯之城』來形容這個世界嗎？

1.沿用亞里斯多德的四因說，即『質料因、形式因、動力因、目的因』。『質料因』即『事物所由產生的、並在事物內部始終存在著的東西』，『形式因』即事物的『原型亦即表達出本質的定義』。

answer which a man might give on the hypothesis of souls continuing to exist. But we must not only think of the number of bodies which are thus buried, but also of the number of animals which are daily eaten by us and the other animals. For what a number is consumed, and thus in a manner buried in the bodies of those who feed on them! And nevertheless this earth receives them by reason of the changes of these bodies into blood, and the transformations into the aerial or the fiery element.

What is the investigation into the truth in this matter? **The division into that which is material and that which is the cause of form, the formal**[1].

Do not be whirled about, but in every movement have respect to justice, and on the occasion of every impression maintain the faculty of comprehension or understanding.

Everything harmonizes with me, which is harmonious to thee, O Universe. Nothing for me is too early nor too late, which is in due time for thee. Everything is fruit to me which thy seasons bring, O Nature: from thee are all things, in thee are all things, to thee all things return. The poet says, Dear **City of Cecrops**[2]; and wilt not thou say, Dear city of Zeus?

2.Cecrops 是傳說中的第一個雅典國王。City of Cecrops 即雅典城。作者在這裏的觀點是：我們應該效忠我們的城邦和宇宙之城。

哲學家說，如果你要活得快樂，就少做些事情。想一下，更好的說法是：只做必然之事，只做社會動物的理性所要求的，並且按照理性所要求的方式去做。這種寧靜不僅來自於做得好，而且來自於做得少。我們所說和所做的絕大部分事情都是不必要的，一個人如果能夠拋開這些事情，他將有更多的閒暇，免去很多煩惱。因而一個人每做一件事都應當問問自己：我現在要做的是不是一件不必要的事情？我們不僅應該減少不必要的行為，而且應該丟棄不必要的想法，這樣，無聊的行為就不會紛至沓來。

努力像一個好人那樣生活，這樣的人對命運給他的一切都感到非常滿意，對自己現在合乎正義的行為及未來人格的完善也感到非常滿意和滿足。

你看到那些事情了嗎？不妨也看看這些事情：不要自尋煩惱；要使你儘量過一種單純的生活。有什麼人行惡嗎？他行惡是害了自己。你遭遇了什麼事情嗎？其實，它是從宇宙設計之初就安排、編造給你的。總之，我們的生命很短促，我們必須藉助理智和正義的指引努力地把握現在的時光，即使在你放鬆時也要保持清醒。

1.這裏指哲學家德謨克利特。
2.sober [`sobə] adj. 冷靜的

Occupy thyself with few things, says **the philosopher**[1], if thou wouldst be tranquil. – But consider if it would not be better to say, Do what is necessary, and whatever the reason of the animal which is naturally social requires, and as it requires. For this brings not only the tranquility which comes from doing well, but also that which comes from doing few things. For the greatest part of what we say and do being unnecessary, if a man takes this away, he will have more leisure and less uneasiness. Accordingly on every occasion a man should ask himself, is this one of the unnecessary things? Now a man should take away not only unnecessary acts, but also, unnecessary thoughts, for thus superfluous acts will not follow after.

Try how the life of the good man suits thee, the life of him who is satisfied with his portion out of the whole, and satisfied with his own just acts and benevolent disposition.

Hast thou seen those things? Look also at these. Do not disturb thyself. Make thyself all simplicity. Does any one do wrong? It is to himself that he does the wrong. Has anything happened to thee? Well, out of the universe from the beginning everything which happens has been apportioned and spun out to thee. In a word, thy life is short. Thou must turn to profit the present by the aid of reason and justice. Be **sober**[2] in thy relaxation.

這個世界不是井然有序，就是由各種東西混雜在一起，雖然混亂，但仍然是一個整體。難道可能你身上有某種秩序，但是作為整體的宇宙卻沒有秩序？既然所有的事物既相互區別，又相互聯繫，那宇宙怎麼可能沒有秩序？

一個陰暗邪惡的性格、一個懦弱的性格、一個頑固的性格，無人性、幼稚、獸性的、愚蠢、虛偽、下流、欺詐、殘暴。

如果他不諳世事，那他在這個世界上就是一個陌生人；如果他對已經發生的事大驚小怪，那他在這個世界上同樣也是個陌生人。這樣的人是一個真正的逃犯，逃離人之所以為社會人的理性，是個無法用心靈之眼來觀察事物的盲人，是一個需要從別人而非從自身汲取生活所需的乞丐。這樣的人對這個世界來說是個膿瘡，他因對自己的命運不滿而失去了人類所共有的理性。同一個自然產生了現實也產生了你，把靈魂與渾然一體的理性動物的靈魂分離開來的人是國家的碎片。

一個哲學家衣不蔽體，另外一個無書可讀，後者也是一個半裸的。有人說，雖然我衣不蔽體，食不果腹，但我還有理智。他說，我沒有麵包，但是我遵守理性。我從我的學識中沒有得到任何東西，我

1.asunder [əˋsʌndɚ] adv. 分離地
2.tunic [ˋtjunɪk] n.（古希臘、古羅馬）長達膝蓋的短袖束腰外衣

Either it is a well-arranged universe or a chaos huddled together, but still a universe. But can a certain order subsist in thee, and disorder in the All? And this too when all things are so separated and diffused and sympathetic.

A black character, a womanish character, a stubborn character, bestial, childish, animal, stupid, counterfeit, scurrilous, fraudulent, tyrannical.

If he is a stranger to the universe who does not know what is in it, no less is he a stranger who does not know what is going on in it. He is a runaway, who flies from social reason; he is blind, who shuts the eyes of the understanding; he is poor, who has need of another, and has not from himself all things which are useful for life. He is an abscess on the universe who withdraws and separates himself from the reason of our common nature through being displeased with the things which happen, for the same nature produces this, and has produced thee too: he is a piece rent **asunder**[1] from the state, who tears his own soul from that of reasonable animals, which is one.

The one is a philosopher without a **tunic**[2], and the other without a book: here is another half naked: Bread I have not, he says, and I abide by reason. – And I do not get the means of living out of my learning, and I abide by my

遵守我的理性。

熱愛你所學習的技藝吧，不管它多麼卑微，要對此滿足。像一個全心全意信賴上帝的人那樣度過你的餘生，既不成為暴君，也不成為任何人的奴隸。

舉個例子，如果回想一下維斯佩申的時代，你將會發現那時的世界和現在沒有什麼不同：有人結婚、有人養育子女、有人生病、有人垂死、有人交戰、有人飲宴、有人貿易、有人耕種、有人阿諛奉承、有人吹噓炫耀、有人多疑、有人狡詐、有人詛咒他人死亡、有人不停地抱怨現狀、有人戀愛、有人斂財、有人夢想著做高官、當國王，而如今他們已不復存在。現在再來想想圖拉真時代吧。你也會看到同樣的情況，他們的生活也蕩然無存。以同樣的方式再來觀察別的朝代和整個國家，你會發現有多少人雖然生前竭盡全力追求世間的東西，但很快就退出了歷史舞臺，分解為各種元素。但是，你應當特別注意你所見過的某些人，他們被虛名所累，而不做合於他本性之事，不堅守本性，也不以此為滿足。在這裏，你要記住，**對每件事情的注意力有其自身的價值和分寸，只要你不過度地關注旁枝末節的事情，你就不會感到不滿**。

1.Vespasian（西元9年～西元79年），是古羅馬第九任皇帝，西元69年～西元79年執政。繼尼祿之後統治羅馬，創立了弗拉維王朝。
2.Trajan（西元53年～西元117年），古羅馬第十三任皇帝，西元97年～西元117

reason.

Love the art, poor as it may be, which thou hast learned, and be content with it; and pass through the rest of life like one who has intrusted to the gods with his whole soul all that he has, making thyself neither the tyrant nor the slave of any man.

Consider, for example, the times of **Vespasian**[1]. Thou wilt see all these things, people marrying, bringing up children, sick, dying, warring, feasting, trafficking, cultivating the ground, flattering, obstinately arrogant, suspecting, plotting, wishing for some to die, grumbling about the present, loving, heaping up treasure, desiring consulship, kingly power. Well then, that life of these people no longer exists at all. Again, remove to the times of **Trajan**[2]. Again, all is the same. Their life too is gone. In like manner view also the other **epochs**[3] of time and of whole nations, and see how many after great efforts soon fell and were resolved into the elements. But chiefly thou shouldst think of those whom thou hast thyself known distracting themselves about idle things, neglecting to do what was in accordance with their proper constitution, and to hold firmly to this and to be content with it. And herein it is necessary to remember that the attention given to everything has its proper value and proportion. For thus thou wilt not be dissatisfied, if thou

---

年執政。在位時兩次對外征伐,建立阿拉伯行省,並向東擴張勢力至兩河流域。
3.epoch [ˋɛpək] n. 時期

　　那些過去被頻繁使用過的詞現在被廢棄了，同樣，那些過去家喻戶曉的名字現在也在某種程度上被忘卻了。例如，克米勒斯、凱撒、沃勒塞斯、利奧拉圖斯以及稍後的西皮奧、加圖，然後是奧古斯都，還有哈德良和安東尼，所有這些名字很快將會過時，變成傳說，淹沒於歷史洪流中。我說這些指的是那些曾經是在他們那個時代呼風喚雨的人，至於其他人，他們一死，就沒人再談起他們了。那麼，有什麼是會永遠被紀念的呢？所有的一切都是虛無。我們要努力追求什麼呢？只有這件事：思想正直，與人為善，不欺瞞，對於發生在我們身上的一切都坦然接受，不管是那些必須發生的，經常發生的，還是稀鬆平常的，它們和你及其他事物一樣有共同的原則和根源。

　　因此，你要心甘情願地把自己交給命運女神，讓她們隨心所欲地安排、編造你的命運吧。

　　一切皆是朝生暮死，記憶者和被記憶者同樣如此。

1.appliest為古英語中apply的第二人稱單數（主語為thou時使用）。　2.Camillus（西元前446年～西元前365年），古羅馬共和國初期獨裁者，被尊為『第二個羅馬締造者』。　3.Volesus，古羅馬共和國初期的英雄。　4.Leonnatus（西元前356年～西元前322年），古羅馬著名的軍事活動家和政治家。　5.Scipio（西元前236年～西元前183年），古羅馬著名統帥。　6.Cato（西元前234年～西元前

appliest[1] thyself to smaller matters no further than is fit.

The words which were formerly familiar are now antiquated: so also the names of those who were famed of old, are now in a manner antiquated, **Camillus**[2], Caeso, **Volesus**[3], **Leonnatus**[4], and a little after also **Scipio**[5] and **Cato**[6], then **Augustus**[7], then also **Hadrian**[8] and **Antoninus**[9]. For all things soon pass away and become a mere tale, and complete oblivion soon buries them. And I say this of those who have shone in a wondrous way. For the rest, as soon as they have breathed out their breath, they are gone, and no man speaks of them. And, to conclude the matter, what is even an eternal remembrance? A mere nothing. What then is that about which we ought to employ our serious pains? This one thing, thoughts just, and acts social, and words which never lie, and a disposition which gladly accepts all that happens, as necessary, as usual, as flowing from a principle and source of the same kind.

Willingly give thyself up to **Clotho**[10], one of the Fates, allowing her to spin thy thread into whatever things she pleases.

Everything is only for a day, both that which remembers and that which

149年），古羅馬政治家、將軍。 7.Augustus（西元前63年～西元14年），古羅馬第一任皇帝。 8.Hadrian（西元76年～西元138年），古羅馬第十四任皇帝，西元117年～西元138年執政，圖拉真的侄子和繼位人。 9.Antoninus（西元86年～西元161年），古羅馬第十五任皇帝，西元138年～西元161年執政，羅馬五賢帝之一。 10.Clotho，古希臘、羅馬神話中命運三女神之一。命運三女神分別指Clotho, Lachesis, and Atropos。

　　要經常觀察所有事物都是透過變化而產生的，因此，要使自己習慣於這樣想：宇宙生性喜歡改變那存在的事物並創造新的類似事物。從某種意義上說，一切現存的事物都是那將要存在的事物的種子。如果你認為只有那些落入大地裏或子宮裏的才是種子，那你就想得過於簡單了。

　　你不久就要離世了，但你還沒有達到完全單純的境界：你還有很多煩惱和不安分的想法，對外界的事物還有害怕和疑慮，也還沒有養成和善地對待所有人的性情，還沒有做到把你的智慧專注於正義的行為中。

　　仔細考察人們，尤其是智者的主宰原則吧，看看他們力圖避開什麼，追求什麼。

　　你的惡並不存在於別人的主宰原則中，也不存在於你軀體的任何轉變和變化中。那麼，它在哪裏呢？存在於你有力量形成惡的意見的部分中。就讓此力量不形成這樣的意見，一切就相安無事。判斷力近鄰那可怕的軀體，就算它被燒毀，腐爛化膿，也要讓做出判斷的部分

1.thyself 為古英語中 yourself 的拼寫方法。
2.corporeal [kɔr`pɔrɪəl] adj. 肉體的

is remembered.

Observe constantly that all things take place by change, and accustom **thyself**[1] to consider that the nature of the Universe loves nothing so much as to change the things which are and to make new things like them. For everything that exists is in a manner the seed of that which will be. But thou art thinking only of seeds which are cast into the earth or into a womb: but this is a very vulgar notion.

Thou wilt soon die, and thou art not yet simple, not free from perturbations, nor without suspicion of being hurt by external things, nor kindly disposed towards all; nor dost thou yet place wisdom only in acting justly.

Examine men's ruling principles, even those of the wise, what kind of things they avoid, and what kind they pursue.

What is evil to thee does not subsist in the ruling principle of another; nor yet in any turning and mutation of thy **corporeal**[2] covering. Where is it then? It is in that part of thee in which subsists the power of forming opinions about evils. Let this power then not form such opinions, and all

保持安靜。也就是說，讓它做出這樣的判斷：在好人和壞人身上都會發生的事情既不是好的也不是惡的。在那些違背自然而生活的人與按照自然而生活的人身上同樣發生的事情，無所謂是有悖於自然還是順應於自然。

常常把宇宙看作一個有生命之物，只有一個本質和一個靈魂，一切事物都與這個有生命之物的知覺相關聯，受到那唯一的衝動的支配。現在的一切事物的總和正是那將來的一切事物的源頭。其中錯綜複雜的聯繫正如同縱橫交錯的網一樣。

埃比克提圖常常說，人是一個帶軀體的小小靈魂。

變化不是壞事，透過變化而保持其存在也不是好事。

時間好像一條由發生的各種事件構成的湍急河流。你剛剛看見了

1.rottenness [`rɑtnnɪs] n. 腐敗

is well. And if that which is nearest to it, the poor body, is burnt, filled with matter and **rottenness**[1], nevertheless let the part which forms opinions about these things be quiet, that is, let it judge that nothing is either bad or good which can happen equally to the bad man and the good. For that which happens equally to him who lives contrary to nature and to him who lives according to nature, is neither according to nature nor contrary to nature.

Constantly regard the universe as one living being, having one substance and one soul; and observe how all things have reference to one perception, the perception of this one living being; and how all things act with one movement; and how all things are the cooperating causes of all things which exist; observe too the continuous spinning of the thread and the contexture of the web.

Thou art a little soul bearing about a corpse, as Epictetus used to say.

It is no evil for things to undergo change, and no good for things to subsist in consequence of change.

Time is like a river made up of the events which happen, and a violent

一個事物，它很快就淹沒在時間的急流裏被帶走，很快又會出現另一個事物來代替它，而這個事物也將很快消失。

這個世界上發生的每一件事都像春天的玫瑰和夏天的果實一樣平常。疾病、死亡、誹謗、背叛以及任何別的使愚蠢的人喜歡或煩惱的事情概莫能外。

所有後發生的事情都自然而然地，而且常常是前面發生的事情的延續。你必須要想到，世界上的事情並不是鬆散的、獨立的事件，而是一個必然的序列，它們有一個理性的聯繫。正如現存的事物都被安排得很和諧，即將產生的事物展示的不僅僅是一個序列，而且是某種奇妙的關聯。

你要始終牢牢銘記赫拉克利特的話：土死變水，水死變氣，氣死變火，然後再倒過來往復迴向。還要記住他說的，有人忘記了腳下的路通向何方，人們與每天相伴的、支配宇宙的理性爭吵。我們也不應該有覺得每日發生的事情似乎對我們來說是陌生的這種感覺；也想想我們說話和做事不應當像個睡著了的人一樣：我們覺得我們說了或做了，但其實不然；也不應當像習慣於受父母管制的孩子一樣，僅僅依據對我們的教誨而行動和言語。

1.treachery [`trɛtʃərɪ] n. 背叛
2.enumeration [ɪ,njumə`reʃən] n. 列舉

stream; for as soon as a thing has been seen, it is carried away, and another comes in its place, and this will be carried away too.

Everything which happens is as familiar and well known as the rose in spring and the fruit in summer; for such is disease, and death, and calumny, and **treachery**[1], and whatever else delights fools or vexes them.

In the series of things those which follow are always aptly fitted to those which have gone before; for this series is not like a mere **enumeration**[2] of disjointed things, which has only a necessary sequence, but it is a rational connection: and as all existing things are arranged together harmoniously, so the things which come into existence exhibit no mere succession, but a certain wonderful relationship.

Always remember the saying of Heraclitus, that the death of earth is to become water, and the death of water is to become air, and the death of air is to become fire, and reversely. And think too of him who forgets whither the way leads, and that men quarrel with that with which they are most constantly in communion, the reason which governs the universe; and the things which daily meet with seem to them strange: and consider that we ought not to act and speak as if we were asleep, for even in sleep we seem

　　即使有神告訴你，你明天或後天就會死去，你不會太在意是明天
還是後天吧，除非你是個無恥又懦弱的人，因為那又有什麼差別呢！
同樣，不要覺得許多年之後再死比起明天就死有什麼了不起。

　　你要經常想想：有多少醫生曾經對著他們的病人皺眉頭，神色凝
重，而現在他們自己卻去逝；有多少占星家預言了別人的死亡，又有
多少哲學家曾滔滔不絕地探討死亡或不朽，有多少英勇的將領曾殺戮
了多少人命，有多少國王和暴君，彷彿他們是永生的一樣，以可怕的
蠻橫手段濫用生殺大權，現在都死去了；有多少城邦及它的居民，比
如赫利斯、龐培、赫庫萊尼恩以及其他不可計數的城邦被完全毀滅。
再想想那些你知道的一個接一個死去的人。一個人在埋葬了別人之後
死了，另一個人又埋葬了他，埋了他的人不久之後也被埋到了土裏，
一個人是這樣，另一個人也是這樣，所有這些都是在很短的時間內
發生。這一切告訴我們要把世間萬物的生命看成只有短暫的一天，而
它們的價值非常低微，不值一提。人是什麼？昨天還只是一攤黏液組
成的軀體，再過幾天就將成為木乃伊或塵埃。因此，**你要遵循自然和**

1.canst [kænst] , 古英語中can的第二人稱單數現在式
2.astrologer [əˋstrɑlədʒɚ] n. 占星家
3.Helice，是Achaio的一座城池，於西元前373年被地震和海嘯所毀。
4.Pompeii，在西元79年維蘇威火山爆發時被岩漿毀滅。

to act and speak; and that we ought not, like children who learn from their parents, simply to act and speak as we have been taught.

If any god told thee that thou shalt die to-morrow, or certainly on the day after to-morrow, thou wouldst not care much whether it was on the third day or on the morrow, unless thou wast in the highest degree mean-spirited; for how small is the difference. So think it no great thing to die after as many years as thou **canst**[1] name rather than to-morrow.

Think continually how many physicians are dead after often contracting their eyebrows over the sick; and how many **astrologers**[2] after predicting with great pretensions the deaths of others; and how many philosophers after endless discourses on death or immortality; how many heroes after killing thousands; and how many tyrants who have used their power over men's lives with terrible insolence as if they were immortal; and how many cities are entirely dead, so to speak, **Helice**[3] and **Pompeii**[4] and **Herculaneum**[5], and others innumerable. Add to the reckoning all whom thou hast known, one after another. One man after burying another has been laid out dead, and another buries him: and all this in a short time. To conclude, always observe how **ephemeral**[6] and worthless human things are, and what was yesterday a little mucus to-morrow will be a mummy or

---

5.Herculaneum，也在維蘇威火山附近，同樣於西元79年被岩漿吞沒。
6.ephemeral [ɪˋfɛmərəl] adj. 短暫的

真理，想想人的生命有多短暫，然後安然地、滿足地離開人世，就像一顆橄欖成熟時掉落一樣，感激承托它的大地，感激它生於其上的樹木。

你要像那屹立於岸邊的礁石，任憑海浪不斷拍打，仍巍然不動，並讓周圍狂暴的海浪平靜下來。

哦，可憐的我啊，這樣的不幸居然發生在我的頭上！不，應該說，我是多麼幸福啊，雖然發生了這件事，但我仍能無憂無慮地繼續生活下去，既不因現在的遭遇而傷心，也不害怕將來發生的事。像這樣的事情可能會發生在任何人身上，但不是每一個人在遇到這種事情的時候都能夠繼續無憂無慮地生活下去。那麼為什麼我們非得把這認為是不幸而不是快樂呢？難道你會把那並不傷害人的本性的東西稱為不幸嗎？難道你能把一個並不違反人的目標和意志的東西看成是對人的本性的不幸嗎？你已經知道了人的本性的意志，那這發生在你身上的事情能夠阻止你做一個正直、高尚、節制、明智、細心、誠實、謙虛、自由的人嗎？難道它將阻止你擁有其他那些與人性相符合的好品性嗎？因為人的本性正是在這些品性中獲得所有屬於它自己的東西。不管你遇到了什麼難過的事，你都要記住這個原則：這件事本身都不是不幸的，如果你能坦然地接受它，就一定能獲得莫大的幸福。

1.deviation [ˌdivɪˋeʃən] n. 越軌

2.knowest為古英語中know的第二人稱單數（主語為thou時使用）。

3.magnanimous [mægˋnænəməs] adj. 寬大的

ashes. Pass then through this little space of time conformably to nature, and end thy journey in content, just as an olive falls off when it is ripe, blessing nature who produced it, and thanking the tree on which it grew.

Be like the promontory against which the waves continually break, but it stands firm and tames the fury of the water around it.

Unhappy am I because this has happened to me. – Not so, but happy am I, though this has happened to me, because I continue free from pain, neither crushed by the present nor fearing the future. For such a thing as this might have happened to every man; but every man would not have continued free from pain on such an occasion. Why then is that rather a misfortune than this a good fortune? And dost thou in all cases call that a man's misfortune, which is not a deviation from man's nature? And does a thing seem to thee to be a **deviation**[1] from man's nature, when it is not contrary to the will of man's nature? Well, thou **knowest**[2] the will of nature. Will then this which has happened prevent thee from being just, **magnanimous**[3], temperate, prudent, secure against inconsiderate opinions and **falsehood**[4]; will it prevent thee from having modesty, freedom, and everything else, by the presence of which man's nature obtains all that is its own? Remember too on every occasion which leads thee to **vexation**[5] to apply this principle: not that

---

4.falsehood [ˋfɔlsˌhʊd] n. 謊言
5.vexation [vɛkˋseʃən] n. 煩惱

想想那些長壽的、拼命享受生活的人，這個方法雖然很普通，但卻能很有效地克服對死亡的恐懼。他們比那些英年早逝的人獲得了更多的東西嗎？他們自己最後不也都回歸塵土嗎？比如克迪斯亞盧斯、費比厄斯、朱利安盧斯、萊皮德斯或任何在活著的時候曾給許多人送葬的人，他們自己最後也被人埋葬。生與死之間的距離是很短的，儘管生命這麼短，還帶著多少苦惱，伴隨著多少人情冷暖，可人們還是要拖著可憐的軀殼走完這段距離！所以不要在意生命的長短，如果你往後看的話，你將看到無盡的時間的混沌；如果你往前看，看到的也是無盡的時間的混沌。在這無盡的時間裏，活三天和活三代有什麼差別呢？

你要總是走捷徑，因為捷徑是最合乎自然的。同理，言行都要遵循健全的理性的指引。這種決心能使人擺脫所有苦惱、爭鬥、詭計和炫耀。

1.tenaciously [tɪˋneʃəslɪ] adv. 堅持地

2.Cadicianus，指長壽者或追求長壽者，生平不詳。

3.Fabius，也指長壽者或追求長壽者，可能指的是古羅馬政治家和將軍，西元前275年～西元前203年，他擔任5次執政官，2次獨裁者。

this is a misfortune, but that to bear it nobly is good fortune.

It is a vulgar, but still a useful help towards contempt of death, to pass in review those who have **tenaciously**[1] stuck to life. What more then have they gained than those who have died early? Certainly they lie in their tombs somewhere at last, **Cadicianus**[2], **Fabius**[3], **Julianus**[4], **Lepidus**[5], or any one else like them, who have carried out many to be buried, and then were carried out themselves. Altogether the interval is small between birth and death; and consider with how much trouble, and in company with what sort of people and in what a feeble body this interval is laboriously passed. Do not then consider life a thing of any value. For look to the immensity of time behind thee, and to the time which is before thee, another boundless space. In this infinity then what is the difference between him who lives three days and him who lives three generations?

Always run to the short way; and the short way is the natural: accordingly say and do everything in conformity with the soundest reason. For such a purpose frees a man from trouble, and warfare, and all artifice and ostentatious display.

4.Julianus，也指長壽者或追求長壽者，所指不明。

5.Lepidus，貪求長生不老，可能是古羅馬三執政之一的一位，全名Marcus Aemilius Lepidus（約西元前90年～西元前13年），三執政的另兩位是屋大維和安東尼。

第五卷

早晨當你不願起床時，你可隨時想到：我起來是去做一個人應該做的工作。難道我不願去做那些我生來要做的事嗎？難道我是為了躲在溫暖的被窩裏睡覺而生的嗎？「可這樣很舒服。」難道你是為了享樂而生的嗎？難道你不是應該一直有所作為嗎？難道你沒有看到世界上的小生靈，一草一木、燕子、螞蟻、蜘蛛和蜜蜂都在辛勤地、有條不紊地盡它們在宇宙中的職分，以保持宇宙的秩序井然嗎？難道你不願做人該做的工作嗎？難道你不應趕快去做那合乎你本性的事嗎？「但你也得休息啊。」對，你是要休息，自然也允許你足夠的休息和吃喝。但如果你超過了這些限制，超出了足夠的休息或吃喝的量，而該做的事卻不做。那麼，你肯定不愛你自己。如果你愛你自己，你就會愛你的本性和本性的意志。那些熱愛他們行業和技藝的人忙得憔悴不堪，廢寢忘食。難道你對你的本性的重視甚至還不如雜耍藝人對雜耍技藝、舞蹈家對舞藝、聚財者對他的金錢，或者虛榮者對他小小虛名的重視嗎？只要是他們喜歡做的事情，他們就願意為了它廢寢忘食。難道那有益於社會的工作比這還令人討厭，不值得你勞心勞力嗎？

1.risest 為古英語中 rise 的第二人稱單數（主語為 thou 時使用）。

2.goest 為古英語中 go 的第二人稱單數（主語為 thou 時使用）。

3.stoppest 為古英語中 stop 的第二人稱單數（主語為 thou 時使用）。

BOOK 5

In the morning when thou **risest**[1] unwillingly, let this thought be present – I am rising to the work of a human being. Why then am I dissatisfied if I am going to do the things for which I exist and for which I was brought into the world? Or have I been made for this, to lie in the bed-clothes and keep myself warm? – But this is more pleasant. – Dost thou exist then to take thy pleasure, and not at all for action or exertion? Dost thou not see the little plants, the little birds, the ants, the spiders, the bees working together to put in order their several parts of the universe? And art thou unwilling to do the work of a human being, and dost thou not make haste to do that which is according to thy nature? – But it is necessary to take rest also. – It is necessary: however nature has fixed bounds to this too: she has fixed bounds both to eating and drinking, and yet thou **goest**[2] beyond these bounds, beyond what is sufficient; yet in thy acts it is not so, but thou **stoppest**[3] short of what thou canst do. So thou **lovest**[4] not thyself, for if thou **didst**[5], thou wouldst love thy nature and her will. But those who love their several arts exhaust themselves in working at them unwashed and without food; but thou **valuest**[6] thy own nature less than the turner values the turning art, or

---

4.lovest 為古英語中 love 的第二人稱單數（主語為 thou 時使用）。

5.didst [dɪdst]，古英語中 did 的第二人稱單數

6.valuest 為古英語中 value 的第二人稱單數（主語為 thou 時使用）。

　　一個人如果拋棄了一切令人苦惱的、無益的念頭，立刻獲得心靈的平靜是多麼容易的事啊！

　　判斷出每一個符合你本性的言行，不要因別人的非議和指指點點而受到影響，從而改變你自己的想法。如果這麼說或這麼做是誠實的、正當的，就不要妄自菲薄。至於別人，他們有自己為人處世的指導原則，也有他們自己的打算。這不是你要考慮的，而是要勇往直前，沿著你自己的本性和人類共同的本性而前進，這兩者原本就是在同一條道路上。

　　我按照我的本性在人生道路上前進，直到我倒下了，向那日日供我呼吸的空氣裏吐出最後一口氣，倒在這塊大地上。這塊土地所提供的禮物和果實讓我父親得以耕種收穫，讓我的母親得以孕育我，讓我的奶媽得以哺育我，在這麼多年裏為我提供了食物和飲料。最後，它

1.vile [vaɪl] adj. 卑鄙的

the dancer the dancing art, or the lover of money values his money, or the vainglorious man his little glory. And such men, when they have a violent affection to a thing, choose neither to eat nor to sleep rather than to perfect the things which they care for. But are the acts which concern society more **vile**[1] in thy eyes and less worthy of thy labour?

How easy it is to repel and to wipe away every impression which is troublesome or unsuitable, and immediately to be in all tranquility.

Judge every word and deed which are according to nature to be fit for thee; and be not diverted by the blame which follows from any people nor by their words, but if a thing is good to be done or said, do not consider it unworthy of thee. For those persons have their peculiar leading principle and follow their peculiar movement; which things do not thou regard, but go straight on, following thy own nature and the common nature; and the way of both is one.

I go through the things which happen according to nature until I shall fall and rest, breathing out my breath into that element out of which I daily draw it in, and falling upon that earth out of which my father collected the seed, and my mother the blood, and my nurse the milk; out of which during

還默默忍受了我對它的踐踏、為所欲為，以及大肆地利用它來滿足自己的行為。

　　如果有人，因為你天生沒有機智雄辯的口才而不欣賞你，那就隨他們去吧。但是你也有許多別的品格，你不能說是你天生沒有的。那麼，展示一下在你力量之內的那些品格吧：真誠、莊重、勤勞、不沉溺享樂、不暴躁、知足常樂、善良、自由、節儉、不虛偽、高尚。難道你沒有看到不以本性無能和不適合為藉口，你可以立刻展示出多少種品德嗎？你還願意自甘墮落嗎？難道說你因為先天不足才被迫抱怨、卑微、諂媚，一會兒抱怨自己的身體，一會兒又要討好它，驕傲自負，做事草率，不得安寧嗎？不（神明作證），你早就應該從這些事情中解脫出來了，如果你沒有，那也只能是你天性遲鈍，不能怨天尤人；但如果真是天性遲鈍，你也要訓練自己，不能忽略你的遲鈍或自甘遲鈍。

　　有一種人，當他為別人做了一件好事之後，就會把它記到賬上，

1.sayest 為古英語中 say 的第二人稱單數（主語為 thou 時使用）。
2.remainest 為古英語中 remain 的第二人稱單數（主語為 thou 時使用）。
3.dulness 為古英語中 dullness 的拼寫方式。

so many years I have been supplied with food and drink; which bears me when I tread on it and abuse it for so many purposes.

Thou **sayest**[1], Men cannot admire the sharpness of thy wits. – Be it so: but there are many other things of which thou canst not say, I am not formed for them by nature. Show those qualities then which are altogether in thy power, sincerity, gravity, endurance of labour, aversion to pleasure, contentment with thy portion and with few things, benevolence, frankness, no love of superfluity, freedom from trifling magnanimity. Dost thou not see how many qualities thou art immediately able to exhibit, in which there is no excuse of natural incapacity and unfitness, and yet thou still **remainest**[2] voluntarily below the mark? Or art thou compelled through being defectively furnished by nature to murmur, and to be stingy, and to flatter, and to find fault with thy poor body, and to try to please men, and to make great display, and to be so restless in thy mind? No, by the gods: but thou mightest have been delivered from these things long ago. Only if in truth thou canst be charged with being rather slow and dull of comprehension, thou must exert thyself about this also, not neglecting it nor yet taking pleasure in thy **dulness**[3].

One man, when he has done a service to another, is ready to set it down

準備以後索取回報。還有人雖然不要求回報，但他們還是覺得別人欠他們人情，他們把自己做過的事記得非常清楚。還有人在做了這樣的好事之後自己並沒有意識到，就像一株葡萄藤一樣，在它結出葡萄之後就感到心滿意足了，並不會再索取什麼回報。正如馬跑完了路程，獵狗追到了獵物，蜜蜂釀好了蜜。所以一個人做了一件好事，不會要求其他人過來看，而是會繼續做另一件好事，正像已經結過葡萄的葡萄藤準備在下一個季節到來的時候繼續結果一樣。一個人必須成為這樣的人，即在某種意義上如此做卻不留意？是的。但是，觀察一個人在做什麼也是必須的，因為有人會說：留意到以群體的方式工作，並且渴望他的同伴也意識到這一點是社會動物的特徵。你說得確實沒錯，但你並沒有理解現在所說的，因此你將成為我前面所說的那些人中的一個，因為他們也是受到似是而非的理性的指引。但如果你願意理解現在所說的話的意義，就不要害怕你會因此忽略任何有益社會的行為。

　　雅典人祈禱的方式是這樣的：降雨吧，降雨吧，親愛的宙斯，使雨降落到屬於雅典人的每一寸土地上吧。我們不是乾脆就不要祈禱，

to his account as a favour conferred. Another is not ready to do this, but still in his own mind he thinks of the man as his debtor, and he knows what he has done. A third in a manner does not even know what he has done, but he is like a vine which has produced grapes, and seeks for nothing more after it has once produced its proper fruit. As a horse when he has run, a dog when he has tracked the game, a bee when it has made the honey, so a man when he has done a good act, does not call out for others to come and see, but he goes on to another act, as a vine goes on to produce again the grapes in season. – Must a man then be one of these, who in a manner act thus without observing it? – Yes. – But this very thing is necessary, the observation of what a man is doing: for, it may be said, it is characteristic of the social animal to perceive that he is working in a social manner, and indeed to wish that his social partner also should perceive it. – It is true what thou sayest, but thou dost not rightly understand what is now said: and for this reason thou wilt become one of those of whom I spoke before, for even they are misled by a certain show of reason. But if thou wilt choose to understand the meaning of what is said, do not fear that for this reason thou wilt omit any social act.

A prayer of the Athenians: Rain, rain, O dear Zeus, down on the ploughed fields of the Athenians and on the plains. – In truth we ought not

不然就要像他們這樣簡單而高尚地祈禱。

　　當醫生讓一個病人練騎馬，讓另一個病人洗冷水浴，讓第三個病人赤腳走路，對此我們都可以理解。同樣地，當宇宙讓這個人生病、失明，或是喪失他所寶貴的東西等諸如此類，對此我們也應該理解。在第一種情況裏，醫生給人開藥方意味著他把一些健康有益的東西給了這個人；在後一種情況裏，每個人身上發生的事情在某種意義上都是都是合乎命運的安排。我們說這些事情適合我們正如此意，就像工匠談起牆上或是金字塔上的方磚一樣，他們以某種方式將方磚聯結在一起，說它們是適合的。總的說來，只有一種適合，即和諧。正如整個宇宙是由無數個體所構成的整體一樣，必然性（命運）也是由所有的原因所構成的一個原因。我現在所說的，就連傻瓜也知道，因為他們經常說：這是他命中註定要發生的事情，因此這件事落到了他的頭上，就好像是醫生特別為他開設的藥方。那麼，讓我們像接受醫生的藥方一樣來接受這些事情吧！雖然我們會發現在他開的藥方中有許多苦口良藥，但為了健康，我們都應接受。共同的本性所斷定的事物的完善和完成是有益的，你也要像斷定健康一樣肯定它。要接受每一件發生的事情，即使它看起來不那麼好，但它歸根結底是為了宇宙的健康與宇宙的幸福和發展。因為如果這件事對整體沒有好處，那它就不會發生了。不論是什麼東西，自然都不會讓任何會引起與支配它的東西不相合的事情發生。下面這兩個理由能使你安心接受發生在你身上

1.Aesculapius，指的是羅馬神話中的神醫，手持靈蛇纏繞的木杖。
2.pyramid [`pɪrəmɪd] n. 金字塔

to pray at all, or we ought to pray in this simple and noble fashion.

Just as we must understand when it is said, That **Aesculapius**[1] prescribed to this man horse-exercise, or bathing in cold water or going without shoes; so we must understand it when it is said, That the nature of the universe prescribed to this man disease or mutilation or loss or anything else of the kind. For in the first case Prescribed means something like this: he prescribed this for this man as a thing adapted to procure health; and in the second case it means: That which happens to (or, suits) every man is fixed in a manner for him suitably to his destiny. For this is what we mean when we say that things are suitable to us, as the workmen say of squared stones in walls or the **pyramids**[2], that they are suitable, when they fit them to one another in some kind of connexion. For there is altogether one fitness, harmony. And as the universe is made up out of all bodies to be such a body as it is, so out of all existing causes necessity (destiny) is made up to be such a cause as it is. And even those who are completely ignorant understand what I mean, for they say, It (necessity, destiny) brought this to such a person. – This then was brought and this was prescribed to him. Let us then receive these things, as well as those which Aesculapius prescribes. Many as a matter of course even among his prescriptions are disagreeable, but we accept them in the hope of health. Let the perfecting and accomplishment

的一切事情：第一，它是為你而做的，是給你開的藥方，並且在宇宙之初就和你的命運緊緊聯繫；第二，對管理宇宙的力量甚至是對宇宙的延續而言，發生在每個人身上的事情都是一種幸福和完善的原因。如果你從各個部分或各個原因的聯結與延續中間打斷任何事情，就破壞了整體的完整。就像你經常對發生的事情感到不滿意並且企圖以某種方式消滅一切時，只要力所能及，你就會破壞。

　　如果你根據正確的原則卻沒有取得成功，不要不滿，不要沮喪，也不要絕望。失敗了就從頭再來，如果你做的大部分合乎你的本性，你應該對此滿足，熱愛你所回歸的家園，但不要像回到老師一樣，而

1.cuttest 為古英語中 cut 的第二人稱單數（主語為 thou 時使用）。
2.triest 為古英語中 try 的第二人稱單數（主語為 thou 時使用）。
3.bast 為古英語中 be 的第二人稱單數（主語為 thou 時使用）。

of the things, which the common nature judges to be good, be judged by thee to be of the same kind as thy health. And so accept everything which happens, even if it seem disagreeable, because it leads to this, to the health of the universe and to the prosperity and felicity of Zeus (the universe). For he would not have brought on any man what he has brought, if it were not useful for the whole. Neither does the nature of anything, whatever it may be, cause anything which is not suitable to that which is directed by it. For two reasons then it is right to be content with that which happens to thee; the one, because it was done for thee and prescribed for thee, and in a manner had reference to thee, originally from the most ancient causes spun with thy destiny; and the other, because even that which comes severally to every man is to the power which administers the universe a cause of felicity and perfection, nay even of its very continuance. For the integrity of the whole is mutilated, if thou **cuttest**[1] off anything whatever from the conjunction and the continuity either of the parts or of the causes. And thou dost cut off, as far as it is in thy power, when thou art dissatisfied, and in a manner **triest**[2] to put anything out of the way.

Be not disgusted, nor discouraged, nor dissatisfied, if thou dost not succeed in doing everything according to right principles; but when thou **bast**[3] failed, return back again, and be content if the greater part of what

要像眼睛腫了的那些人看到海綿或雞蛋那樣，或者像那些想得到一塊膏藥，或一次熱敷的病人一樣。這樣你就不會覺得遵循理性是虛有其表，就能從中得到從容自在。記住，哲學僅要求你的本性所要求的事情，你所要求的卻是悖於你本性的東西。你可能反駁，還有什麼事比我現在做的更使人愉悅呢？但是這不正是快樂欺騙我們之所在嗎？再想想慷慨、真正的自由、真正的簡單、平靜、虔誠，這些是不是更讓人快樂。當你想到那依賴於理解和認識能力去解決一切問題是多麼自在和快樂的時候，還能有什麼比智慧本身更令人愉悅呢？

至於這世界上的事物，它們的真實面目在一定程度上總是模糊不清的，以致在許多哲學家（並非庸俗的哲學家）看來，它們幾乎無法理解，即使是斯多噶派哲學家，他們也很難理解。我們的認同都是變化無常的，哪有人從來不變呢？從你的思想再到事物本身，它們的存在是多麼短促和卑微，可能被一個卑鄙的可憐蟲、娼妓或強盜所佔有。再想想那些你經常見面的人的性格，我們就連那些個性最可愛最親切的人都很難忍受，更不必說容忍我們自己了。一切都是如此的黑

1.doest 為古英語中 do 的第二人稱單數（主語為 thou 時使用）。

2.sore [sor] adj. 悲痛的

3.sponge [spʌndʒ] n. 海綿

thou **doest**[1] is consistent with man's nature, and love this to which thou returnest; and do not return to philosophy as if she were a master, but act like those who have **sore**[2] eyes and apply a bit of **sponge**[3] and egg, or as another applies a plaster, or **drenching**[4] with water. For thus thou wilt not fail to obey reason, and thou wilt repose in it. And remember that philosophy requires only the things which thy nature requires; but thou wouldst have something else which is not according to nature. – It may be objected, Why what is more agreeable than this which I am doing? – But is not this the very reason why pleasure deceives us? And consider if magnanimity, freedom, simplicity, equanimity, piety, are not more agreeable. For what is more agreeable than wisdom itself, when thou **thinkest**[5] of the security and the happy course of all things which depend on the faculty of understanding and knowledge?

Things are in such a kind of envelopment that they have seemed to philosophers, not a few nor those common philosophers, altogether unintelligible; nay even to the Stoics themselves they seem difficult to understand. And all our assent is changeable; for where is the man who never changes? Carry thy thoughts then to the objects themselves, and consider how short-lived they are and worthless, and that they may be in the possession of a filthy wretch or a whore or a robber. Then turn to the

---

4.drench [drɛntʃ] vt. 熱敷
5.thinkest 為古英語中 think 的第二人稱單數（主語為 thou 時使用）。

暗和骯髒，時間在永無休止的流動，事物在不停地變化。人的一切行為也處在不停地變化之中，很難想像有什麼值得高度讚揚甚或值得認真追求的東西。相反，你的責任是必須安心等待自然的分解，同時也不要迫不及待，而是要想著這兩點讓自己得到安寧：一是有悖宇宙本性的事情是不會發生在你身上；二是你有能力不做有悖神和內在神性的事情，沒有人可以迫使你如此做。

我現在把我自己的靈魂用於什麼事情上呢？不管在什麼場合你都必須不時問自己這個問題；我身上的被人們稱為主宰原則的那部分現在有些什麼呢？我現在擁有的靈魂屬於什麼人呢？是孩子的靈魂？抑或是年輕人的、婦人的、暴君的、家畜的還是野獸的？

從這段話中，你可以看出那些在絕大部分人看來是好的事物本質為何。如果有人受到像謹慎、節制、正義、堅定這些好品格──它們也確實是好的──的耳濡目染之後，他就無法忍受聽到別的其他東西。一個人把大多數人認為是好的當作是好的，他就會傾聽並且樂於接受喜劇作家所說的。因而，大多數人都意識到這種差別。不然的話，當我們聽到追求財富、追求奢侈和名聲 這樣的俏皮話時就不會惱怒反駁而是樂於接受。接著問問我們自己，你是否會重視這些事物，是否會認

morals of those who live with thee, and it is hardly possible to endure even the most agreeable of them, to say nothing of a man being hardly able to endure himself. In such darkness then and dirt and in so constant a flux both of substance and of time, and of motion and of things moved, what there is worth being highly prized or even an object of serious pursuit, I cannot imagine. But on the contrary it is a man's duty to comfort himself, and to wait for the natural dissolution and not to be vexed at the delay, but to rest in these principles only: the one, that nothing will happen to me which is not conformable to the nature of the universe; and the other, that it is in my power never to act contrary to my god and daemon: for there is no man who will compel me to this.

About what am I now employing my own soul? On every occasion I must ask myself this question, and inquire, what have I now in this part of me which they call the ruling principle? And whose soul have I now? That of a child, or of a young man, or of a feeble woman, or of a tyrant, or of a domestic animal, or of a wild beast?

What kind of things those are which appear good to the many, we may learn even from this. For if any man should conceive certain things as being really good, such as prudence, temperance, justice, fortitude, he would not after having first conceived these endure to listen to anything which should not be in harmony with what is really good. But if a man has first conceived as good the things which appear to the many to be good, he will listen and readily receive as very applicable that which was said by the comic writer.

為它們是好的？是否在心裏抱有對它們的成見之後喜劇作家的話還可以恰當地應用於它們？喜劇作家筆下的那個人，我們可以說他什麼都不缺，但基於純粹的富足卻沒有辦法使自己得到安寧。

我是由形式和物質組成的，它們都不會完全消失，歸於虛無，因為我也不是來自虛無。我身上的每一部分都將發生轉變，轉移到宇宙的某一部分，在一段時間之後再轉移到宇宙的另一部分，如此生生不息。我之所以存在也是經過了這種變化，那些生我的人也是這樣，我們可以這樣無止盡地向上追溯。換句話說，即使是宇宙的支配也終有確定的期限。

理智和理性的藝術（哲學）對於它們自身和自身的工作是一種自足的力量。它們是以它們自己的第一原則作為起點的，它們遵從這種原則開闢著它們的道路，直到達到那規定給它們的終點。也就是因為這個原因，這種行為被稱為正確的，這表示這樣的行為是沿著正確的道路行進的。

人不應擁有那些他作為人不應擁有的東西。它們不是人所需求

Thus even the many perceive the difference. For were it not so, this saying would not offend and would not be rejected in the first case, while we receive it when it is said of wealth, and of the means which further luxury and fame, as said fitly and wittily. Go on then and ask if we should value and think those things to be good, to which after their first conception in the mind the words of the comic writer might be aptly applied – that he who has them, through pure abundance has not a place to ease himself in.

I am composed of the formal and the material; and neither of them will perish into non-existence, as neither of them came into existence out of non-existence. Every part of me then will be reduced by change into some part of the universe, and that again will change into another part of the universe, and so on for ever. And by consequence of such a change I too exist, and those who begot me, and so on for ever in the other direction. For nothing hinders us from saying so, even if the universe is administered according to definite periods of revolution.

Reason and the reasoning art (philosophy) are powers which are sufficient for themselves and for their own works. They move then from a first principle which is their own, and they make their way to the end which is proposed to them; and this is the reason why such acts are named catorthoseis or right acts, which word signifies that they proceed by the right road.

None of these things ought to be called a man's, which do not belong

的，也不符合人的本性，這些行為的完成對於人性毫無益處。人的目標不在於這些事情上，達成人生目標（即善）也不在於這些事情上。如果這些外在的俗事有利於人，那一個人輕視和反對它們就是不對的，沒有這些俗事纏身的人也就不值得讚揚；如果這些事物確是好的，那麼自願擺脫它們的人也就很難說是好的。相反，我們看到一個人越是將自己從這些外在的事物或光環中抽離出來，越是能耐心地忍受這損失，那他就愈是值得嘉獎。

你的思想和平時的思考將會決定你的心靈，因為靈魂會受到思想的薰陶。經常用這些想法去影響你的靈魂吧！不管你住在哪裡，你都有能力讓自己過得幸福快樂。你必須生活在王宮中，好吧，你在王宮中也可以活得很好。再想想每個事物產生的目的是什麼，因為這個目的它產生，並朝向這個目的前進，它的目的就在於它前進的地方，它的目的也是事物優勢及好處。理性動物的善就在於社會，因為我們是為社會而造的，這個道理前文已經闡明。難道還會有人問：是不是低等的東西都要服從高等的東西？有生命的東西要優於沒有生命的東西？有理性的生命又要優於那些沒有理性的生命？

to a man, as man. They are not required of a man, nor does man's nature promise them, nor are they the means of man's nature attaining its end. Neither then does the end of man lie in these things, nor yet that which aids to the accomplishment of this end, and that which aids towards this end is that which is good. Besides, if any of these things did belong to man, it would not be right for a man to despise them and to set himself against them; nor would a man be worthy of praise who showed that he did not want these things, nor would he who stinted himself in any of them be good, if indeed these things were good. But now the more of these things a man deprives himself of, or of other things like them, or even when he is deprived of any of them, the more patiently he endures the loss, just in the same degree he is a better man.

Such as are thy habitual thoughts, such also will be the character of thy mind; for the soul is dyed by the thoughts. Dye it then with a continuous series of such thoughts as these: for instance, that where a man can live, there he can also live well. But he must live in a palace – well then, he can also live well in a palace. And again, consider that for whatever purpose each thing has been constituted, for this it has been constituted, and towards this it is carried; and its end is in that towards which it is carried; and where the end is, there also is the advantage and the good of each thing. Now the good for the reasonable animal is society; for that we are made for society has been shown above. Is it not plain that the inferior exist for the sake of the superior? But the things which have life are superior to those which have not life, and of those which have life the superior are those which have

瘋子會想要那些他不可能得到的東西，惡人也可能這樣做。

　　沒有什麼發生在人身上的事情是他本性所不能承擔的。同樣的事情也會發生在別人身上，若不是因為他沒有意識到這件事的發生，就是因為他故意要表現得很堅定，竟不因此而受到傷害。無知和自負竟能壓倒智慧，難道不是令人很難過的事情嗎？

　　至於事情本身，它們不會影響到靈魂，即使是最低程度上的；它們既不能支配靈魂，也沒有任何辦法可以左右它或者駕馭它。只有**靈魂自己才能改變和駕馭自己**；而且它還能確保它做出一切判斷都是適合的，對於呈現於面前的事物都如此判斷。

　　從某一方面來看，別人與我們的關係最為密切，所以我們必須要對他們行善並忍受他們。但如果有人反對我們合理的行為時，那我就會對他毫不在乎，就像面對太陽、面對風或某種野獸一樣。他們有時候可能確實能阻礙我的行動，但他們並不能改變我的想法和性情，因為我的想法和性情能夠見機行事。由於心靈把每一障礙扭轉為對它活

1.conceit [kən`sit] n. 自負；自滿

reason.

To seek what is impossible is madness: and it is impossible that the bad should not do something of this kind.

Nothing happens to any man which he is not formed by nature to bear. The same things happen to another, and either because he does not see that they have happened or because he would show a great spirit he is firm and remains unharmed. It is a shame then that ignorance and **conceit**[1] should be stronger than wisdom.

Things themselves touch not the soul, not in the least degree; nor have they admission to the soul, nor can they turn or move the soul: but the soul turns and moves itself alone, and whatever judgments it may think proper to make, such it makes for itself the things which present themselves to it.

In one respect man is the nearest thing to me, so far as I must do good to men and endure them. But so far as some men make themselves obstacles to my proper acts, man becomes to me one of the things which are indifferent, no less than the sun or wind or a wild beast. Now it is true that these may impede my action, but they are no **impediments**[1] to my affects and

動有幫助的事物，使它們成為有利於實現目標的動力，這樣原本是障礙的東西卻變成幫助我們在這條路上行進的事物。

　　尊重那宇宙中最主要、最強大的力量吧，就是這種力量在利用、掌控著萬事萬物。同樣，也要尊重你心中那個最主要、最強大的力量，它和我們現在所說的那種力量具有同樣的性質。它支配著你的一切，控制著你的生活。

　　那不損害城邦的事情，不會損害任何公民。每個傷害都適用這種規則：如果整個城邦不會因此而受到損害，那我當然也不會！如果整個城邦受到傷害，切莫遷怒於那個傷害城邦之人，而是指出錯誤所在，讓他們明白。

　　要經常想想所有存在的事物消失得多麼迅速，瞬間就不見蹤影。所有的事物在我們看來就像是處在川流不息的河流中，所有的行為都在不斷變化，各種因果也有萬千的變化，世上幾乎沒有什麼可以說是永恆穩定的。再想想你身邊的事物，都消失於過去和未來的無限深淵之中。那麼，那些因為這些事物而自得或分心、長時間受到困擾的

1.impediment [ɪmˋpɛdəmənt] n. 阻礙

disposition, which have the power of acting conditionally and changing: for the mind converts and changes every hindrance to its activity into an aid; and so that which is a hindrance is made a furtherance to an act; and that which is an obstacle on the road helps us on this road.

Reverence that which is best in the universe; and this is that which makes use of all things and directs all things. And in like manner also reverence that which is best in thyself; and this is of the same kind as that. For in thyself also, that which makes use of everything else, is this, and thy life is directed by this.

That which does no harm to the state, does no harm to the citizen. In the case of every appearance of harm apply this rule: if the state is not harmed by this, neither am I harmed. But if the state is harmed, thou must not be angry with him who does harm to the state. Show him where his error is.

Often think of the rapidity with which things pass by and disappear, both the things which are and the things which are produced. For substance is like a river in a continual flow, and the activities of things are in constant change, and the causes work in infinite varieties; and there is hardly anything which stands still. And consider this which is near to thee, this

人，似乎顯得愚昧？

想想你只是整個宇宙微不足道的一部分；你的生命與整個宇宙的時間相比是非常短暫的；你的命運在整個宇宙的命運中又是多麼渺小的一部分啊！

還要想想：如果別人對我言行不佳，那是他的事情；他有自己的性情，有自己的行為。同時，宇宙的本性要我有的我均擁有，我現在所為都是我的本性要我做的。

不要讓你靈魂中首要和支配的力量受肉體的痛苦或快樂所左右，也不要讓它和肉體的痛苦、快樂混在一起，而是要讓它限定自己的活動範圍，讓那些感受留在它們應該在的地方。不過，你畢竟是一個靈魂和肉體統一的生物，當這些感情反映在你的思想和靈魂的時候，你不要急著抗拒這種感覺，因為它是自然的。你要注意的是不要讓支配你的那一部分對這一感覺加上好壞的判斷。

1.abyss [ə`bɪs] n. 深淵

boundless **abyss**[1] of the past and of the future in which all things disappear. How then is he not a fool who is puffed up with such things or plagued about them and makes himself miserable? for they vex him only for a time, and a short time.

Think of the universal substance, of which thou hast a very small portion; and of universal time, of which a short and indivisible interval has been assigned to thee; and of that which is fixed by destiny, and how small a part of it thou art.

Does another do me wrong? Let him look to it. He has his own disposition, his own activity. I now have what the universal nature wills me to have; and I do what my nature now wills me to do.

Let the part of thy soul which leads and governs be undisturbed by the movements in the flesh, whether of pleasure or of pain; and let it not unite with them, but let it circumscribe itself and limit those affects to their parts. But when these affects rise up to the mind by virtue of that other sympathy that naturally exists in a body which is all one, then thou must not strive to resist the sensation, for it is natural: but let not the ruling part of itself add to the sensation the opinion that it is either good or bad.

　　我們要和神靈生活在一起。和神靈生活在一起的人會一直檢視自己的靈魂，欣然接受命運的安排，並遵照內在的神性行事。這個內在的神性即宙斯指派給人的守護者和引領者，同時也是你自身的一部分。這就是人的理解力和理性。

　　不要對那些患有狐臭或口臭的人生氣。他們也莫何奈何？他天生會呼吸，有腋下，所以必然會有氣味。可能你會說：「啊，可是那個人應該有自知之明，應該知道他一靠近就會令人難受。」而你（願神保佑你！）也有理性，那就用你的理性來引導他的理性吧，告訴他他錯在哪裏，勸誡他。如果他肯聽你的話，你就能醫治他，沒必要生氣。你既非悲劇演員，亦非娼妓⋯⋯

　　正如你離開時打算繼續生活，你有能力生活在此。但是如果別人不允許，你就放棄生命吧，但是要像沒有受到傷害一樣離開。房裏有煙，我就離開這裏這有何困難呢？除非我被趕出去，不然我就會自由地生活下去；亦沒有人能阻止我做我想做的事，我會按照一個理性的和社會動物的本性去做我想做的事。

1.armpit [ˋɑrm͵pɪt] n. 腋下
2.emanation [͵ɛməˋneʃən] n. 發射物
3.admonish [ədˋmɑnɪʃ] vt. 勸告
4.intendest為古英語中intend的第二人稱單數（主語為thou時使用）。

Live with the gods. And he does live with the gods who constantly shows to them, his own soul is satisfied with that which is assigned to him, and that it does all that the daemon wishes, which Zeus hath given to every man for his guardian and guide, a portion of himself. And this is every man's understanding and reason.

Art thou angry with him whose **armpits**[1] stink? Art thou angry with him whose mouth smells foul? What good will this danger do thee? He has such a mouth, he has such arm-pits: it is necessary that such an **emanation**[2] must come from such things; but the man has reason, it will be said, and he is able, if he takes pain, to discover wherein he offends; I wish thee well of thy discovery. Well then, and thou hast reason: by thy rational faculty stir up his rational faculty; show him his error, **admonish**[3] him. For if he listens, thou wilt cure him, and there is no need of anger. Neither tragic actor nor whore.

As thou **intendest**[4] to live when thou art gone out, ...so it is in thy power to live here. But if men do not permit thee, then get away out of life, yet so as if thou wert suffering no harm. **The house is smoky, and I quit it**[5]. Why dost thou think that this is any trouble? But so long as nothing of the kind drives me out, I remain, am free, and no man shall hinder me from doing what I choose; and I choose to do what is according to the nature of the

---

5.這是指一句諺語:「有三種東西可以把人趕出屋子:煙霧、屋頂漏水、吵架的妻子。」

控制宇宙的理智是社會性的。它為高等的事物創造出低等的事物，並使他們與高等的事物相互適應。難道你沒看到它使事物高下有序，相互合作嗎？它分配給每一事物以適當的份額使它們各得其所，它把事物相互結合使這些事物和諧相處。

你是怎樣對待神靈、父母、兄弟、妻子、孩子、老師、那些從小照顧你的人、朋友、同胞以及奴隸的呢？你是不是從來沒有在言行上傷害過他們呢？要記住你已經經歷了多少事，忍受了多少磨難，現在你的生命已經圓滿了，你的使命也已經完成。還有，你做過了多少好事？你看淡過多少你所經歷的快樂和痛苦？你輕視過多少被世人認為是榮耀的事？你又和善謹慎地面對過多少不理性的人呢？

衝動、無知的靈魂怎麼會困擾那些謹慎博學的人呢？什麼靈魂才是謹慎博學的呢？這種靈魂知道事物的因果，知道那隱含在整個宇宙

1.hast [hæst]，古英語中 have 的第二人稱單數現在式
2.hitherto [ˌhɪðɚˋtu] adv. 至此

rational and social animal.

The intelligence of the universe is social. Accordingly it has made the inferior things for the sake of the superior, and it has fitted the superior to one another. Thou seest how it has subordinated, coordinated and assigned to everything its proper portion, and has brought together into concord with one another the things which are the best.

How hast thou behaved hitherto to the gods, thy parents, brethren, children, teachers, to those who looked after thy infancy, to thy friends, kinsfolk, to thy slaves? Consider if thou **hast**[1] **hitherto**[2] behaved to all in such a way that this may be said of thee: "Never has wronged a man in deed or word". And call to recollection both how many things thou hast passed through, and how many things thou hast been able to endure and that the history of thy life is now complete and thy service is ended: and how many beautiful things thou hast seen: and how many pleasures and pains thou hast despised; and how many things called honourable thou hast spurned; and to how many ill-minded folks thou hast shown a kind disposition.

Why do unskilled and ignorant souls disturb him who has skill and knowledge? What soul then has skill and knowledge? That which knows

物質中的理性所在，知道這理性能夠支配整個宇宙的循環往復，生生不息。

　　在很短的時間內，你將化為灰塵、骷髏或只是一個名字，甚至可能連名字都沒有。名字只是空洞的聲音和回聲而已。**那些你今生最重視的東西本身都是虛無、易朽和不值一提的。**這些事情也不過像小狗一樣互相撕咬，或像沒有教養的孩子們一樣一會笑、一會哭。至於信仰、謙虛、正義和真理，正如某一位詩人所說，它們早已拋開了塵世，隱居到了天上。

　　那是什麼讓你留戀這個塵世呢？既然我們可感知的東西是如此多變，如此不定，既然我們的感官既遲鈍又容易犯錯，我們的靈魂不過是從血液中升騰出來的一股煙氣，名聲榮耀也不過是一場空虛，那麼留在這個世界是為了什麼呢？是心滿意足地安心等待生命的消逝或**轉變**。但是當那一刻來臨的時候，什麼能使你心滿意足呢？只有敬奉和頌揚神明，與人為善，要忍受他們，並堅持不傷害他們才能感到滿足。至於屬於你可憐的軀殼或是生命的所有外在物質，你要記住它們既不是你的，也不是你所能掌控的。

　　如果你能選擇正確的道路，用正確的方法思考和行動，你就能寧

1.thine 為古英語中 thou 的所有格代名詞（＝ yours）。

beginning and end, and knows the reason which pervades all substance and through all time by fixed periods (revolutions) administers the universe.

Soon, very soon, thou wilt be ashes, or a skeleton, and either a name or not even a name; but name is sound and echo. And the things which are much valued in life are empty and rotten and trifling, and like little dogs biting one another, and little children quarrelling, laughing, and then straightway weeping. But fidelity and modesty and justice and truth are fled up to Olympus from the wide-spread earth.

What then is there which still detains thee here? If the objects of sense are easily changed and never stand still, and the organs of perception are dull and easily receive false impressions; and the poor soul itself is an exhalation from blood. But to have good repute amidst such a world as this is an empty thing. Why then dost thou not wait in tranquility for thy end, whether it is extinction or removal to another state? And until that time comes, what is sufficient? Why, what else than to venerate the gods and bless them, and to do good to men, and to practise tolerance and self-restraint; but as to everything which is beyond the limits of the poor flesh and breath, to remember that this is neither **thine**[1] nor in thy power.

Thou canst pass thy life in an equable flow of happiness, if thou canst go

靜、幸福地度過你的一生。這兩樣東西共同存在於神、人以及所有理
性的靈魂中：首先，不被別人所阻礙；其次，堅持並施行正義以尋求
善，慾望也因此而得以消除。

如果這不是我自己的惡，也不是源自我的惡，公眾利益也沒有因
此受到損害，那我為什麼要為它苦惱呢？什麼行為會對公眾利益造成
損害呢？

不要總是被假象和大眾的看法牽著鼻子走，而是要根據你的能力
和情況幫助別人。如果他們蒙受的是一些無關緊要的物質上的損失，
不要認為他們會因此真正受到損害。這是不對的，你應該像喜劇裏的
老僕人一樣，在他即將離開人世的時候，回顧他撫育的孩子的巔峰時
期，記住這是巔峰時期。你也要這樣做。

在講壇上大聲叫喊又有何用呢？人啊，難道你忘記了這些事物
是什麼嗎？是的，別人很關心也很重視它們。所以你也要做一個傻瓜
嗎？

by the right way, and think and act in the right way. These two things are common both to the soul of God and to the soul of man, and to the soul of every rational being, not to be hindered by another; and to hold good to consist in the disposition to justice and the practice of it, and in this to let thy desire find its termination.

If this is neither my own badness, nor an effect of my own badness, and the common weal is not injured, why am I troubled about it? And what is the harm to the common weal?

Do not be carried along inconsidera- tely by the appearance of things, but give help to all according to thy ability and their fitness; and if they should have sustained loss in matters which are indifferent, do not imagine this to be a damage. For it is a bad habit. But as the old man, when he went away, asked back his foster-child's top, remembering that it was a top, so do thou in this case also.

When thou art calling out on the Rostra, hast thou forgotten, man, what these things are? – Yes; but they are objects of great concern to these people – wilt thou too then be made a fool for these things?

　　我曾經很幸運，但是卻被我搞砸了，而且我還不知道我如何丟失的。但是所謂幸運，就是給自己安排運氣，而好運氣就是靈魂好的意向、好的情緒和好的行動。

I was once a fortunate man, but I lost it, I know not how. – But fortunate means that a man has assigned to himself a good fortune: and a good fortune is good disposition of the soul, good emotions, good actions.

第六卷

宇宙的本質是馴良、順服的，那支配著它的理性自身沒有任何原因行惡。因為它本身毫無惡意。它不會行惡，也不會傷害任何事物，所有的事物都是根據這一理性產生和完善的。

如果你在履行你的職責，那麼不管你是凍得發抖還是感到非常溫暖；不管你是正在昏睡還是剛從美夢中醒來；不管你是被人指責還是被人讚揚；也不管你是正在死亡的邊緣或是做別的什麼事情，你都不要在意。因為這是我們的一種活動，透過這種活動我們死去：在這種活動中，做好手中的事也就足夠了。

要反觀自身，不要讓任何正當的品質或有價值的東西在你真正意識到它們的價值之前就被錯過。

所有存在的事物很快都要改變，或者將回歸於氣體（如果這樣的話，那麼所有事物都將合而為一）；或者將被分解，散落到世界各地。

1.malice [`mælɪs] n. 惡意
2.drowsy [`draʊzɪ] adj. 昏昏欲睡的
3.vapour [`vepɚ] n. 水汽

BOOK 6

The substance of the universe is obedient and compliant; and the reason which governs it has in itself no cause for doing evil, for it has no **malice**[1], nor does it do evil to anything, nor is anything harmed by it. But all things are made and perfected according to this reason.

Let it make no difference to thee whether thou art cold or warm, if thou art doing thy duty; and whether thou art **drowsy**[2] or satisfied with sleep; and whether ill-spoken of or praised; and whether dying or doing something else. For it is one of the acts of life, this act by which we die: it is sufficient then in this act also to do well what we have in hand.

Look within. Let neither the peculiar quality of anything nor its value escape thee.

All existing things soon change, and they will either be reduced to **vapour**[3], if indeed all substance is one, or they will be dispersed.

那支配萬事萬物的理性知道自己的意向，知道該做什麼、用什麼原料做。

報復的最好方式就是不要變成一個像作惡者一樣的人。

在接連不斷的社會活動中，讓心念神明成為你獲取快樂和慰藉的唯一源泉。

因為支配人的原則能自我激勵與改變，所以，它可以使自己以及所有發生的事情看起來像是如願以償。

每一單個事物的完成都是按照宇宙的本性來決定的，而不是按照任何別的性質而決定的——既不是包含宇宙本性的道理，也不是包含在宇宙本性之內的道理，更不是獨立於宇宙本性之外的道理。

宇宙若不是是由各種事物複雜地糾結在一起，且最終都會被再次分解散落到各地；就是一個有秩序、由神統治的整體。如果是前者，為什麼我還想繼續留在這一由各事物偶然結合的無秩序的宇宙中呢？為什麼我除了關心我最終將怎樣化為泥土之外還要關心別的事情呢？為什麼我還要繼續煩擾自己呢？因為不管我做什麼，不論我做什麼，我最終都會化為塵土。但如果是後者，那我的信仰就不是虛幻的，我就會崇敬、堅信、信賴那萬事萬物的主宰。

The reason which governs knows what its own disposition is, and what it does, and on what material it works.

The best way of avenging thyself is not to become like the wrong doer.

Take pleasure in one thing and rest in it, in passing from one social act to another social act, thinking of God.

The ruling principle is that which rouses and turns itself, and while it makes itself such as it is and such as it wills to be, it also makes everything which happens appear to itself to be such as it wills.

In conformity to the nature of the universe every single thing is accomplished, for certainly it is not in conformity to any other nature that each thing is accomplished, either a nature which externally comprehends this, or a nature which is comprehended within this nature, or a nature external and independent of this.

The universe is either a confusion, and a mutual involution of things, and a dispersion; or it is unity and order and providence. If then it is the former, why do I desire to tarry in a fortuitous combination of things and such a disorder? And why do I care about anything else than how I shall at last become earth? And why am I disturbed, for the dispersion of my elements will happen whatever I do. But if the other supposition is true, I venerate, and I am firm, and I trust in him who governs.

不論何時，當你因為某些現實的困境而煩惱時，你要迅速地回歸自身，不要過多地停留在這種強迫性衝動中。透過不斷地回到內心的和諧，你會有更大的控制力量。

如果你同時有一繼母和親生母親，你要尊敬繼母，但你還是要經常回到親生母親的身邊，求助於她。假設宮廷和哲學分別是你的繼母和親生母親。你要經常求助於哲學，在它那裏得到安寧，它能讓你忍受在宮廷中遇到的事情，不至於在宮廷中被別人討厭。

當肉類以及其他可食用的東西擺在我們面前，我們會有這樣的印象：這是一條魚的屍體，這是一隻鳥的屍體，而這是一頭豬的屍體。以此類推，這種飲料，這種人人讚頌的美酒只是普通葡萄的汁液而已；這件紫色袍子只是一些以貝的血染紅的羊毛而已。這些對事物的印象如此透徹、一針見血，對我們認識事物真正的本質是多麼有幫助啊！你必須一生時時刻刻都貫徹這一法則，尤其是當某些事物被認為是非常有價值，深受人們尊敬的時候，你必須小心地發現它們邪惡的一面，剝去那些煞有介事的外衣。外表是非常富有欺騙性的，當別人認為你在從事值得你努力的事情時，也就是你最有可能被欺騙的時

1.meetest 為古英語中 meet 的第二人稱單數（主語為 thou 時使用）。
2.appearest為古英語中 appear 的第二人稱單數（主語為 thou 時使用）。

When thou hast been compelled by circumstances to be disturbed in a manner, quickly return to thyself and do not continue out of tune longer than the compulsion lasts; for thou wilt have more mastery over the harmony by continually recurring to it.

If thou hadst a step-mother and a mother at the same time, thou wouldst be dutiful to thy step-mother, but still thou wouldst constantly return to thy mother. Let the court and philosophy now be to thee step-mother and mother: return to philosophy frequently and repose in her, through whom what thou **meetest**[1] with in the court appears to thee tolerable, and thou **appearest**[2] tolerable in the court.

When we have meat before us and such eatables we receive the impression, that this is the dead body of a fish, and this is the dead body of a bird or of a pig; and again, that this Falernian is only a little grape juice, and this purple robe some sheep's wool dyed with the blood of a shell-fish: such then are these impressions, and they reach the things themselves and penetrate them, and so we see what kind of things they are. Just in the same way ought we to act all through life, and where there are things which appear most worthy of our approbation, we ought to lay them bare and look at their worthlessness and strip them of all the words by which they

候。想想克拉蒂斯本人對色諾克拉蒂斯所說的話吧。

普通人讚頌的那些事物絕大部分都是非常普通的，可以透過凝聚或是自然組織而聚在一起——例如石頭、木材、無花果樹、葡萄樹和橄欖樹。那些更為謙虛和內斂的人讚揚的事物則可歸之於被一個生命原則結為一體的東西，如鳥群和獸群。那些更有教養的人們所讚揚的事物往往是那些理性的靈魂，這裏所說的理性靈魂，並不是指宇宙的靈魂，之所以說它是理性的，僅僅因為它在某一方面技藝嫻熟，很擅長，抑或擁有很多奴隸。而那尊重理性靈魂的人——一個普通且適合政治生活的人，除了以下的事以外，不看重任何事情：他首要的事情是努力保持自己的靈魂處於符合理性和社會生活的一種狀態和活動中，並且與同道中人攜手奔赴目標。

一些事物急著存在，而另一些事物則忙於消失，甚至現在存在的，其中的某一些也已經消亡。永恆的運動和變化讓這個世界保持常

1.perverter n. =pervert 反常者，背叛者

2.Crates（約西元前365年～西元前285年），古希臘犬儒派哲學家。

3.Xenocrates（約西元前396年～西元前314年），古希臘哲學家，柏拉圖的弟子。

are exalted. For outward show is a wonderful **perverter**[1] of the reason, and when thou art most sure that thou art employed about things worth thy pains, it is then that it cheats thee most. Consider then what **Crates**[2] says of **Xenocrates**[3] himself.

Most of the things which the multitude admire are referred to objects of the most general kind, those which are held together by cohesion or natural organization, such as stones, wood, fig-trees, vines, olives. But those which are admired by men who are a little more reasonable are referred to the things which are held together by a living principle, as flocks, herds. Those which are admired by men who are still more instructed are the things which are held together by a rational soul, not however a universal soul, but rational so far as it is a soul skilled in some art, or expert in some other way, or simply rational so far as it possesses a number of slaves. But he who values rational soul, a soul universal and fitted for political life, regards nothing else except this; and above all things he keeps his soul in a condition and in an activity conformable to reason and social life, and he co-operates to this end with those who are of the same kind as himself.

Some things are hurrying into existence, and others are hurrying out of it; and of that which is coming into existence part is already extinguished.

新，正像永恆的時間之流讓這世界（無止盡的世界）的時間總是顯得年輕而新鮮。既然在這永恆變化的萬事萬物中沒有什麼事情是人能夠牢牢抓住的，什麼是人應該關注的呢？這正像一個人竟然愛上身邊的一隻普通的麻雀一樣，麻雀眨眼之間就不見了。這就是我們的生命，只是血液的蒸發和普通的呼吸。我們每天都在吸入空氣，再把它呼出來。事情就是如此，正像我們每時每刻做的那樣，我們吸入空氣，又馬上把它呼出，在你吸入第一口氣的時候，你的生命也就開始了。

植物的葉面蒸發，家畜和野獸的呼吸和存在對我們而言都不是值得尊重的事；透過事物現象得到印象也不是那麼重要；我們像木偶一樣被感官所驅使，採集食物，群居生活，或餵養動物，也不那麼重要——這就像切割並分離出食物當中對我們沒用的事物一樣，對我們而言都不是那麼重要。那麼，什麼才是重要的呢？是聽到眾人的鼓掌嗎？不，不會是人們口舌的稱讚。因為眾人的讚揚事實上只是鼓舌。如果不是眾人的讚揚，還有什麼東西是重要的呢？我的意見是，你的一切活動和行動都要按照你的本性和能力來進行，有所取捨。就連普通的技藝和職業也是這麼教導我們的。每一技藝的目標都是如此，被

1.sparrow [`spæro] n. 麻雀
2.exhalation [ˌɛksə`leʃən] n. 散發，蒸發

Motions and changes are continually renewing the world, just as the
uninterrupted course of time is always renewing the infinite duration of
ages. In this flowing stream then, on which there is no abiding, what is there
of the things which hurry by on which a man would set a high price? It
would be just as if a man should fall in love with one of the **sparrows**[1] which
fly by, but it has already passed out of sight. Something of this kind is the
very life of every man, like the **exhalation**[2] of the blood and the respiration
of the air. For such as it is to have once drawn in the air and to have given
it back, which we do every moment, just the same is it with the whole
respiratory power, which thou didst receive at thy birth yesterday and the
day before, to give it back to the element from which thou didst first draw it.

Neither is transpiration, as in plants, a thing to be valued, nor respiration,
as in domesticated animals and wild beasts, nor the receiving of impressions
by the appearances of things, nor being moved by desires as puppets by
strings, nor assembling in herds, nor being nourished by food; for this is just
like the act of separating and parting with the useless part of our food. What
then is worth being valued? To be received with clapping of hands? No.
Neither must we value the clapping of tongues, for the praise which comes
from the many is a clapping of tongues. Suppose then that thou hast given
up this worthless thing called fame, what remains that is worth valuing?

創造的事物應當適應於它因此而被造的工作；葡萄種植者、馴馬師、馴狗者都追求這一目的。而對孩童的教育和其他需要知識的職業難道還有什麼別的目的嗎？你將不會再想追求任何別的東西。但是，難道你能不停止重視許多別的東西了嗎？這樣的話，你就失去了自由，不滿足於幸福，不能擺脫激情。你可能會羨慕、嫉妒、猜疑那些你認為能奪走這些東西的人，還可能會暗地策劃反對那些擁有你所重視的這些東西的人。簡而言之，那些想要這些東西的人必定會自我迷失，常常抱怨神靈。如果你只尊重和讚頌你自己的心靈，你就會滿足於自身，順從朋友，與神靈保持一致，帶著頌揚的心接受所有他們賜予和命令你的東西。

元素向上下左右的方向運動，美德的運動卻不是如此：它更神聖、更高級，以一種無法被人輕易理解的方式加速前進。

人們的行為是多麼奇怪啊：他們不讚揚那些與自己同時代、與自己一起生活的人，卻極為重視那些他們從未見過，也永遠不會見到的後代將會讚揚他們。如同一個人竟然因為生活在你前面的人沒有讚揚

This in my opinion, to move thyself and to restrain thyself in conformity to thy proper constitution, to which end both all employments and arts lead. For every art aims at this, that the thing which has been made should be adapted to the work for which it has been made; and both the vine-planter who looks after the vine, and the horse-breaker, and he who trains the dog, seek this end. But the education and the teaching of youth aim at something. In this then is the value of the education and the teaching. And if this is well, thou wilt not seek anything else. Wilt thou not cease to value many other things too? Then thou wilt be neither free, nor sufficient for thy own happiness, nor without passion. For of necessity thou must be envious, jealous, and suspicious of those who can take away those things, and plot against those who have that which is valued by thee. Of necessity a man must be altogether in a state of perturbation who wants any of these things; and besides, he must often find fault with the gods. But to reverence and honour thy own mind will make thee content with thyself, and in harmony with society, and in agreement with the gods, that is, praising all that they give and have ordered.

Above, below, all around are the movements of the elements. But the motion of virtue is in none of these: it is something more divine, and advancing by a way hardly observed it goes happily on its road.

How strangely men act. They will not praise those who are living at the same time and living with themselves; but to be themselves praised by posterity, by those whom they have never seen or ever will see, this they set

你而感到悲哀一樣荒謬。

　　不要認為你無法完成的事對別人來說也是無法完成，或是難以完成的。如果你覺得有什麼事是人類能夠完成的，並且合乎他本性，那麼你也應該認為自己也能夠做到。

　　假設在體育競賽中有人用指甲抓傷了你，或是打破了你的頭，讓你受了傷。別惱怒，不要覺得受到了冒犯，也不要懷疑他是故意要傷害你。然而，你要提防他，不是把他看作是一個敵人，也不是出於猜忌，而是善意地躲避。在生活中別的方面你也要這樣做，因為有許多事情，我們必須用對付體育場上的對手一樣的態度來處理。正如我所說，雖然我們既不猜疑，也不仇恨，但還是要盡可能避免紛爭，對對手敬而遠之。

　　如果有人責備我，讓我明白我的言行哪裡錯了，我將非常愉快地改正。因為我尋求真理，我相信任何人都不會受到真理的傷害；同樣肯定的是，那些繼續犯錯或是不知道自己錯了的人則會因此受到傷害。

　　就我自己而言，我會履行我的義務，至於其他的事物，它們不會使我苦惱，因為它們不是沒有生命，就是沒有理性，或者就算是有理性，也是誤入歧途或不明白道路的存在。

much value on. But this is very much the same as if thou shouldst be grieved because those who have lived before thee did not praise thee.

If a thing is difficult to be accomplished by thyself, do not think that it is impossible for man: but if anything is possible for man and conformable to his nature, think that this can be attained by thyself too.

In the gymnastic exercises suppose that a man has torn thee with his nails, and by dashing against thy head has inflicted a wound. Well, we neither show any signs of vexation, nor are we offended, nor do we suspect him afterwards as a treacherous fellow; and yet we are on our guard against him, not however as an enemy, nor yet with suspicion, but we quietly get out of his way. Something like this let thy behaviour be in all the other parts of life; let us overlook many things in those who are like antagonists in the gymnasium. For it is in our power, as I said, to get out of the way, and to have no suspicion nor hatred.

If any man is able to convince me and show me that I do not think or act right, I will gladly change; for I seek the truth by which no man was ever injured. But he is injured who abides in his error and ignorance.

I do my duty: other things trouble me not; for they are either things without life, or things without reason, or things that have rambled and know not the way.

對於那沒有理性的動物和一般的事物和物件，由於你有理性而它們沒有，你要以一種大方和慷慨的精神對待它們。對於人來說，由於他們有理性，你要以一種友愛的精神對待他們。不管你做什麼，你都要記得向神靈禱告，不要對於你將花多長時間做這件事而感到困擾，因為即使三個小時也是情有可原的。

馬其頓的亞歷山大和他的馬夫在死後就毫無區別了，因為他們或者是被納入宇宙的同一繁衍本源，或者是以同樣的方式被分解為原子。

考慮一下我們每個人的身體或靈魂在同一時間會發生多少事，那麼，對於在唯一的普遍的宇宙中同時有更多事物，甚至存在萬事萬物，你就不會感到驚奇了。

如果有人向你提出這個問題——『安東尼』這個名字要怎樣寫，難道你不會馬上集中注意力，一個字母一個字母地念出來嗎？如果有人開始否認你的說法，並和你吵起來，你是會繼續和他吵，還是會繼續鎮定地把所有的字母一個個說出來。記住，在生活中也是這樣，人的義務都是由某些部分組成的。遵循它們是你的義務，對待那些生你氣的人，不要煩惱和生氣，繼續走你的路，完成擺在你面前的既定目標。

As to the animals which have no reason and generally all things and objects, do thou, since thou hast reason and they have none, make use of them with a generous and liberal spirit. But towards human beings, as they have reason, behave in a social spirit. And on all occasions call on the gods, and do not perplex thyself about the length of time in which thou shalt do this; for even three hours so spent are sufficient.

Alexander the Macedonian and his groom by death were brought to the same state; for either they were received among the same seminal principles of the universe, or they were alike dispersed among the atoms.

Consider how many things in the same indivisible time take place in each of us, things which concern the body and things which concern the soul: and so thou wilt not wonder if many more things, or rather all things which come into existence in that which is the one and all, which we call Cosmos, exist in it at the same time.

If any man should propose to thee the question, how the name Antoninus is written, wouldst thou with a straining of the voice utter each letter? What then if they grow angry, wilt thou be angry too? Wilt thou not go on with composure and number every letter? just so then in this life also remember that every duty is made up of certain parts. These it is thy duty to observe and without being disturbed or showing anger towards those who are angry with thee to go on thy way and finish that which is set before thee.

　　禁止人們努力追求那些在他們看來是適合他們本性的和對他們有利的事物，難道不是殘忍的嗎？但當你因他們的過錯而生氣時，還是要以某種方式不允許他們做這些事。他們被推動做這些事確實是因為他們假設這些事是適合於他們本性的，是對他們有利的，然而情況並非如此。你將教育他們，讓他們看到自己的錯誤，但不要生他們的氣。

　　死亡意味著感官印象的中止、慾望統治的中斷，思想不再犯錯，不再為肉體服務。

　　如果在生活中你的身體很健康，但你的靈魂卻先暈厥過去，開始衰退，這就是種羞愧。

　　注意不要讓自己變成凱撒，並染上那種習氣。如果你不注意的話，這樣的事情可能會發生。要使你自己保持樸素、善良、真誠、嚴肅、不做作、愛正義、崇敬神靈、和善、溫柔、行事果斷積極。努力保持哲學想把你塑造成的樣子，崇敬神靈，為人類帶來福祉。生命是短暫的，這一塵世的生命只有一個果實：虔誠的精神和友善的行為。

1.cessation [sɛ`seʃən] n. 停止；中止

How cruel it is not to allow men to strive after the things which appear to them to be suitable to their nature and profitable! And yet in a manner thou dost not allow them to do this, when thou art vexed because they do wrong. For they are certainly moved towards things because they suppose them to be suitable to their nature and profitable to them. – But it is not so. – Teach them then, and show them without being angry.

Death is a **cessation**[1] of the impressions through the senses, and of the pulling of the strings which move the appetites, and of the discursive movements of the thoughts, and of the service to the flesh.

It is a shame for the soul to be first to give way in this life, when thy body does not give way.

Take care that thou art not made into a Caesar, that thou art not dyed with this dye; for such things happen. Keep thyself then simple, good, pure, serious, free from affectation, a friend of justice, a worshipper of the gods, kind, affectionate, strenuous in all proper acts. Strive to continue to be such as philosophy wished to make thee. Reverence the gods, and help men. Short is life. There is only one fruit of this terrene life, – a pious disposition and social acts.

　　做任何事情都要像安東尼爾斯的信徒一樣。要記住他在符合理性的每一行為中的一貫堅定，他對所有事物的一視同仁，他的虔誠，他令人愉悅的面容，他的溫柔，他的毫無虛榮之心。他對他著手的事是如何小心地加以瞭解，獲得真知。在沒有努力地完全瞭解一件事情以前，他是絕對不會放手的。對那些不公正地責備他的人，他會耐心地接受他們，不會與他們爭吵。他從不倉促行事，不信謠言誹謗，而是仔細觀察人們的各種言行和性情。他不會在背後誹謗人、不輕易膽怯、不多疑、言談不做作，也不窺探別人的隱私。在住處、睡床、衣服、日常食物和僕人方面，他很容易就能滿足。他能夠耐心而不辭辛勞地工作。他可以靠著粗茶淡飯從早晨堅持到夜晚，除了在必要的時候之外不需要任何休息。他對待朋友一貫堅定並始終如一。他能夠容忍那些隨意反對他意見的人。當有人能提出更好的建議時，他甚至會感到快樂。最後，他雖然信奉神明，卻不迷信。你要記住所有這些有關他的事，不論最後的時刻何時來臨，你的心都會像他一樣善良、高尚。

　　喚醒你的意識，從你的睡夢中醒來，你就會明白那使你苦惱的只是虛幻，現在你看待這些俗事就像一個剛從夢中醒來的人看待那些

1.這裏的安東尼爾斯指的是作者的繼父安東尼‧派厄斯，第一卷中有介紹。

Do everything as a disciple of **Antoninus**[1]. Remember his constancy in every act which was conformable to reason, and his evenness in all things, and his piety, and the serenity of his countenance, and his sweetness, and his disregard of empty fame, and his efforts to understand things; and how he would never let anything pass without having first most carefully examined it and clearly understood it; and how he bore with those who blamed him unjustly without blaming them in return; how he did nothing in a hurry; and how he listened not to calumnies, and how exact an examiner of manners and actions he was; and not given to reproach people, nor timid, nor suspicious, nor a sophist; and with how little he was satisfied, such as lodging, bed, dress, food, servants; and how laborious and patient; and how he was able on account of his sparing diet to hold out to the evening, not even requiring to relieve himself by any evacuations except at the usual hour; and his firmness and uniformity in his friendships; and how he tolerated freedom of speech in those who opposed his opinions; and the pleasure that he had when any man showed him anything better; and how religious he was without superstition. Imitate all this that thou mayest have as good a conscience, when thy last hour comes, as he had.

Return to thy sober senses and call thyself back; and when thou hast roused thyself from sleep and hast perceived that they were only dreams

（夢）一樣。

我是由肉體和靈魂組成的。所有的事物對我的肉體而言都是不重要的，因為它無法意識到各個事物之間的差別。但對於我的靈魂而言，所有那些與它自身活動無關的事物都是不重要的，而所有與它有關的事物都依賴於它。然而，在這些事物中又只有那些現在所做的事在其力量範圍之內，至於心靈將來和過去的活動，對於現在的活動來說也是不重要的。

只要腳做腳的工作，手做手的工作，那不管它們做什麼，都絕不會違反本性。所以，只要一個人做的事合乎人性，那麼他的工作就絕不會違反本性。如果這項工作不違反自然，那它就不會對這個人造成傷害。

那些臭名昭著的強盜、骯髒而令人憎惡的弒父者、暴君享受了多少快樂！

難道你沒有看到那些工匠在某些時候可以向不精通他們手藝的人做出妥協，但仍然堅持他們手藝的理性（原則），而不忍心拋棄它們嗎？如果建築師和醫生對於自己手藝理性（原則）的尊重超過人對於自己理性（神人共有的）的重視，這不是很奇怪嗎？

which troubled thee, now in thy waking hours look at these (the things about thee) as thou didst look at those (the dreams).

I consist of a little body and a soul. Now to this little body all things are indifferent, for it is not able to perceive differences. But to the understanding those things only are indifferent, which are not the works of its own activity. But whatever things are the works of its own activity, all these are in its power. And of these however only those which are done with reference to the present; for as to the future and the past activities of the mind, even these are for the present indifferent.

Neither the labour which the hand does nor that of the foot is contrary to nature, so long as the foot does the foot's work and the hand the hand's. So then neither to a man as a man is his labour contrary to nature, so long as it does the things of a man. But if the labour is not contrary to his nature, neither is it an evil to him.

How many pleasures have been enjoyed by robbers, patricides, tyrants.

Dost thou not see how the handicraftsmen accommodate themselves up to a certain point to those who are not skilled in their craft, – nevertheless they cling to the reason (the principles) of their art and do not endure to depart from it? Is it not strange if the architect and the physician shall have more respect to the reason (the principles) of their own arts than man to his

　　亞細亞、歐羅巴不過是宇宙的小角落；所有的海洋也只是宇宙的一滴水；崇峻的阿陀斯山也只是宇宙的一小塊塵土，所有現存的時間只是永恆時間中的一點。所有的事物都是微小的，瞬息萬變，轉瞬即逝的。萬事萬物都只有一個源頭，從宇宙的統治力量中直接產生或者作為後繼物出現。因此，獅子可怕的下顎，所有有毒的物質，像荊棘、泥沼等所有有害的東西，都是好的和美麗的事物的副產品。不要以為它們與你尊崇的事物相反，而是要對事物的來源有一個恰當的意見。

　　那些看見了現在事物的人也看見了以前發生過或將要發生的一切，因為所有的事物都是一樣的。

　　要經常思考宇宙中所有事物之間的關聯和它們相互之間的關係。所有事物都以某種方式互相聯繫，並透過這些方式和諧地存在。一事物在另一事物之後出現，這是由主動的運動和相互的協作以及實體的統一性造成的。

1.Athos，在愛琴海北部，希臘的東北部，後為希臘東正教的聖地。
2.thorn [θɔrn] n. 荊刺；棘
3.connexion [kəˈnɛkʃən] n. 聯繫，連結

own reason, which is common to him and the gods?

Asia, Europe are corners of the universe: all the sea a drop in the universe; **Athos**[1] a little clod of the universe: all the present time is a point in eternity. All things are little, changeable, perishable. All things come from thence, from that universal ruling power either directly proceeding or by way of sequence. And accordingly the lion's gaping jaws, and that which is poisonous, and every harmful thing, as a **thorn**[2], as mud, are after-products of the grand and beautiful. Do not then imagine that they are of another kind from that which thou dost venerate, but form a just opinion of the source of all.

He who has seen present things has seen all, both everything which has taken place from all eternity and everything which will be for time without end; for all things are of one kin and of one form.

Frequently consider the **connexion**[3] of all things in the universe and their relation to one another. For in a manner all things are implicated with one another, and all in this way are friendly to one another; for one thing comes in order after another, and this is by virtue of the active movement and mutual conspiration and the unity of the substance.

　　要使你自己適應命中註定屬於你的事物，還要愛那些你註定要一起生活的人，而且要真正愛他們。

　　每一件器具、工具、器皿，如果實現了它被製作的目的，儘管它的製作者可能已經離世，它還是好的。但是，對靠自然形成的事物而言，那製造它們的力量仍會與它們共存。正因為這一原因，我們更應尊重這一力量，並且認為：如果你真是按照其意志生活。那麼，你的一切也都是符合理智的。宇宙中屬於它的事物都符合理智。

　　如果你對那些你能力之外的事物假定好或壞，必然出現這種情況：如果你陷入你所認為的厄運中，或是錯過了你認為好的事物，你必然會抱怨神靈，也恨那些給你造成不幸或讓你錯失良機的人們，卻不管是不是確有其事，還是只是你憑空猜疑。我們的確做了許多不公正的事情，因為我們或多或少都對這些事物做出了好與壞的區分。但如果我們只對我們能力之內的事物判斷好壞，我們就沒有理由怨天尤人。

　　我們都是朝著同一個目標而工作的。有些人是自覺的，清楚地知道自己在做什麼，而另一些人卻不知道。我想到赫拉克利特在某個地方曾說過，這些人儘管也在從事他們的工作，為整個宇宙的運轉做出貢獻，但他們就像在沉睡一樣。不過，每個人合作的方式不同：甚至

Adapt thyself to the things with which thy lot has been cast: and the men among whom thou hast received thy portion, love them, but do it truly, sincerely.

Every instrument, tool, vessel, if it does that for which it has been made, is well, and yet he who made it is not there. But in the things which are held together by nature there is within and there abides in them the power which made them; wherefore the more is it fit to reverence this power, and to think, that, if thou dost live and act according to its will, everything in thee is in conformity to intelligence. And thus also in the universe the things which belong to it are in conformity to intelligence.

Whatever of the things which are not within thy power thou shalt suppose to be good for thee or evil, it must of necessity be that, if such a bad thing befall thee or the loss of such a good thing, thou wilt blame the gods, and hate men too, those who are the cause of the misfortune or the loss, or those who are suspected of being likely to be the cause; and indeed we do much injustice, because we make a difference between these things. But if we judge only those things which are in our power to be good or bad, there remains no reason either for finding fault with God or standing in a hostile attitude to man.

We are all working together to one end, some with knowledge and design, and others without knowing what they do; as men also when they are asleep, of whom it is Heraclitus, I think, who says that they are labourers

是那些對發生的事情不滿或極力阻撓的人，也都進行了充分的合作，因為這個世界也需要這樣一些人。現在，你認為自己是哪種人呢？對宇宙萬物的統治者來說，他會讓你物盡其用，接納你為合作者的一部分，接納你到有共同目標的勞動者中去。但是不要像克內西帕斯在某個場合曾經說過的經驗，去扮演類似戲劇中滑稽可笑的角色。

太陽承擔了雨的工作，或者是艾斯庫累普承擔了豐收的工作？那具體到每個星星又是怎樣呢？儘管它們各不相同，卻致力於同一目的嗎？

如果神靈對於那些應該發生在我身上的事情都經過了仔細的考慮，那麼，我就相信他們經過了審慎的、明智的思考，因為人們很難想像神會草率從事。而且，他們為什麼要傷害我呢？這樣做對他們，或者對他們特別眷顧的整體會有什麼好處呢？但是假如他們沒有特別考慮發生在我身上的事情，那他們也肯定是從大局出發，因此，那些為了顧全大局而發生在我身上的事情，我都應該欣然接受。但如果他們完全沒有經過思考——相信這一點是對神明的褻瀆，因為如果我們

1.placest 為古英語中 place 的第二人稱單數（主語為 thou 時使用）。
2.Chrysippus（約西元前280年～西元前207年），斯多噶派哲學的重要理論家，使該派哲學成為當時希臘和羅馬最有影響的哲學派別之一。他說的與此相關的話被普塔克記載在自己的著作裏：「詩人們把荒謬的笑話寫進他們的喜劇裏，其本

and co-operators in the things which take place in the universe. But men co-operate after different fashions: and even those co-operate abundantly, who find fault with what happens and those who try to oppose it and to hinder it; for the universe had need even of such men as these. It remains then for thee to understand among what kind of workmen thou **placest**[1] thyself; for he who rules all things will certainly make a right use of thee, and he will receive thee among some part of the co-operators and of those whose labours conduce to one end. But be not thou such a part as the mean and ridiculous verse in the play, which **Chrysippus**[2] speaks of.

Does the sun undertake to do the work of the rain, or **Aesculapius**[3] the work of the Fruit-bearer (the earth)? And how is it with respect to each of the stars, are they not different and yet they work together to the same end?

If the gods have determined about me and about the things which must happen to me, they have determined well, for it is not easy even to imagine a deity without forethought; and as to doing me harm, why should they have any desire towards that? For what advantage would result to them from this or to the whole, which is the special object of their providence? But if they have not determined about me individually, they have certainly determined about the whole at least, and the things which happen by way of sequence in

身固然微不足道,但對於整篇作品卻帶來一種美妙,同樣的,罪惡本身固然可惡,但對於非罪惡的部分仍然有其用處。」

3.Aesculapius,古希臘醫藥之神,同時也是帶來豐收之神。

真這樣想，就會不祭祀、不祈禱、不尊重自己的誓言，也不做任何好像神靈在面前，並且和我們生活在一起時所做的事情——假如神靈真的沒有考慮過那些發生我們人身上的事情，我有能力思考有關自身利益的事情，我就能思考什麼是對我最有利的，符合一個人的能力和本性的事情就是對其最有利的。而我的本性是理性的、社會的。就我安東尼爾斯來說，羅馬就是我的城邦與國家；但作為一個人，整個世界也是我的城邦與國家。因此，對這些城邦有利的事物，對我而言才是好的、有用的事物。

無論誰身上發生了什麼事情，都是出於整體的利益，這就足夠了。如果你經常仔細觀察的話，你將發現一項真理：對一個人有益的，對其他人也有益。但是此處的『有益』這個詞應該被廣義地理解為那些我們通常說的中性的事物，既不好也不壞。

如果你看慣了在劇場和其他諸如此類的地方的平常演出，這些千篇一律的表演會使你厭倦；那些我們看了一輩子的事情也會讓我們感到厭倦。所有的事物，天上的、地下的，都是同樣的，來自同一個地

1.amphitheatre [`æmfə‚θiətɚ] n. 羅馬圓形露天劇場，建於西元80年。

this general arrangement I ought to accept with pleasure and to be content with them. But if they determine about nothing, – which it is wicked to believe, or if we do believe it, let us neither sacrifice nor pray nor swear by them nor do anything else which we do as if the gods were present and lived with us, – but if however the gods determine about none of the things which concern us, I am able to determine about myself, and I can inquire about that which is useful; and that is useful to every man which is conformable to his own constitution and nature. But my nature is rational and social; and my city and country, so far as I am Antoninus, is Rome, but so far as I am a man, it is the world. The things then which are useful to these cities are alone useful to me.

Whatever happens to every man, this is for the interest of the universal: this might be sufficient. But further thou wilt observe this also as a general truth, if thou dost observe, that whatever is profitable to any man is profitable also to other men. But let the word profitable be taken here in the common sense as said of things of the middle kind, neither good nor bad.

As it happens to thee in the **amphitheatre**[1] and such places, that the continual sight of the same things and the uniformity make the spectacle wearisome, so it is in the whole of life; for all things above, below, are the

方。那麼，還要看多久呢？

　　你要不斷地思考各種各樣的人、各種追求以及各個國家是如何消失的，甚至回溯到腓力斯遜、菲伯斯和奧里更尼安。現在再想想別的時代，經過諸多變化之後，那兒有如此多的雄辯家，如此多高貴的哲學家：赫拉克利特、畢達哥拉斯、蘇格拉底，如此多以往的英雄，以及隨後出現的英勇將領和君王。除此之外，還有尤多克烏斯、希帕爾克斯、阿基米德和別的思維敏捷、胸襟博大、勤奮、敏銳和充滿威嚴的人，甚至還有那些嘲弄短暫和速朽生命的人，如門尼帕斯及其他像他一樣的人。在想起他們的時候，你也要想到他們都早已化為塵土。這對他們有什麼損失呢？這對那些名字完全被人遺忘的人們又有什麼損失呢？在短暫的生命中，只有一件事值得我們努力追求，即要追求真理和正義，對說謊者和不公正的人也應持仁愛的態度。

　　如果你想安慰自己，讓自己開心，那就想想那些每天都和你在一起相處的人的才能和美德，例如這個人很勤奮、那個人很謙虛、另一個人很慷慨，以及其他人另外的優點。沒有什麼能比身邊的人的美德更能讓你開心了，尤其是當它們一下子都呈現在你面前時，我們必須

1.Philistion，Phoebus，Origanion這3個都是人名，生平不詳。
2.Eudoxus（約西元前410年～西元前355年），古希臘著名天文學家和數學家，柏拉圖的學生。
3.Hipparchus（約西元前190年～西元前120年），古希臘天文學家和數學家。

same and from the same. How long then?

Think continually that all kinds of men and of all kinds of pursuits and of all nations are dead, so that thy thoughts come down even to **Philistion and Phoebus and Origanion**[1]. Now turn thy thoughts to the other kinds of men. To that place then we must remove, where there are so many great orators, and so many noble philosophers, Heraclitus, Pythagoras, Socrates; so many heroes of former days, and so many generals after them, and tyrants; besides these, **Eudoxus**[2], **Hipparchus**[3], **Archimedes**[4], and other men of acute natural talents, great minds, lovers of labour, versatile, confident, mockers even of the perishable and ephemeral life of man, as **Menippus**[5] and such as are like him. As to all these consider that they have long been in the dust. What harm then is this to them; and what to those whose names are altogether unknown? One thing here is worth a great deal, to pass thy life in truth and justice, with a **benevolent**[6] disposition even to liars and unjust men.

When thou **wishest**[7] to delight thyself, think of the virtues of those who live with thee; for instance, the activity of one, and the modesty of another, and the liberality of a third, and some other good quality of a fourth. For nothing delights so much as the examples of the virtues, when they are

---

4.Archimedes（西元前287年～西元前212年），古希臘數學家和發明家。

5.Menippus，西元前3世紀古希臘犬儒派哲學家和諷刺作家。

6.benevolent [bə`nɛvələnt] adj.仁慈的

7.wishest為古英語中wish的第二人稱單數（主語為thou時使用）。

時時把它們記在心裏。

難道你會因你體重只有這麼少磅而不是300磅感到難過嗎？同樣，也不要因為你只能活這幾年而不能活得更久而傷心。正像你滿足於分派給你的物質數額一樣，你也應滿足於分派給你的時間。

讓我們盡自己最大的努力說服他們吧，儘管違背他們的意志，但如果正義的原則指引你這麼做，你就去做吧。如果有人用武力阻攔你，不讓你做，那你就要使自己的心靈變得滿足、平靜，同時用阻攔你的事物來鍛煉你別的美德。請記住，你的嘗試要有所保留，留有餘地，不要想著不可能實現的事情。你想要什麼呢？不要想做不可能的事情。一旦引領你的東西完成了，你就實現了自己的目標。

貪圖虛名的人把自己的幸福建立在別人的行為上；沉溺酒色的人把自己的幸福建立在感官的滿足上；智者則把幸福建立在自己的行為上。

1.weighest，為古英語中 weigh 的第二人稱單數（主語為 thou 時使用）。
2.litrae，古希臘的重量單位，等於12盎司。
3.attainest，為古英語中 attain 的第二人稱單數（主語為 thou 時使用）。

exhibited in the morals of those who live with us and present themselves in abundance, as far as is possible. Wherefore we must keep them before us.

Thou art not dissatisfied, I suppose, because thou **weighest**[1] only so many **litrae**[2] and not three hundred. Be not dissatisfied then that thou must live only so many years and not more; for as thou art satisfied with the amount of substance which has been assigned to thee, so be content with the time.

Let us try to persuade them (men). But act even against their will, when the principles of justice lead that way. If however any man by using force stands in thy way, betake thyself to contentment and tranquility, and at the same time employ the hindrance towards the exercise of some other virtue; and remember that thy attempt was with a reservation, that thou didst not desire to do impossibilities. What then didst thou desire? – Some such effort as this. – But thou **attainest**[3] thy object, if the things to which thou wast moved are accomplished.

He who loves fame considers another man's activity to be his own good; and he who loves pleasure, his own sensations; but he who has understanding, considers his own acts to be his own good.

你完全有能力對事物不做出主觀臆斷，你也完全有能力讓你的靈魂不受干擾，因為事物本身沒有自然能力形成我們的判斷。

當有人對你說話的時候，你要仔細地傾聽，盡可能地觸及他的靈魂深處。

不利於蜂群的東西也不可能對蜜蜂有利。

乘客會對載他渡江的船夫挑三揀四嗎？病人會對治癒他的醫生說三道四嗎？他們關心的只有一件事：乘客只關心船夫能讓他們安全上岸，而病人只關心醫生能使他們痊癒。

和我一起來到這世界的人有多少已經離開了人世？

對於黃疸病患者來說，蜜嚐起來是苦的；對於狂犬病患者來說，水顯得很可怕；對於孩子來說，一顆小球看起來就有吸引力。那麼我為什麼生氣呢？你是否認為一個錯誤的意見不如黃疸病患者體內的膽汁，或狂犬病患者體內的毒素有力量？

1.helmsman [`hɛlmzmən] n. 舵手
2.jaundiced [`dʒɔndɪst] adj. 患黃疸病的

It is in our power to have no opinion about a thing, and not to be disturbed in our soul; for things themselves have no natural power to form our judgments.

Accustom thyself to attend carefully to what is said by another, and as much as it is possible, be in the speaker's mind.

That which is not good for the swarm, neither is it good for the bee.

If sailors abused the **helmsman**[1] or the sick the doctor, would they listen to anybody else; or how could the helmsman secure the safety of those in the ship or the doctor the health of those whom he attends?

How many together with whom I came into the world are already gone out of it.

To the **jaundiced**[2] honey tastes bitter, and to those bitten by mad dogs water causes fear; and to little children the ball is a fine thing. Why then am I angry? Dost thou think that a false opinion has less power than the bile in the jaundiced or the poison in him who is bitten by a mad dog?

　　沒有人能阻止你按照自己的本性生活；沒有一件違反宇宙本性的事情會發生在你頭上。

　　人們想要討好什麼樣的人呢？是為了什麼目的，透過什麼行為來討好他們呢？這一切很快都將會被時間淹沒，而且時間的洪流已經淹沒了多少事物啊！

No man will hinder thee from living according to the reason of thy own nature: nothing will happen to thee contrary to the reason of the universal nature.

What kind of people are those whom men wish to please, and for what objects, and by what kind of acts? How soon will time cover all things, and how many it has covered already.

第七卷

什麼是惡？它是你司空見慣的一個東西。在任何事發生的時候，都要抱持此想法：它是你司空見慣的。你將在上上下下一切地方都發現它，這同樣的事物充滿了從古至今的歷史；也充斥著城邦和家庭。沒有什麼新事物，所有事物都是熟悉的，也是短暫的。

我們的原則怎麼能死去呢？除非那符合它們的印象（思想）熄滅了。但是不斷地把這些思想搧成旺盛的火焰是在你的力量範圍之內的。我對任何事情都能形成正確的意見。如果我能做到，我為什麼要煩惱呢？我心靈之外的事物跟我的心靈沒有任何關係。永遠保持這種心態，你就能堅定地站立起來。恢復你的生命是在你力量範圍之內的，用你過去慣常的眼光看待事物，因為你生命的恢復就在於此。

無聊的展覽，舞臺上的表演，羊群牛群，還有打打殺殺；一根投

1.standest 為古英語中 stand 的第二人稱單數（主語為 thou 時使用）。

BOOK 7

What is badness? It is that which thou hast often seen. And on the occasion of everything which happens keep this in mind, that it is that which thou hast often seen. Everywhere up and down thou wilt find the same things, with which the old histories are filled, those of the middle ages and those of our own day; with which cities and houses are filled now. There is nothing new: all things are both familiar and short-lived.

How can our principles become dead, unless the impressions (thoughts) which correspond to them are extinguished? But it is in thy power continuously to fan these thoughts into a flame. I can have that opinion about anything, which I ought to have. If I can, why am I disturbed? The things which are external to my mind have no relation at all to my mind. – Let this be the state of thy affects, and thou **standest**[1] erect. To recover thy life is in thy power. Look at things again as thou didst use to look at them; for in this consists the recovery of thy life.

The idle business of show, plays on the stage, flocks of sheep, herds,

向小狗的骨頭，一點丟在魚塘裏的麵包，螞蟻的勞作和搬運，驚嚇後奔跑的老鼠，被人操縱的木偶，置身於諸如此類事物之中擺正自己的位置，端正自己的心態而不鄙薄這些瑣碎是你的職責。要懂得一個人的價值和他所做事情的價值是等量齊觀的。

在談話中要留意所說的話，在行為中要觀察所做的事。在後一種情況下你應當直接洞察它所指向的目的，而在前一種情況下你應當仔細觀察事物所表示的意義。

我的理智足以勝任這一工作嗎？如果能勝任，那麼我在這一工作中就把它作為宇宙本性給予的一個工具來使用。但如果不能勝任，那麼，我或者放棄這一工作，把它讓給能夠較好地做它的人，除非有某種理由使我不應這樣做；或者我盡力而為，接受他人的幫助。我在他的幫助下，運用自己的理性去做那些現在是恰當並對公共利益有用的事。無論是我做的事還是我和別人一起做的事，目的只有一個，即對社會有用和適用於社會。

有多少人在享受赫赫聲名之後被人遺忘，又有多少人在稱頌別人的聲名之後與世長辭。

不要因受人幫助而感到羞愧，因為像一個戰士在攻池掠地中一

exercises with spears, a bone cast to little dogs, a bit of bread into fish-ponds, labourings of ants and burden-carrying, runnings about of frightened little mice, puppets pulled by strings – all alike. It is thy duty then in the midst of such things to show good humour and not a proud air; to understand however that every man is worth just so much as the things are worth about which he busies himself.

In discourse thou must attend to what is said, and in every movement thou must observe what is doing. And in the one thou shouldst see immediately to what end it refers, but in the other watch carefully what is the thing signified.

Is my understanding sufficient for this or not? If it is sufficient, I use it for the work as an instrument given by the universal nature. But if it is not sufficient, then either I retire from the work and give way to him who is able to do it better, unless there be some reason why I ought not to do so; or I do it as well as I can, taking to help me the man who with the aid of my ruling principle can do what is now fit and useful for the general good. For whatsoever either by myself or with another I can do, ought to be directed to this only, to that which is useful and well suited to society.

How many after being celebrated by fame have been given up to oblivion; and how many who have celebrated the fame of others have long been dead.

Be not ashamed to be helped; for it is thy business to do thy duty like

樣，履行職責正是你的本分。如果因為瘸拐使你不能獨立走上城牆，而靠其他士兵的幫助你卻能時，怎麼辦呢？

不要為將來的事憂慮，如果那是必然要發生的話，你將帶著與對待當前事物同樣的理性去對待它。

所有的事物都是相互聯結的，這一紐帶是神聖的，幾乎沒有一個事物能獨立存在。事物都是相互聯結的，它們結合起來形成同一有秩序的宇宙。只有一個由所有事物組成的宇宙，只有一個存在於所有事物的神，只有一個實體、一種法、一個所有理智動物所擁有的共同理性、一個真理。對於這些來自同一根源，分享同一理性的生靈來說，如果該事物確實存在，那麼也有一個臻於完美的境界。

一切材質的東西不久就要消失於作為整體的實體之中，一切形式（原因）也很快要回到宇宙的理性之中，對一切事物的記憶也很快要淹沒在時間中。

對於理性動物來說，同樣的行為既符合本性，也符合理性。

1.usest 為古英語中 use 的第二人稱單數（主語為 thou 時使用）。
2.holy [`holɪ] adj. 神聖的，聖潔的

a soldier in the assault on a town. How then, if being lame thou canst not mount up on the battlements alone, but with the help of another it is possible?

Let not future things disturb thee, for thou wilt come to them, if it shall be necessary, having with thee the same reason which now thou **usest**[1] for present things.

All things are implicated with one another, and the bond is **holy**[2]; and there is hardly anything unconnected with any other thing. For things have been co-ordinated, and they combine to form the same universe (order). For there is one universe made up of all things, and one God who pervades all things, and one substance, and one law, one common reason in all intelligent animals, and one truth; if indeed there is also one perfection for all animals which are of the same stock and participate in the same reason.

Everything material soon disappears in the substance of the whole; and everything formal (causal) is very soon taken back into the universal reason; and the memory of everything is very soon overwhelmed in time.

To the rational animal the same act is according to nature and according

自己站直，否則被別人扶直。

　　正像身體中各個部分是統一體一樣，各有理性的人也是合而為一的，因為他們是為合作而生的。如果你經常對自己說我是理性社會中的一個成員。那麼，你將更清楚地察覺到這一點。但如果你說是一個部分，你就還沒有從心裏熱愛人們，你就還沒有從仁愛本身中得到歡樂，你就還僅僅將行善作為一件合宜的事情來做，而尚未把它看成也是對你自己行善。

　　讓那要從外部降臨的事情落在那可以感覺這降臨效果的部分吧。那些感覺得到的部分，如果願意，將要抱怨，但是，除非我認為發生的事情是一種惡，我不會受到傷害。而我有能力不這麼想。

　　不管任何人做什麼或說什麼，我必須做個好人，正像綠寶石（或黃金，或紫袍）總是這樣說：無論一個人做什麼或說什麼，我還是綠寶石，保持我的本色。

1.erect [ɪˋrɛkt] adj. 直立的，豎立的，筆直的
2.emerald [ˋɛmərəld] n. 翡翠，綠寶石

to reason.

Be thou **erect**[1], or be made erect.

Just as it is with the members in those bodies which are united in one, so it is with rational beings which exist separate, for they have been constituted for one co-operation. And the perception of this will be more apparent to thee, if thou often sayest to thyself that I am a member of the system of rational beings. But if (using the letter r) thou sayest that thou art a part thou dost not yet love men from thy heart; beneficence does not yet delight thee for its own sake; thou still doest it barely as a thing of propriety, and not yet as doing good to thyself.

Let there fall externally what will on the parts which can feel the effects of this fall. For those parts which have felt will complain, if they choose. But I, unless I think that what has happened is an evil, am not injured. And it is in my power not to think so.

Whatever any one does or says, I must be good, just as if the gold, or the **emerald**[2], or the purple were always saying this, Whatever any one does or says, I must be emerald and keep my colour.

我的內心主宰部分並不打擾自身。我的意思是：不嚇唬自己或造成自身痛苦。但如果有什麼別的人能嚇唬它或使它痛苦，讓他這樣做吧。因為這一能力本身並不因此走向這條道路。如果身體能夠做到，讓它自己照顧自己不受苦吧；如果它受苦，就讓它表現出來。而容易受到恐嚇和痛苦的靈魂本身，完全有力量對這些事作出判斷的靈魂，將不受任何痛苦，因為它將不會偏向這種判斷。靈魂的指導原則是本身無所需求，除非它自己製造需求。所以它免除打擾，不受阻礙，只要它不被擾亂、阻礙自己。

幸福是一個好神，或一個好事物。那麼，你正在做什麼呢？噢，想像嗎？當你來時，我以神靈名義懇求你，像來時那樣離去吧，因為我不需要你。但你又按照舊習慣來了，我不生你的氣，只是要你離開。

有人害怕變化嗎？沒有變化，事物怎麼能發生呢？又怎麼能使宇宙本性更愉悅或對它更適合呢？木柴不經歷一種變化你能洗澡嗎？食物不經歷一種變化你能吸收到營養嗎？沒有變化，其他任何有用的東西能夠形成嗎？你難道沒看到，你的變化也是一樣的，這對於宇宙本性同樣都是必需的？

1.impede [ɪm`pid] v. 妨礙，阻礙，阻止
2.Eudaemonia（happiness），源於古希臘。在古希臘思想中，幸福同好的外在環境（神賜）是一致的；在大多數古希臘哲學家那裏，幸福同內心的品德（例

The ruling faculty does not disturb itself; I mean, does not frighten itself or cause itself pain. But if any one else can frighten or pain it, let him do so. For the faculty itself will not by its own opinion turn itself into such ways. Let the body itself take care, if it can, that is suffer nothing, and let it speak, if it suffers. But the soul itself, that which is subject to fear, to pain, which has completely the power of forming an opinion about these things, will suffer nothing, for it will never deviate into such a judgment. The leading principle in itself wants nothing, unless it makes a want for itself; and therefore it is both free from perturbation and unimpeded, if it does not disturb and **impede**[1] itself.

Eudaemonia[2] (happiness) is a good daemon, or a good thing. What then art thou doing here, O imagination? Go away, I entreat thee by the gods, as thou didst come, for I want thee not. But thou art come according to thy old fashion. I am not angry with thee: only go away.

Is any man afraid of change? Why what can take place without change? What then is more pleasing or more suitable to the universal nature? And canst thou take a bath unless the wood undergoes a change? And canst thou be nourished, unless the food undergoes a change? And can anything else that is useful be accomplished without change? Dost thou not see then

---

如，德性）是一致的。這裏所強調的是對自己內心的良好支配能力和守護精神，
不要被外在印象（impression）所驅使。

透過宇宙實體就像通過一道急流，所有東西都被帶走了，它們按其本性與整體相統一合作，就像我們身體各部分的統一與合作一樣。時間已經吞沒了多少個克里西普，多少個蘇格拉底，多少個埃庇克太德？讓你以同樣的思想來看待每一個人和每一件事吧。

我只為一件事而苦惱，唯恐自己做出人的本性不允許做的事情：或者是以不當的方式；或者是在不當的時候。

你忘記所有東西的時刻已經臨近，你被所有人忘記的時候也已經臨近。

愛及那些做錯事的人，是人特有的性質。如果當他們做錯事時，你想到他們是你的同胞，你就會去愛他們。他們是因為無知和不自覺而做錯事的，你們都不久就要死去，特別是，做錯事者沒有造成任何傷害，因為他們沒有使你的自我支配能力變得比以前更糟。

1.Chrysippus，早期斯多噶派的代表。

that for thyself also to change is just the same, and equally necessary for the universal nature?

Through the universal substance as through a furious torrent all bodies are carried, being by their nature united with and cooperating with the whole, as the parts of our body with one another. How many a **Chrysippus**[1], how many a Socrates, how many an Epictetus has time already swallowed up? And let the same thought occur to thee with reference to every man and thing.

One thing only troubles me, lest I should do something which the constitution of man does not allow, or in the way which it does not allow, or what it does not allow now.

Near is thy forgetfulness of all things; and near the forgetfulness of thee by all.

It is peculiar to man to love even those who do wrong. And this happens, if when they do wrong it occurs to thee that they are kinsmen, and that they do wrong through ignorance and unintentionally, and that soon both of you will die; and above all, that the wrong-doer has done thee no harm, for he

在宇宙實體之外的宇宙本性類似於蠟，現在塑一匹馬，當它打破時，它用這質料造一棵樹，然後是一個人，然後又是別的什麼東西，每樣都只存在短短瞬間。對於容器來說，打破它並不是什麼難事，正像組裝它也不是什麼難事一樣。

愁眉苦臉的神態是不自然的，如果經常這樣，其結果是所有的美麗清秀都消散，最後蕩然無存以致完全不可能再恢復。試著從這一事實得出結論吧：它是違反理性的，如果做了錯事還渾然不知，那繼續活下去還有什麼理由呢？

支配著整體的理性不久將改變你見到的所有事物，而別的事物將從現存事物中產生，這些事物又再被另一些事物取代，依此進行，世界就可以永遠是新的。

當一個人對你做了什麼錯事時，馬上考慮：他是抱一種什麼善惡觀做這些事。當你明白了他的善惡觀，你將憐憫他，而不是驚訝或生氣。你或者會有與他相同的善惡觀，或者你認為另一件同樣性質的事

1.scowling [skaʊlɪŋ] adj. 不悅的，有怒容的

has not made thy ruling faculty worse than it was before.

The universal nature out of the universal substance, as if it were wax, now moulds a horse, and when it has broken this up, it uses the material for a tree, then for a man, then for something else; and each of these things subsists for a very short time. But it is no hardship for the vessel to be broken up, just as there was none in its being fastened together.

A **scowling**[1] look is altogether unnatural; when it is often assumed, the result is that all comeliness dies away, and at last is so completely extinguished that it cannot be again lighted up at all. Try to conclude from this very fact that it is contrary to reason. For if even the perception of doing wrong shall depart, what reason is there for living any longer?

Nature which governs the whole will soon change all things which thou seest, and out of their substance will make other things, and again other things from the substance of them, in order that the world may be ever new.

When a man has done thee any wrong, immediately consider with what opinion about good or evil he has done wrong. For when thou hast seen this, thou wilt pity him, and wilt neither wonder nor be angry. For either

是善的，那麼你有義務寬恕他。如果你認為這樣的事情是無所謂善的還是惡的，你將更樂於友好對待那還在錯誤中的人。

不要老想擁有你沒有的東西，而要想想你所擁有的東西，挑出你認為最好的，然後思考如果你尚未擁有它們，要多麼熱切地追求它們。請注意，不能因為喜愛它們就習慣於過分看重它們，以致於失去它們就感到煩躁不堪。

退回自身。那支配的理性原則有此一本性，做正當的事時就自我滿足，從而獲得了寧靜。

驅散幻想，不要再成為情感的傀儡。好好地理解發生在你或是別人身上的事，把每一物體劃分為原因的（形式的）和物質的。想著你最後的時刻。對別人所犯的錯既往不咎。

你要注意所說的話，細心理解正在發生的事以及做這些事的人。

用樸實、謙虛來裝飾你自己，不關心介乎善惡之間的事物。熱

thou thyself thinkest the same thing to be good that he does or another thing of the same kind. It is thy duty then to pardon him. But if thou dost not think such things to be good or evil, thou wilt more readily be well disposed to him who is in error.

Think not so much of what thou hast not as of what thou hast: but of the things which thou hast select the best, and then reflect how eagerly they would have been sought, if thou hadst them not. At the same time however take care that thou dost not through being so pleased with them accustom thyself to overvalue them, so as to be disturbed if ever thou shouldst not have them.

Retire into thyself. The rational principle which rules has this nature, that it is content with itself when it does what is just, and so secures tranquility.

Wipe out the imagination. Stop the pulling of the strings. Confine thyself to the present. Understand well what happens either to thee or to another. Divide and distribute every object into the causal (formal) and the material. Think of thy last hour. Let the wrong which is done by a man stay there where the wrong was done.

Direct thy attention to what is said. Let thy understanding enter into the things that are doing and the things which do them.

Adorn thyself with simplicity and modesty and with indifference towards

愛人類，追隨神靈。詩人說，法能統治著一切，記住萬物有法就足夠了。

　　關於死亡：它或者消散、分解為原子，或者徹底消滅；它不是毀滅，就是改變。

　　關於痛苦：那不可忍受的痛苦奪去我們的生命，而那長期持續的痛苦是可以忍受的；心靈透過隱入自身而保持著它自己的寧靜，支配的能力並不因此虧損。至於被痛苦傷害的部分，如果它們能夠，那就讓它們給予關於痛苦的意見吧。

　　關於名聲：注意那些追求名聲者的內心，觀察他們是什麼人，他們避開什麼，追求什麼。想想那沖積而來的沙，逐漸掩埋以前的沙，在生命中，也是先前的事物被後來的事物迅速掩埋。

　　引自柏拉圖：那種有崇高心靈並觀照全部時間和整體的人，你想他會認為人的生命是一種偉大的東西嗎？那是不可能的。這樣一個心靈也不會把死看作是惡，肯定不會。

1.此處指德謨克利特。
2.annihilation [ə,naɪə`leʃən] n. 徹底消滅

the things which lie between virtue and vice. Love mankind. Follow God. **The poet**[1] says that Law rules all. – And it is enough to remember that Law rules all.

About death: Whether it is a dispersion, or a resolution into atoms, or **annihilation**[2], it is either extinction or change.

About pain: The pain which is intolerable carries us off; but that which lasts a long time is tolerable; and the mind maintains its own tranquility by retiring into itself, and the ruling faculty is not made worse. But the parts which are harmed by pain, let them, if they can, give their opinion about it.

About fame: Look at the minds of those who seek fame, observe what they are, and what kind of things they avoid, and what kind of things they pursue. And consider that as the heaps of sand piled on one another hide the former sands, so in life the events which go before are soon covered by those which come after.

From **Plato**[3]: The man who has an elevated mind and takes a view of all time and of all substance, dost thou suppose it possible for him to think that human life is anything great? it is not possible, he said. – Such a man then

---

3.Plato（約西元前427年～西元前347年），古希臘哲學家，蘇格拉底的學生。這段話出自柏拉圖《理想國》。

引自安提斯坦尼：國王的職責就是行善事而遭惡譽。

面容要服從心靈的召喚，按照心靈的要求管制、調整自身。如果心靈自己不能調節和鎮定自己，便是一件可恥的事。

因事物而使我們自己煩惱是不對的。
因事物對此並不在乎。

以快樂給不朽的神靈和我們。

生命必須像收割成熟的麥穗一樣，
一個人誕生，另一個人離去。

如果神靈不關心我和我的孩子，
自然有它的道理。

善與我同在，正義與我同在。

1.Antisthenes（西元前445年～西元前365年），古希臘犬儒學派哲學創始者。
2.nought [nɔt] n. 無
3.出自 Euripides 戲劇中的片段。
4.出處不詳。

will think that death also is no evil. – Certainly not.

From **Antisthenes**[1]: It is royal to do good and to be abused.

It is a base thing for the countenance to be obedient and to regulate and compose itself as the mind commands, and for the mind not to be regulated and composed by itself.

It is not right to vex ourselves at things,
*For they care **nought**[2] about it.*[3]

To the immortal gods and us give joy. [4]

Life must be reaped like the ripe ears of corn.
One man is born; another dies.[5]

If gods care not for me and for my children,
There is a reason for it.[6]

For the good is with me, and the just.[7]

5.出自 Euripides 戲劇中的片段。
6.出自 Euripides 戲劇中的片段。
7.出自 Euripides 戲劇中的片段。
8.出處不詳。

不要跟著別人哭泣，不要有太強烈的感情。

引自柏拉圖：但是我將給這個人一個滿意的回答，那就是：你錯了！如果你認為一個對所有事情都擅長的人應當計算生或死的可能性，而不是在他做的事情中注意他是否做得正當，做的是否是一個善良人的工作。

雅典人啊，事實就是這樣：一個人無論置身於什麼地方，無論那是他最佳的地方也好，或者是由一個主宰者將他放置的地方也罷。在我看來，他應當堅守那裡，順從這偶然，即使面臨險境，也不盤算死或任何別的事情。

我的好朋友，且想想那高貴的、和善的事情是不是某種與拯救和得救不同的事情。對一個真正的人來說，不應只關注生活如此或那麼長，而是要考慮是否應該想想這種事情：不要眷戀生命，至於這些事情，一個人必須把它們託付給神，並相信女人所說的，沒有誰能逃脫自己的命運。接著要探究的是：**在有生之年如何才能最好地度過這一段時間。**

1.出自柏拉圖《申辯篇》。
2.出自柏拉圖《高爾吉亞篇》。

No joining others in their wailing, no violent emotion. [8]

From Plato: But I would make this man a sufficient answer, which is this: Thou sayest not well, if thou thinkest that a man who is good for anything at all ought to compute the hazard of life or death, and should not rather look to this only in all that he does, whether he is doing what is just or unjust, and the works of a good or a bad man[1].

For thus it is, men of Athens, in truth: wherever a man has placed himself thinking it the best place for him, or has been placed by a commander, there in my opinion he ought to stay and to abide the hazard, taking nothing into the reckoning, either death or anything else, before the baseness of deserting his post.

But, my good friend, reflect whether that which is noble and good is not something different from saving and being saved; for as to a man living such or such a time, at least one who is really a man, consider if this is not a thing to be dismissed from the thoughts: and there must be no love of life: but as to these matters a man must intrust them to the deity and believe what the women say, that no man can escape his destiny, the next inquiry being how he may best live the time that he has to live[2].

環視星球的運動，彷彿你是和它們一起運行，不斷地考慮元素的嬗遞變化，這種思想將濯去塵世生命的污穢。

柏拉圖這話說得實在好：談論世人的人，也應當居高臨下來觀察世事。諸如人群、軍事、農耕、婚姻、談判、生死、法庭的喧鬧、不毛之地、各種野蠻民族、飲宴、哀慟、市場等等，它們複雜交錯卻有秩序地聯繫在一起。

想想過去政治霸權的巨變，你也可以預見將要發生的事情，它們在形式上肯定是相似的。它們不可能偏離現在發生事物的秩序，不管是思考四十年還是一萬年，你所見到的人類生活都差不多。因為，還有什麼別的東西可看呢？

那從地球生長的東西要回到地球，

而那從神聖的種子誕生的，

也將回到天國。

1.wert [wɜt]，古英語中 be 的第二人稱單數過去式。

2.purge [pɜdʒ] v. 淨化

3.terrene [tɛˋrin] adj.世俗的，塵世的

Look round at the courses of the stars, as if thou **wert**[1] going along with them; and constantly consider the changes of the elements into one another; for such thoughts **purge**[2] away the filth of the **terrene**[3] life.

This is **a fine saying of Plato**[4]: That he who is discoursing about men should look also at earthly things as if he viewed them from some higher place; should look at them in their assemblies, armies, agricultural labours, marriages, treaties, births, deaths, noise of the courts of justice, desert places, various nations of barbarians, feasts, **lamentations**[5], markets, a mixture of all things and an orderly combination of contraries.

Consider the past, – such great changes of political **supremacies**[6]. Thou mayest foresee also the things which will be. For they will certainly be of like form, and it is not possible that they should deviate from the order of the things which take place now: accordingly to have contemplated human life for forty years is the same as to have contemplated it for ten thousand years. For what more wilt thou see?

That which has grown from the earth to the earth,
But that which has sprung from heavenly seed,
Back to the heavenly realms returns.

4.該段落此句之後其實並不是柏拉圖所說的話。
5.lamentations [ˌlæmənˈteʃənz] n. [pl.]耶利米哀歌
6.supremacy [səˈprɛməsɪ] n. 霸權

這不是原子的相互結合的分解，就是無知覺的元素的類似消散。

帶著食物、酒和巧妙的魔術，
躡步通過窄道，想逃脫一死，
而天國送出來的微風，
我們必須忍受，辛苦而不抱怨。

一個人可能更善於摔倒他的對手，可是他並非更友善、更謙虛。他沒有得到更好的訓練來待人接物，也沒有更慎重地對待他鄰居的過錯。

在任何工作都能按照符合於神和人的理性完成的地方，沒有任何東西值得我們害怕。只要我們能夠按照我們自己的方向努力，並繼續進行活動，使自己得益，在這種地方，無疑不會有任何傷害。

在任何場合，這些都在你的力量範圍之內：虔誠地默認你現在的條件；公正地對待你周圍的人；努力完善你現在的思想，不讓任何未經仔細考察的東西潛入。

1.出自 Euripides 戲劇中的片段。
2.古喜劇中，為了韻律，常常省略單詞的一些音節。

This is either a dissolution of the mutual involution of the atoms, or a similar dispersion of the unsentient elements. [1]

With food and drinks and cunning magic arts
Turning the channel's course to **'scape** [2] *from death.*
The breeze which heaven has sent.
We must endure, and toil without complaining. [3]

Another may be more expert in casting his opponent; but he is not more social, nor more modest, nor better disciplined to meet all that happens, nor more considerate with respect to the faults of his neighbours.

Where any work can be done conformably to the reason which is common to gods and men, there we have nothing to fear: for where we are able to get profit by means of the activity which is successful and proceeds according to our constitution, there no harm is to be suspected.

Everywhere and at all times it is in thy power **piously** [4] to acquiesce in thy present condition, and to behave justly to those who are about thee, and to exert thy skill upon thy present thoughts, that nothing shall steal into them without being well examined.

3.出自 Euripides 戲劇中的片段。
4.piously [ˈpaɪəslɪ] adv. 虔誠地

不要環顧四周去發現別人的指導原則，而要直接注意那引導你的本性，注意是什麼樣的本性引領你，這種本性既指那透過發生在你身上的事而表現的宇宙本性，又指透過必須由你採取的行為而表現出你的本性。每一個人都應當做合乎他本性的事情，所有其他事物都是為了理性存在物而構成的。在無理性的事物中，低等事物是為了高等事物而存在的；但理性動物是為了彼此而存在。

在人的本性中首要的原則是社會性，其次是不要屈服於感官的引誘。因為身體只是有理性者和理智活動確定自己範圍的特殊場所；不要被感官或嗜慾的活動壓倒，這兩者都是動物的，理智活動卻要取得一種至高無上性，不允許自己被其他運動凌駕。保持健全的理性，它天生是為了運用所有事物而形成的。理性動物的第三個原則是：擺脫錯誤和欺騙。把握這些原則並前進吧，你就能得到屬於你的東西。

想到你終究要死亡的，現在你的生命已經要結束了，那麼按照本性度過留給你的時光。

熱愛那僅僅發生於你的事情，熱愛僅僅為你紡的命運之線，還有什麼比這更適合於你呢？

Do not look around thee to discover other men's ruling principles, but look straight to this, to what nature leads thee, both the universal nature through the things which happen to thee, and thy own nature through the acts which must be done by thee. But every being ought to do that which is according to its constitution; and all other things have been constituted for the sake of rational beings, just as among irrational things the inferior for the sake of the superior, but the rational for the sake of one another.

The prime principle then in man's constitution is the social. And the second is not to yield to the persuasions of the body, for it is the peculiar office of the rational and intelligent motion to circumscribe itself, and never to be overpowered either by the motion of the senses or of the appetites, for both are animal; but the intelligent motion claims superiority and does not permit itself to be overpowered by the others. And with good reason, for it is formed by nature to use all of them. The third thing in the rational constitution is freedom from error and from deception. Let then the ruling principle holding fast to these things go straight on, and it has what is its own.

Consider thyself to be dead, and to have completed thy life up to the present time; and live according to nature the remainder which is allowed thee.

Love that only which happens to thee and is spun with the thread of thy destiny. For what is more suitable?

　　面對發生的一切事情，回憶一下這樣一些人，同樣的事也曾對他們發生，他們曾是多麼煩惱啊，把這些事情看作奇怪的、不滿於它們的，而現在他們到哪裡去了？無處可尋。那麼，你為什麼願意以同樣的方式行動呢？你為什麼不把這些與本性相異的焦慮，留給那些引起它們並被它們推動的人呢？你為什麼不完全專注於對待你遭遇事物的正確方式呢？那樣你將好好地利用它們，它們將給你的工作提供質料。僅僅傾聽自身，在你做的一切行為裡都決心做一個好人，記住……

　　觀照內心。善的源泉在內心，如果你挖掘，它將汩汩湧出。

　　身體應當是強壯的，無論活動還是態度，都不能有散漫之態。心靈透過面容表現的理智和合宜也應當體現在整個身體之中，所有這些都應當毫不矯揉造作。

　　較之舞蹈者的藝術，生活的藝術更像鬥士的藝術：堅定地站立，準備對付突如其來的進攻。

　　總是觀察那些你希望得到他們嘉許的人，看看他們擁有什麼樣的

In everything which happens keep before thy eyes those to whom the same things happened, and how they were vexed, and treated them as strange things, and found fault with them: and now where are they? Nowhere. Why then dost thou too choose to act in the same way? And why dost thou not leave these agitations which are foreign to nature, to those who cause them and those who are moved by them? And why art thou not altogether intent upon the right way of making use of the things which happen to thee? For then thou wilt use them well, and they will be a material for thee to work on. Only attend to thyself, and resolve to be a good man in every act which thou doest: and remember...

Look within. Within is the fountain of good, and it will ever bubble up, if thou wilt ever dig.

The body ought to be compact, and to show no irregularity either in motion or attitude. For what the mind shows in the face by maintaining in it the expression of intelligence and propriety, that ought to be required also in the whole body. But all of these things should be observed without affectation.

The art of life is more like the wrestler's art than the dancer's, in respect of this, that it should stand ready and firm to meet onsets which are sudden and unexpected.

Constantly observe who those are whose approbation thou wishest to

支配原則。這樣你將不會譴責那些無意中冒犯你的人，只要你看清了他們的意見和慾望的根源，你也不會想要得到他們的嘉許。

　　哲學家說，每一個靈魂都會不由自主地偏離真理，因而也同樣不由自主地偏離正義、節制、仁愛等品格。把這牢記在心是很有必要的，因為這樣你就將對所有人更和藹。

　　在任何痛苦中都讓這一思想出現，在痛苦中就不會感到恥辱，它並不使支配的理智虧損，因為就理智是理性或社會的而言，它並不損害理智。的確，在痛苦之際也可以讓伊比鳩魯的這些話來幫助你：痛苦不是不可忍受或永遠持續的，只要你記住它有它的界限，只要你不在想像中增加任何東西給它。也記住這一點，我們並沒有覺察，我們感覺許多使我們不愜意的事情是痛苦，像瞌睡、燥熱和失去胃口，當你不滿於這些事情時，你就對自己說，我是在屈服於痛苦。

1.lookest 為古英語中 look 的第二人稱單數（主語為 thou 時使用）。
2.Epicurus（約西元前341年～西元前270年），花園學派的創始人。這段是出自伊比鳩魯關於快樂和痛苦的學說之中。
3.bearest 為古英語中 bear 的第二人稱單數（主語為 thou 時使用）。

have, and what ruling principles they possess. For then thou wilt neither blame those who offend involuntarily, nor wilt thou want their approbation, if thou **lookest**[1] to the sources of their opinions and appetites.

Every soul, the philosopher says, is involuntarily deprived of truth; consequently in the same way it is deprived of justice and temperance and benevolence and everything of the kind. It is most necessary to bear this constantly in mind, for thus thou wilt be more gentle towards all.

In every pain let this thought be present, that there is no dishonour in it, nor does it make the governing intelligence worse, for it does not damage the intelligence either so far as the intelligence is rational or so far as it is social. Indeed in the case of most pains let this remark of **Epicurus**[2] aid thee, that pain is neither intolerable nor everlasting, if thou **bearest**[3] in mind that it has its limits, and if thou **addest**[4] nothing to it in imagination: and remember this too, that we do not perceive that many things which are disagreeable to us are the same as pain, such as excessive **drowsiness**[5], and the being **scorched**[6] by heat, and the having no appetite. When then thou art discontented about any of these things, say to thyself, that thou art yielding to pain.

4.addest 為古英語中 add 的第二人稱單數（主語為 thou 時使用）。
5.drowsiness [ˋdraʊzɪnɪs] n. 假寐

注意，對薄情寡義的人，不要像他們對待別人那樣對待他們。

我們怎麼知道泰拉格斯在品格上不如蘇格拉底優秀呢？因為僅下面這些論點還是不夠的：蘇格拉底有更高貴的死亡；更巧妙地與智者辯論；更能忍耐寒冷的冬夜；當他被命令去逮捕薩拉米的萊昂時，他認為拒絕是更高尚的；他在街上昂首闊步地走過——雖然人們懷疑這一事實人其真實性。此外我們還應當探究：蘇格拉底擁有一個什麼樣的靈魂，他是否能夠滿足於公正地對待人和虔誠地對待神，不無益地為人們的犯罪苦惱，同時也不使自己屈服於任何人的無知，不把從宇宙降臨於他的任何事情看作是奇怪的，不把它作為不可忍受的東西，不允許他的理智與可憐的肉體的愛好發生共鳴。

自然並沒有如此混合你的靈魂與軀體，以致你難以控制、把握自己；因為成為一個神聖的人，卻不被人如此承認是很有可能的。請把這牢記在心：過一種幸福生活所需要的東西確實是很少的。不要因為你無望變成一個自然知識領域中的辯證家和能手，就放棄成為一個自由、謙虛、友善和遵從神的人的希望。

1.Telauges，是畢達哥拉斯（Pythagoras）之子，關於他的資料很少，曾經出現在由 Aeschines 所寫的蘇格拉底對話中，這篇對話現已遺失。
2.蘇格拉底受『三十人暴政』之命去逮捕此人，但他認為此人無辜，就冒險抗命。

Take care not to feel towards the inhuman, as they feel towards men.

How do we know if **Telauges**[1] was not superior in character to Socrates? For it is not enough that Socrates died a more noble death, and disputed more skilfully with the sophists, and passed the night in the cold with more endurance, and that when he was bid to arrest **Leon of Salamis**[2], he considered it more noble to refuse, and that he walked in a **swaggering**[3] way in the streets – though as to this fact one may have great doubts if it was true. But we ought to inquire, what kind of a soul it was that Socrates possessed, and if he was able to be content with being just towards men and pious towards the gods, neither idly vexed on account of men's villainy, nor yet making himself a slave to any man's ignorance, nor receiving as strange anything that fell to his share out of the universal, nor enduring it as intolerable, nor allowing his understanding to sympathize with the affects of the miserable flesh.

Nature has not so **mingled**[4] the intelligence with the composition of the body, as not to have allowed thee the power of circumscribing thyself and of bringing under subjection to thyself all that is thy own; for it is very possible to be a divine man and to be recognised as such by no one. Always bear this in mind; and another thing too, that very little indeed is necessary for living

3.swagger [`swægɚ] n. 昂首闊步
4.mingle [`mɪŋɡl] vt. 使混合，使相混

你有能力免除所有壓力，保持內心的最大寧靜，即使全世界的人都聲嘶力竭地反對你，即使野獸把裹著你的這一捏製的皮囊撕成碎片。因為置身於所有阻礙物中的心靈，獲得內心的寧靜，正確判斷周圍的事物，可以正確運用展示給它的物件。判斷可以對落入它的視線的事物說：你確實存在（是一現實），然而在人們的意見中你可以呈現為另一種不同的模樣；這運用也將對落入它手中的事物說：你是我追求的事物，對於我來說，那出現的事物始終是有助於理智和政治德性的質料。概言之，是可屬於人或神的藝術訓練的質料。發生的一切事情都或者與神或者與人有一種聯繫，絕不是新的和難於把握的，而是有用和容易處理的。

道德品格的完善在於，把每一天都作為最後一天度過，既不過於

1.dialectician [ˌdaɪəlɛk`tɪʃən] n. 辯證學家

a happy life. And because thou hast despaired of becoming a **dialectician**[1] and skilled in the knowledge of nature, do not for this reason renounce the hope of being both free and modest and social and obedient to God.

It is in thy power to live free from all compulsion in the greatest tranquility of mind, even if all the world cry out against thee as much as they choose, and even if wild beasts tear in pieces the members of this kneaded matter which has grown around thee. For what hinders the mind in the midst of all this from maintaining itself in tranquility and in a just judgment of all surrounding things and in a ready use of the objects which are presented to it, so that the judgment may say to the thing which falls under its observation: This thou art in substance (reality), though in men's opinion thou mayest appear to be of a different kind; and the use shall say to that which falls under the hand: Thou art the thing that I was seeking; for to me that which presents itself is always a material for virtue both rational and political, and in a word, for the exercise of art, which belongs to man or God. For everything which happens has a relationship either to God or man, and is neither new nor difficult to handle, but usual and apt matter to work on.

The perfection of moral character consists in this, in passing every day as

激動，也不麻木不仁或者表現虛偽。

　　不朽的神不會因為在如此長的時間裏必須不斷地忍受人們中的許多惡人而煩惱，而是從各個方面關心他們。作為註定很快要死去的人，你厭倦了忍受惡人嗎，當你是他們當中的一員時，反應亦同嗎？

　　對一個人來說這是件可笑的事情：他不從自己的惡逃開——這的確是可能的；他竟要從別人的惡逃開——而這是不可能的。

　　凡是理性的和政治（社會）能力認為『既不合於理性也不合於社會的東西』，它一定是認定那東西低於它自身。

　　當你做了一件好事使別人得益，你為什麼還要像傻瓜一樣尋求名聲或獲得回報呢？

　　沒有人會因為有用的東西太多而感到厭倦。按照本性行動是有用的，那麼就不厭倦地多做些利己利人的事吧。

1.torpid [`tɔrpɪd] adj. 遲鈍的

the last, and in being neither violently excited nor **torpid**[1] nor playing the hypocrite.

The gods who are immortal are not vexed because during so long a time they must tolerate continually men such as they are and so many of them bad; and besides this, they also take care of them in all ways. But thou, who art destined to end so soon, art thou wearied of enduring the bad, and this too when thou art one of them?

It is a ridiculous thing for a man not to fly from his own badness, which is indeed possible, but to fly from other men's badness, which is impossible.

Whatever the rational and political (social) faculty finds to be neither intelligent nor social, it properly judges to be inferior to itself.

When thou hast done a good act and another has received it, why dost thou look for a third thing besides these, as fools do, either to have the reputation of having done a good act or to obtain a return?

No man is tired of receiving what is useful. But it is useful to act according to nature. Do not then be tired of receiving what is useful by doing it to

_____

　　宇宙的整個本性產生了宇宙。現在發生的一切事物或者是作為結果、或者是作為後果出現的，甚或那宇宙支配力量本身的運動所指向的主要事物也不受理性原則的支配。如果記住這一點，你將在很多事情中反應更為寧靜。

others.

The nature of the All moved to make the universe. But now either everything that takes place comes by way of consequence or continuity; or even the chief things towards which the ruling power of the universe directs its own movement are governed by no rational principle. If this is remembered it will make thee more tranquil in many things.

第八卷

你難以像哲學家一樣生活，或者至少青年之後不能，這種反思有助於你擺脫虛名。你已經遠離哲學，對大多數人和你自己來說這都是顯而易見的。於是你變得很混亂，以致重獲一個哲學家的名號和讚譽不再那麼容易，而且你生活的計畫也與之相悖。如果你真正明白問題所在，就不要想你在別人眼中是什麼樣子，如果你能按照自己本性所希望的度過餘生，你應對此感到滿足。你應該不辭辛苦地注意你的本性想要什麼，不要為任何別的東西分心。你在哪裏也沒有找到幸福，並為此徘徊迷茫。在三段論中沒有，在財富中沒有，在榮譽和名聲中沒有，在享樂中也沒有，哪裏都沒有。幸福在哪裏？就在做那些人的本性所要求的事情之中。一個人將如何做這些事呢？如果他的情感和行為來自於他的原則，那麼那些原則是什麼？即那些與善惡相關的東西：凡是不能讓人變得公正、節制、堅毅、自由的事皆非善事；凡是不能讓人背離上述品德的事皆非惡事。

在採取任何行動時都問自己，這件事與我有關嗎？我以後會後悔做這事嗎？還有一點點時間我就要死去，一切也都要消逝。如果我現在做的事是一個有理智的人、一個符合社會利益的人、一個與神遵循

BOOK 8

This reflection also tends to the removal of the desire of empty fame, that it is no longer in thy power to have lived the whole of thy life, or at least thy life from thy youth upwards, like a philosopher; but both to many others and to thyself it is plain that thou art far from philosophy. Thou hast fallen into disorder then, so that it is no longer easy for thee to get the reputation of a philosopher; and thy plan of life also opposes it. If then thou hast truly seen where the matter lies, throw away the thought, How thou shalt seem to others, and be content if thou shalt live the rest of thy life in such wise as thy nature wills. Observe then what it wills, and let nothing else distract thee; for thou hast had experience of many wanderings without having found happiness anywhere, not in syllogisms, nor in wealth, nor in reputation, nor in enjoyment, nor anywhere. Where is it then? In doing what man's nature requires. How then shall a man do this? If he has principles from which come his affects and his acts. What principles? Those which relate to good and bad: the belief that there is nothing good for man, which does not make him just, temperate, manly, free; and that there is nothing bad, which does not do the contrary to what has been mentioned.

On the occasion of every act ask thyself, How is this with respect to me? Shall I repent of it? A little time and I am dead, and all is gone. What more do I seek, if what I am now doing is work of an intelligent living being, and a

同樣法則的人做的工作，那麼我還有何求呢？

　　亞歷山大、凱撒和龐培與第歐根尼、赫拉克利特、蘇格拉底比較起來，算得上什麼呢？由於後者能看到事物的本質，熟知各種原因（形式）和質料，這些人的支配原則是相同的。至於前者，他們必須照管多少事物，他們是多少事情的奴隸啊！

　　考慮一下，即使你勃然大怒，人們無論如何也要做同樣的事情。

　　關鍵在於：不要為此而煩惱，因為所有的事物，無論好與壞，都是合乎宇宙本性的，很快就都將化為烏有，再沒有人會記得，就像哈德良、奧古斯都那樣。其次，要聚精會神地考察事情本身，同時記住你應該成為一個好人。做你本性所要求的事，不要逃避；說你看來是最公正的話，只是要以一種好的語氣，以謙虛和毫不虛偽的態度說出來。

　　宇宙的本性有這一工作要做，即把這個地方的事物移到那個地方，改變它們，然後又把它們帶到其他地方。我們沒有必要害怕任何

1.第歐根尼、赫拉克利特、蘇格拉底都是古希臘哲學家，凱撒和龐培是古羅馬大將及政治家，軍功顯赫。

social being, and one who is under the same law with God?

Alexander and Gaius and Pompeius, what are they in comparison with Diogenes and Heraclitus and Socrates[1]? For they were acquainted with things, and their causes (forms), and their matter, and the ruling principles of these men were the same. But as to the others, how many things had they to care for, and to how many things were they slaves?

Consider that men will do the same things nevertheless, even though thou shouldst burst.

This is the chief thing: Be not perturbed, for all things are according to the nature of the universal; and in a little time thou wilt be nobody and nowhere, like **Hadrian and Augustus**[2]. In the next place having fixed thy eyes steadily on thy business look at it, and at the same time remembering that it is thy duty to be a good man, and what man's nature demands, do that without turning aside; and speak as it seems to thee most just, only let it be with a good disposition and with modesty and without hypocrisy.

The nature of the universal has this work to do, to remove to that place the things which are in this, to change them, to take them away hence, and

---

2.Hadrian，哈德良，羅馬皇帝；Augustus，奧古斯都，羅馬第一任皇帝。

新事物。所有的事物都是我們所熟悉的，而且其分佈也是一樣的。

每一本性，當它在循自己合適的路時，都是滿足於自身的。當一個理性的本性不贊成任何錯誤的或不確定的東西，使自己所有的行動都有益於社會時；當它把它的慾望和厭惡限制屬於自己力量範圍之內的事物上時；當它願意並樂於接受那普遍本性分配給它的一切事物時，我們就說它循自己合適的路行進。每一特殊本性都是其共同本性的一部分，正如葉子的本性是草木共同本性的一部分。但草木，葉子的本性作為共同本性的一部分，這種共同本性沒有理性和知覺，它可能會受到阻礙。然而，涵蓋人本性的共同本性卻不能受到阻礙，它是理性的、公正的。它根據事物的價值，以時間、質料、原因（形式）、活動和事件平等地給予一切事物。我們在對任何一個事物和別的事物進行比較和考察時，並不在於要發現它們的各個方面是否平等，而是要對組合成這些事物的所有方面的整體進行相應的比較。

你沒有閱讀的時間或能力，但你有時間或能力來杜絕傲慢，你有時間可以來超越肉體的快樂和痛苦，你有時間來超越對虛名的熱愛。不要惱怒於那些冷漠和忘恩負義的人們，也不必理會他們。

to carry them there. All things are change, yet we need not fear anything new. All things are familiar to us; but the distribution of them still remains the same.

Every nature is contented with itself when it goes on its way well; and a rational nature goes on its way well, when in its thoughts it assents to nothing false or uncertain, and when it directs its movements to social acts only, and when it confines its desires and aversions to the things which are in its power, and when it is satisfied with everything that is assigned to it by the common nature. For of this common nature every particular nature is a part, as the nature of the leaf is a part of the nature of the plant; except that in the plant the nature of the leaf is part of a nature which has not perception or reason, and is subject to be impeded; but the nature of man is part of a nature which is not subject to impediments, and is intelligent and just, since it gives to everything in equal portions and according to its worth, times, substance, cause (form), activity, and incident. But examine, not to discover that any one thing compared with any other single thing is equal in all respects, but by taking all the parts together of one thing and comparing them with all the parts together of another.

Thou hast not leisure or ability to read. But thou hast leisure or ability to check arrogance: thou hast leisure to be superior to pleasure and pain: thou hast leisure to be superior to love of fame, and not to be vexed at stupid and ungrateful people, nay even to care for them.

不要再讓人聽到你對宮廷生活或者你自己吹毛求疵。

你後悔，是因為你沒有做你本來可以做的事情、對你有用的事情，所以你在內心斥責自我。而凡是善的東西必定也是有用的，誠實善良的人應當追求它。但誠實善良的人從來不會因拒絕了肉體的快樂而後悔，因為這樣的快樂既非善的，亦非有用的。

事物本身是什麼，自身的結構是什麼？它的質料和原料是什麼？用途何在？它的原因的本性（或形式）又是什麼？它存在這個世界上做什麼？它要繼續存在多久？

當你不情願地從床上起來時，提醒自己這是按照你的情況和人的本性去從事社會活動，而睡眠卻是對非理智的動物也是同樣的。有什麼事物能比屬於每個個體的本性的東西更為合適、更符合你的本性並讓人愉悅呢？

如果可能的話，常常把物理學、倫理學和邏輯學的原則應用到靈魂收到的每一個印象中。

無論遇到什麼人，你都應該立即問自己：這個人對善惡持什麼態度？如果他對苦樂及其原因，對榮辱、生死持如此這般的態度，對我來說就沒有任何值得奇怪和不可理解的地方了。如果他有這般的行為，我要時刻記住他是不得不那樣做的。

Let no man any longer hear thee finding fault with the court life or with thy own.

Repentance is a kind of self-reproof for having neglected something useful; but that which is good must be something useful, and the perfect good man should look after it. But no such man would ever repent of having refused any sensual pleasure. Pleasure then is neither good nor useful.

This thing, what is it in itself, in its own constitution? What is its substance and material? And what its causal nature (or form)? And what is it doing in the world? And how long does it subsist?

When thou risest from sleep with reluctance, remember that it is according to thy constitution and according to human nature to perform social acts, but sleeping is common also to irrational animals. But that which is according to each individual's nature is also more peculiarly its own, and more suitable to its nature, and indeed also more agreeable.

Constantly and, if it be possible, on the occasion of every impression on the soul, apply to it the principles of Physic, of Ethic, and of Dialectic.

Whatever man thou meetest with, immediately say to thyself: What opinions has this man about good and bad? For if with respect to pleasure and pain and the causes of each, and with respect to fame and ignominy, death and life, he has such and such opinions, it will seem nothing

　　記住：正像對無花果樹結出了無花果感到大驚小怪應當羞愧一樣，對這世界產生了它本應該產生的事物大驚小怪也應當羞愧。如果一個醫生對某人發熱大驚小怪，或者一個舵手對風向不遂人願大驚小怪，對他們來說都是可羞愧的。

　　記住：改變你的意見、追隨糾正你缺點的人，和堅持你的錯誤一樣都不違背你的自由。它是按照你的動機、判斷做出的行為，而且也確實符合你的理解力。

　　如果一件事是在你的力量範圍之內，為什麼做它呢？但如果它不在你的力量範圍之內，你能責怪誰呢？責怪原子嗎？或者責怪神靈？不論怪誰都是愚蠢的。**你絕不要責怪任何人。**如果你能夠做到，就糾正事情的起因；如果你不能辦到這個，那麼至少糾正事物本身；但如果你連這個都做不到，那你抱怨又有什麼用呢？沒有什麼事是不帶有某種目的就完成的。

　　任何死亡和衰落都不會落到宇宙之外。如果它逗留在這裏，它就會在這裏改變，被分解為適當的部分——即組成宇宙和你自身的元素。那些元素也發生改變，並不低聲抱怨。

　　一切事物的存在都有某種目的，如一匹馬、一棵葡萄樹。那你為

wonderful or strange to me, if he does such and such things; and I shall bear in mind that he is compelled to do so.

Remember that as it is a shame to be surprised if the fig-tree produces figs, so it is to be surprised if the world produces such and such things of which it is productive; and for the physician and the helmsman it is a shame to be surprised, if a man has a fever, or if the wind is unfavourable.

Remember that to change thy opinion and to follow him who corrects thy error is as consistent with freedom as it is to persist in thy error. For it is thy own, the activity which is exerted according to thy own movement and judgment, and indeed according to thy own understanding too.

If a thing is in thy own power, why dost thou do it? But if it is in the power of another, whom dost thou blame, – the atoms (chance) or the gods? Both are foolish. Thou must blame nobody. For if thou canst, correct that which is the cause; but if thou canst not do this, correct at least the thing itself; but if thou canst not do even this, of what use is it to thee to find fault? For nothing should be done without a purpose.

That which has died falls not out of the universe. If it stays here, it also changes here, and is dissolved into its proper parts, which are elements of the universe and of thyself. And these too change, and they murmur not.

Everything exists for some end, – a horse, a vine. Why dost thou wonder?

什麼覺得奇怪呢？甚至太陽如是說，我存在是有某種目的的，其他的神靈也都有自己特定的職責。那麼你是為什麼而存在的呢？享樂嗎？看看常理是否允許這樣的說法。

自然在對每一事物完結時的關心不亞於在其開始或中途對它的關心，就像一個人擲球一樣。對於球來說，被向上投有什麼好處呢？或者向下投甚至落到地面對它又有什麼損害呢？對於一個氣泡來說，形成對它有什麼好處，爆裂對它又有什麼壞處呢？這個道理同樣也適用於一盞燈。

把肉體朝外翻轉過來，看看它是什麼樣子；當它變老時，又變成什麼樣子；當它生病時，又變成什麼樣子？

讚頌者和被讚頌者、記憶者和被記憶者都將很快化為塵土。所有這些活動都只是發生在這世界的一部分的一個小角落裏，甚至對此也不是所有人都持相同的意見，甚至任何一個人他自身的意見也不是一直不變的。整個地球也只是一個點。

留心呈現給你的事物，不論它是一種意見、一種行為，還是一句話語。

Even the sun will say, I am for some purpose, and the rest of the gods will say the same. For what purpose then art thou, – to enjoy pleasure? See if common sense allows this.

Nature has had regard in everything no less to the end than to the beginning and the continuance, just like the man who throws up a ball. What good is it then for the ball to be thrown up, or harm for it to come down, or even to have fallen? And what good is it to the bubble while it holds together, or what harm when it is burst? The same may be said of a light also.

Turn it (the body) inside out, and see what kind of thing it is; and when it has grown old, what kind of thing it becomes, and when it is diseased.

Short-lived are both the praiser and the praised, and the rememberer and the remembered: and all this in a nook of this part of the world; and not even here do all agree, no, not any one with himself: and the whole earth too is a point.

Attend to the matter which is before thee, whether it is an opinion or an act or a word.

你活該受這樣的報應！因為你寧願明天才成為一個好人，而不願今天就成為一個好人。

我在做什麼呢？我做對人類有益的事。有什麼事發生在我身上嗎？我接受它，把它歸於神靈——所有事物的根源，所有發生的事物都來源於它們。

正如洗澡呈現給你的：油漬、汗漬、污漬，一切都令人厭惡。而我們生活中的每一個部分和塵世的一切事物皆是如此。

露西拉見證維魯斯死了，然後露西拉死了；瑟孔達見證馬克沁斯死了，然後瑟孔達死了；埃皮梯恩查努斯見證戴奧梯莫斯死了，然後埃皮梯恩查努斯死了；安東尼皮爾斯見證他的妻子福斯蒂娜死了，然後安東尼皮爾斯死了。這就是世界運行的規律。塞勒爾見證哈德良死了，然後塞勒爾死了。那些苦行者、預言家和趾高氣揚的人，他們現在到哪裏去了呢？比如說苦行者沙哈克斯、柏拉圖主義者迪米特裏烏斯、尤德蒙及別的與他們類似的人。所有的人都是朝生暮死，早已辭世。有一些人甚至一死就馬上被人忘記，還有一些人變成了神話故事中的英雄，還有一些人即便是載入了神話故事，現在也被人忘記了。你必須記住的是：作為小小的混合物終將被分解消散，你的呼吸將停止，或者被移到其他某個地方。

1.sufferest 為古英語中 suffer 的第二人稱單數（主語為 thou 時使用）。
2.choosest 為古英語中 choose 的第二人稱單數（主語為 thou 時使用）。
3.Lucilla，作者的母親。　4.Verus，作者的親生父親或者是作者的兄弟。
5.Secunda，Maximus的妻子。　6.Maximus，斯多噶派哲學家，較受作者敬愛。
7.Epitynchanus，可能是哈德良的隨從。　8.Diotimus，哈德良的寵奴。

Thou **sufferest**[1] this justly: for thou **choosest**[2] rather to become good tomorrow than to be good to-day.

Am I doing anything? I do it with reference to the good of mankind. Does anything happen to me? I receive it and refer it to the gods, and the source of all things, from which all that happens is derived.

Such as bathing appears to thee, – oil, sweat, dirt, filthy water, all things disgusting, – so is every part of life and everything.

Lucilla[3] saw **Verus**[4] die, and then Lucilla died. **Secunda**[5] saw **Maximus**[6] die, and then Secunda died. **Epitynchanus**[7] saw **Diotimus**[8] die, and Epitynchanus died. **Antoninus**[9] saw **Faustina**[10] die, and then Antoninus died. Such is everything. **Celer**[11] saw Hadrian die, and then Celer died. And those sharp-witted men, either seers or men inflated with pride, where are they, – For instance the sharp-witted men, **Charax**[12] and **Demetrius**[13] the Platonist and **Eudaemon**[14], and any one else like them. All ephemeral, dead long ago. Some indeed have not been remembered even for a short time, and others have become the heroes of fables, and again others have disappeared even from fables. Remember this then, that this little compound, thyself, must either be dissolved, or thy poor breath must be

---

9.Antoninus，作者的養父，古羅馬第十五任皇帝。

10.Faustina，作者養父安東尼的妻子，她的女兒與她同名，是作者的妻子。

11.Celer，哈德良的秘書，教授作者修辭學。　12.Charax，可能是一個哲學家。

13.Demetrius，可能是犬儒派哲學家，被Vespasian流放。

14.Eudaemon，可能是作者之前的希臘語秘書。

一個人做適合自己做的工作時才會感到真正的快樂。這都是適合的工作：友好對待同胞，輕視感官的意向，正確判斷所有看似可信的表象，對宇宙的本性和發生於其中的事物進行全盤調查。

你和別的事物之間有三種聯繫：一種是與你身體之間的聯繫，一種是你與所有事物最初起源的神聖原因的聯繫，一種是與那些和你一起生活的人之間的聯繫。

痛苦對身體是一種惡，那就讓身體說出它的想法；痛苦對靈魂也是一種惡，但是，靈魂卻可以憑其力量使自己保持安寧和平靜，而不把痛苦作為一種惡。因為所有判斷、思考、活動和厭惡都是發生在內心，沒有惡可以爬上高峰。

消除你的想像要經常對自己說：我有能力把所有的邪惡、慾望以及所有的紛擾都拋在靈魂之外。相反地，根據事物的本性來看待和思考它們，根據其價值來運用它們，然後記住這是本性賦予你的力量。

不論是在元老院中還是對任何一個人講話，都要使你的言詞恰當而不矯飾，均要用實在的話。

extinguished, or be removed and placed elsewhere.

It is satisfaction to a man to do the proper works of a man. Now it is a proper work of a man to be benevolent to his own kind, to despise the movements of the senses, to form a just judgment of plausible appearances, and to take a survey of the nature of the universe and of the things which happen in it.

There are three relations between thee and other things: the one to the body which surrounds thee; the second to the divine cause from which all things come to all; and the third to those who live with thee.

Pain is either an evil to the body – then let the body say what it thinks of it – or to the soul; but it is in the power of the soul to maintain its own serenity and tranquility, and not to think that pain is an evil. For every judgment and movement and desire and aversion is within, and no evil ascends so high.

Wipe out thy imaginations by often saying to thyself: now it is in my power to let no badness be in this soul, nor desire nor any perturbation at all; but looking at all things I see what is their nature, and I use each according to its value. – Remember this power which thou hast from nature.

Speak both in the senate and to every man, whoever he may be, appropriately, not with any affectation: use plain discourse.

奧古斯都的宮廷、妻子、女兒、外甥、女婿、姐妹、阿格裏珀（軍政大臣）、親屬、傭人、朋友、阿利烏（哲學家）、米西納斯（政治家）、祭司，整個宮廷裏的人都死了。奧古斯都死後，其他的也都陸陸續續死了。他們曾經多麼高貴地活著，然而現在還是死了，每個人不都是如此嗎？考慮一下整個家族的死，像龐培的家族，墓碑上銘刻著——他是他的家族中最後死去的一個。再考慮他們的祖先為了有一個後代怎樣的煞費苦心，但是必然要有一個人會成為最後一個人。在此再考慮一下整個家族的死。

在每一項活動中都使你的生活井然有序是你的職責，如果在每一項活動中都盡你所能地履行了這一職責，那你就該滿足。無人能夠阻止你在每一項活動中履行這種職責，但某些外部的事物可能會成為障礙。沒有什麼能夠阻擋這種正當的、嚴肅的、審慎的活動，但是其他活動的能力也許會被阻礙。默許這種阻礙，並且把精力用到那些允許的事情上，另外一種機會將呈現在你面前，代替那被阻礙了的活動，人應該調適自己迎合我們剛剛所談的秩序。

當財富和幸運降臨，毫不炫耀地接受這短暫的賜福，同時也隨時準備好放棄它們。

1.Augustus，指屋大維（西元前63年～西元14年），全名Gaius Julius CaesarOctavianus，在他的統治下，羅馬帝國進入相當長的和平時期。西元前27年，他被元老院授予『奧古斯都』的稱號，這個稱號源於宗教，意味著超越人的權威和崇高的地位。

Augustus'[1] court, wife, daughter, descendants, ancestors, sister, **Agrippa**[2], kinsmen, intimates, friends, **Areius**[3], **Maecenas**[4], physicians and sacrificing priests, – the whole court is dead. Then turn to the rest, not considering the death of a single man, but of a whole race, as of the Pompeii; and that which is inscribed on the tombs, – The last of his race. Then consider what trouble those before them have had that they might leave a successor; and then, that of necessity some one must be the last. Again here consider the death of a whole race.

It is thy duty to order thy life well in every single act; and if every act does its duty, as far as is possible, be content; and no one is able to hinder thee so that each act shall not do its duty. – But something external will stand in the way.- Nothing will stand in the way of thy acting justly and soberly and considerately. – But perhaps some other active power will be hindered. – Well, but by acquiescing in the hindrance and by being content to transfer thy efforts to that which is allowed, another opportunity of action is immediately put before thee in place of that which was hindered, and one which will adapt itself to this ordering of which we are speaking.

Receive wealth or prosperity without arrogance; and be ready to let it go.

2.Agrippa（西元前63年～西元前12年），奧古斯都之軍政大臣，羅馬政治家和將軍。　3.Areius，斯多噶派哲學家，供職於奧古斯都的宮中。
4.Maecenas（西元前70年～西元前8年），古羅馬政治家，資助Horace、Virgil等詩人。

那些對所有事情都抱怨不滿並使自己脫離社會的人，那些不遵守社會準則的人，還有那些過分挑剔苛刻的人，都是他們自作自受把自己變成這樣的。如果你曾經看到過被砍斷的一隻手、一隻腳或者一顆頭躺在地上，那麼你應該能明白那些人脫離群體的感覺。你生來是一個整體中的一部分，而現在你卻把自己從自然的整體中脫離出來。值得高興的是，你還有可能和整體統一起來。上帝並沒有把這種能力，即分離後再統一的能力施予其他任何一種動物，他卻把這種能力賜予了人類。這對人而言是多大的恩惠！因為，上帝讓人有能力不同宇宙徹底分離，即使已經脫離了整體，如果他自己願意，人也可以再回到整體中去，恢復以前的身份和地位，仍然是宇宙的一部分。

大自然幾乎把它所有的其他能力賜予了所有的理性生物，因而我們也從它那裏獲得了這種力量：宇宙本性能夠轉化一切阻礙和反對它的事物，並且把它們固定在預定的地方。所有的理性生物也能夠把阻礙變成自身的質料，根據預先設定的計畫的目的來使用它。

不要讓自己苦於思索整個人生，不要馬上考慮你可能遇到的各種麻煩，而是在每種情況下，問自己一個問題：到底什麼是我不能忍受和難以承受的呢？這個時候你將恥於承認。然後記住：無論將來還是過去都不可能使你痛苦，只有現在才會讓你痛苦。而你只要稍微控制，這種痛苦也會大大減輕。如果你的心靈連這都不能承受，那就責

If thou didst ever see a hand cut off, or a foot, or a head, lying anywhere apart from the rest of the body, such does a man make himself, as far as he can, who is not content with what happens, and separates himself from others, or does anything unsocial. Suppose that thou hast detached thyself from the natural unity, – for thou wast made by nature a part, but now thou hast cut thyself off, – yet here there is this beautiful provision, that it is in thy power again to unite thyself. God has allowed this to no other part, after it has been separated and cut asunder, to come together again. But consider the kindness by which he has distinguished man, for he has put it in his power not to be separated at all from the universal; and when he has been separated, he has allowed him to return and to be united and to resume his place as a part.

As the nature of the universal has given to every rational being all the other powers that it has, so we have received from it this power also. For as the universal nature converts and fixes in its predestined place everything which stands in the way and opposes it, and makes such things a part of itself, so also the rational animal is able to make every hindrance its own material, and to use it for such purposes as it may have designed.

Do not disturb thyself by thinking of the whole of thy life. Let not thy thoughts at once embrace all the various troubles which thou mayest expect to befall thee: but on every occasion ask thyself, What is there in this which is intolerable and past bearing? For thou wilt be ashamed to confess. In the next place remember that neither the future nor the past pains thee, but only

備它吧。

潘瑟和帕加穆斯現在還守在他們主人的陵墓旁？喬內阿斯和戴奧梯莫斯現在還守在哈德良的陵墓旁？真是荒唐！即使他們還守在旁邊，他們的主人能感覺得到嗎？即使他們可以感覺到，他們會高興嗎？即使他們很高興，這些會永恆嗎？不管是男是女，所有人都會變老，然後死去，這不是命運的安排嗎？這些人死後，他們所悼念的那些人該怎麼辦呢？這一切都是臭氣與一包污血。

聖人說，如果你有敏銳的觀察力，那麼你也將擁有明智的判斷力。

在理性動物的構成上，我找不到任何與正義相悖的品質，而只能找到貪圖享樂的剋星：節制。

如果你可以去除帶給你痛苦的那些意見，那麼你的自我將獲得最大的安全。自我？這又是什麼？自我就是你的理性。你也許會說：

---

1. circumscribest 為古英語中 circumscribe 的第二人稱單數（主語為 thou 時使用）。

2.Panthea，作者兄弟 Verus 的情婦。

3.Pergamus，可能是作者兄弟 Verus 的寵奴。

the present. But this is reduced to a very little, if thou only **circumscribest**[1] it, and chidest thy mind, if it is unable to hold out against even this.

Does **Panthea**[2] or **Pergamus**[3] now sit by the tomb of Verus? Does **Chaurias**[4] or Diotimus sit by the tomb of Hadrian? That would be ridiculous. Well, suppose they did sit there, would the dead be conscious of it? And if the dead were conscious, would they be pleased? And if they were pleased, would that make them immortal? Was it not in the order of destiny that these persons too should first become old women and old men and then die? What then would those do after these were dead? All this is foul smell and blood in a bag.

If thou canst see sharp, look and judge wisely, says the philosopher.

In the constitution of the rational animal I see no virtue which is opposed to justice; but I see a virtue which is opposed to love of pleasure, and that is temperance.

If thou **takest**[5] away thy opinion about that which appears to give thee pain, thou thyself standest in perfect security. – Who is this self? – The

---

4.Chaurias，哈德良的寵奴。

5.takest 為古英語中 take 的第二人稱單數（主語為 thou 時使用）。

「但是，我不是理性啊。」暫且這樣。不要讓你的理性煩擾自身。但是如果你身體的某部分感到痛苦，那就讓那它自己表達對痛苦的意見吧。

感覺障礙對動物本性來說是一種惡，運動（慾望）障礙對動物本性來說也是一種惡。對植物本性而言，也存在某方面的障礙和惡。同樣，理解障礙是理性的惡。把這些應用於你自己身上。痛苦或快樂會影響你嗎？讓感官去感受。在你為目標奮鬥時遇到過挫折嗎？如果你絕對努力（無條件，無保留），對於你這個理性動物而言，這種障礙的確是一種惡。但是如果你能把通常的進程都考慮到，你就不會受傷，也不會受到阻撓。因為思想的合理屬物是不會被任何人阻礙的，無論是炙火還是鋼鐵，無論是暴君還是誹謗都不能影響它。球體一旦造成，就永遠是球體。

我怎麼會使我自己痛苦，我甚至從來沒有故意讓別人痛苦過。

不同之物取悅不同之人。對我來說，快樂就是：健全我支配能力，既不背離任何人，也不拒絕任何事；以慈悲的目光看待和接受一切；按照事物的價值來使用它們。

reason. – But I am not reason. – Be it so. Let then the reason itself not trouble itself. But if any other part of thee suffers, let it have its own opinion about itself.

Hindrance to the perceptions of sense is an evil to the animal nature. Hindrance to the movements (desires) is equally an evil to the animal nature. And something else also is equally an impediment and an evil to the constitution of plants. So then that which is a hindrance to the intelligence is an evil to the intelligent nature. Apply all these things then to thyself. Does pain or sensuous pleasure affect thee? The senses will look to that. Has any obstacle opposed thee in thy efforts towards an object? if indeed thou wast making this effort absolutely (unconditionally, or without any reservation), certainly this obstacle is an evil to thee considered as a rational animal. But if thou takest into consideration the usual course of things, thou hast not yet been injured nor even impeded. The things however which are proper to the understanding no other man is used to impede, for neither fire, nor iron, nor tyrant, nor abuse, touches it in any way. When it has been made a sphere, it continues a sphere.

It is not fit that I should give myself pain, for I have never intentionally given pain even to another.

Different things delight different people. But it is my delight to keep the ruling faculty sound without turning away either from any man or from any of the things which happen to men, but looking at and receiving all with

　　只有現在是你的。那些追求身後聲名的人沒有考慮到：後來的人和那些他們現在不能忍受的人一樣。兩者都會死去。別人怎麼說你，怎麼評價你，又與你有何關係？

　　隨便你把我扔到什麼地方，我都不在乎。如果我能按照恰當的本性去感覺和行動，我就能使我神性的部分保持寧靜和滿足。換了地方，就能使得靈魂痛苦，比原來更糟，沮喪，膨脹，畏縮，驚恐嗎？這個世上有什麼東西值得它如此？

　　不符合人之常理的事情是不會發生在你身上的。正如一頭公牛、一根常春藤、一塊石頭，那些不符合它們自然本質的事情是不會發生在它們身上的。如果發生在你身上的事情都是合乎常理的、順應自然的，那你為什麼抱怨呢？共同的本性是不會帶來你所不能承受的事情的。

1.shouldst 為古英語中 should 的第二人稱單數形式（主語為 thou 時使用）。

welcome eyes and using everything according to its value.

See that thou secure this present time to thyself: for those who rather pursue posthumous fame do consider that the men of after time will be exactly such as these whom they cannot bear now; and both are mortal. And what is it in any way to thee if these men of after time utter this or that sound, or have this or that opinion about thee?

Take me and cast me where thou wilt; for there I shall keep my divine part tranquil, that is, content, if it can feel and act conformably to its proper constitution. Is this change of place sufficient reason why my soul should be unhappy and worse than it was, depressed, expanded, shrinking, affrighted? And what wilt thou find which is sufficient reason for this?

Nothing can happen to any man which is not a human accident, nor to an ox which is not according to the nature of an ox, nor to a vine which is not according to the nature of a vine, nor to a stone which is not proper to a stone. If then there happens to each thing both what is usual and natural, why **shouldst**[1] thou complain? For the common nature brings nothing which may not be borne by thee.

　　如果外物讓你悲傷，你應該明白真正讓你悲傷的不是外物，而是你自己對外物的判斷。你有能力清除這些判斷。如果是你自己內在本身讓你悲傷，那誰會阻礙你改正你的觀念呢？如果因為沒有做某件看似正確的事而悲傷，為什麼不行動而把時間浪費在抱怨上呢？也許你會說有一個你無法克服的困難阻撓著你。如果是這樣，那你也不必悲傷，因為不能完成那件事並不是你的錯。你也許又會說：「可是，這件事情如果不能完成的話，我活著也沒什麼意義了。」如果是這樣的話，那麼就安心地走吧，就像諸事順遂的人一樣，接納所有的阻礙。

　　記住：你的主宰能力是不可征服的，只要它是鎮定的，滿足於自身，不做不情願的事情，即使是固執也不能征服它。如果藉助謹慎和理性來進行判斷又會是怎樣的情況呢？所以，**擺脫了激情的心靈就是你的堡壘**，再沒有比這更安全、更堅固的**堡壘**了。不能明白這一點的人是無知的人；明白但是不飛往這一堡壘的人則是不幸的人。

1.inexpugnable [ˌɪnɪks`pʌgnəb!] adj. 不能攻佔的，不能駁倒的

If thou art pained by any external thing, it is not this thing that disturbs thee, but thy own judgment about it. And it is in thy power to wipe out this judgment now. But if anything in thy own disposition gives thee pain, who hinders thee from correcting thy opinion? And even if thou art pained because thou art not doing some particular thing which seems to thee to be right, why dost thou not rather act than complain? – But some insuperable obstacle is in the way? – Do not be grieved then, for the cause of its not being done depends not on thee. – But it is not worth while to live if this cannot be done. – Take thy departure then from life contentedly, just as he dies who is in full activity, and well pleased too with the things which are obstacles.

Remember that the ruling faculty is invincible, when self-collected it is satisfied with itself, if it does nothing which it does not choose to do, even if it resist from mere obstinacy. What then will it be when it forms a judgment about anything aided by reason and deliberately? Therefore the mind which is free from passions is a citadel, for man has nothing more secure to which he can fly for, refuge and for the future be **inexpugnable**[1]. He then who has not seen this is an ignorant man; but he who has seen it and does not fly to this refuge is unhappy.

　　保持對事物的第一印象，不要添加任何東西。如果別人告訴你有人說你的壞話，並沒有告訴你你因此而受到了傷害。我看到我的小孩生病了，而並不知道他生命有危險。因此，你必須保持自己對事物的直接印象。不要從心裏填充任何東西，那麼你就不會發生什麼事。或者可以說，像知曉一切的人一樣補充一些東西。

　　黃瓜是苦的——扔了它。路上有荊棘——避開它。這樣就足夠了。不要再問世界上為什麼會有這些東西？如果你這樣問了，那些懂得自然的人肯定會嘲笑你，這和你在木匠鋪或者鞋鋪發現削屑或碎料而責備木匠或鞋匠時遭到他們嘲笑是一樣的道理。更何況木匠和鞋匠尚且還有可以扔削屑和碎料的地方，而大自然根本就沒有這樣的空間。這就是大自然的奇妙所在。雖然她也限定了自己的範圍，但是她可以把那些腐爛的、陳舊的或者沒用的東西再加以利用，並創造出新的東西。這樣大自然就不需要從外部獲取物質和材料，也不需要在外部找一個投放垃圾的空間。因此，不管是空間、材料還是技藝，大自然都可以自給自足。

1.cucumber [`kjukəmbɚ] n. 黃瓜

Say nothing more to thyself than what the first appearances report. Suppose that it has been reported to thee that a certain person speaks ill of thee. This has been reported; but that thou hast been injured, that has not been reported. I see that my child is sick. I do see; but that he is in danger, I do not see. Thus then always abide by the first appearances, and add nothing thyself from within, and then nothing happens to thee. Or rather add something, like a man who knows everything that happens in the world.

A **cucumber**[1] is bitter. – Throw it away. – There are briars in the road. – Turn aside from them. – This is enough. Do not add, And why were such things made in the world? For thou wilt be ridiculed by a man who is acquainted with nature, as thou wouldst be ridiculed by a carpenter and shoemaker if thou didst find fault because thou seest in their workshop shavings and cuttings from the things which they make. And yet they have places into which they can throw these shavings and cuttings, and the universal nature has no external space; but the wondrous part of her art is that though she has circumscribed herself, everything within her which appears to decay and to grow old and to be useless she changes into herself, and again makes other new things from these very same, so that she requires neither substance from without nor wants a place into which she may cast that which decays. She is content then with her own space, and her

　　行動不能慵懶散漫；言談不能粗魯衝動；思想不能漫無邊際；靈魂不可只傾注於本身，亦不可過於激動；生活不能過於忙碌，要留有閒暇。

　　「他們殺我，把我切成碎片，詛咒我。」那又怎樣？難道這些可以阻止你的心靈保持純淨、謹慎、溫和和公正嗎？例如，一泓清澈的甘泉，即使被路人詛咒，泉水仍然清澈甘甜。如果有人往裏扔垃圾，泉水也會馬上把垃圾沖散，仍然乾淨，不會受到污染。應該怎麼做才能擁有一泓汩汩不息的泉水？而不是只是一口乾涸的井呢？磨練你自己，努力實現真正的自由、寬厚、樸實，和謙虛。

　　不瞭解世界的人不會知道自己的位置。不知道世界為什麼存在的人也不可能知道自己是誰，這個世界又是誰。對這些一無所知的人不會知道自己的生存目的。對於那些不知道自己在哪，是誰的人，還有人逃避或渴望他們的讚美，你對此有什麼看法？

　　1.sluggish [`slʌgɪʃ] adj. 偷懶的；懶惰的；遲鈍的

own matter and her own art.

Neither in thy actions be **sluggish**[1] nor in thy conversation without method, nor wandering in thy thoughts, nor let there be in thy soul inward contention nor external effusion, nor in life be so busy as to have no leisure.

Suppose that men kill thee, cut thee in pieces, curse thee. What then can these things do to prevent thy mind from remaining pure, wise, sober, just? For instance, if a man should stand by a limpid pure spring, and curse it, the spring never ceases sending up potable water; and if he should cast clay into it or filth, it will speedily disperse them and wash them out, and will not be at all polluted. How then shalt thou possess a perpetual fountain and not a mere well? By forming thyself hourly to freedom conjoined with contentment, simplicity and modesty.

He who does not know what the world is, does not know where he is. And he who does not know for what purpose the world exists, does not know who he is, nor what the world is. But he who has failed in any one of these things could not even say for what purpose he exists himself. What then dost thou think of him who avoids or seeks the praise of those who applaud, of men who know not either where they are or who they are?

　　一個人每小時詛咒自己三次，你希望得到他的讚美嗎？你希望取悅一個從不會取悅自己的人嗎？一個整天懊悔自己所做事情的人會取悅自己嗎？

　　不要僅滿足於與周圍的空氣呼吸一致，而要讓你的理智與周圍的事物相合。對於願意接納它的人，理智的力量如同呼吸空氣的力量一樣無處不在，遍佈萬物之中。

　　一般而言，惡行是不會傷害到宇宙的。尤其是一個人的惡行不會傷害到別人，只會傷害到那些想擺脫它的人。

　　鄰人的自由意志就像他的呼吸和身體一樣，於我的自由意志而言是無關緊要的。雖然我們都是為彼此而生，但是我們的支配力量都有各自的職能，否則鄰人的惡即是對我的傷害，這不是上帝的意願，上帝不會讓我的不幸依賴於他人。

1.aerial [`ɛrɪəl] adj. 空中的；航空的

Dost thou wish to be praised by a man who curses himself thrice every hour? Wouldst thou wish to please a man who does not please himself? Does a man please himself who repents of nearly everything that he does?

No longer let thy breathing only act in concert with the air which surrounds thee, but let thy intelligence also now be in harmony with the intelligence which embraces all things. For the intelligent power is no less diffused in all parts and pervades all things for him who is willing to draw it to him than the **aerial**[1] power for him who is able to respire it.

Generally, wickedness does no harm at all to the universe; and particularly, the wickedness of one man does no harm to another. It is only harmful to him who has it in his power to be released from it, as soon as he shall choose.

To my own free will the free will of my neighbour is just as indifferent as his poor breath and flesh. For though we are made especially for the sake of one another, still the ruling power of each of us has its own office, for otherwise my neighbour's wickedness would be my harm, which God has not willed in order that my unhappiness may not depend on another.

陽光向四面八方擴散，但它並沒有流溢，因為這種擴散是擴展。什麼是光線呢？你可以透過觀察陽光通過一個小孔透入一間黑暗的房子發現：光線永遠是筆直的。當它遇到空氣不能透過的固體時，光線就會中斷。但光線絕不會滑脫或者跌落，它仍然在那兒。

思想的散佈也應該如此，不是流出，而是擴展。不管遇到什麼阻礙，都不應該激烈地對抗，也不應該跌落，而應該固定不變、選擇照亮那些接受它的人。對於那些不接受它的人，那是他們自己的損失，是他們自己剝奪了得到光亮的機會。

害怕死亡的人或者是害怕他們從此再無感覺，或者是害怕死後的感覺和現在不同。其實，死亡並不可怕。如果死後沒有感覺，那自然也感覺不到失去的痛苦；如果死後有另一種感覺，那就是另一個生命的開始，依然是生命。

人的存在都是為了他人，不是教導別人，就是容忍別人。

The sun appears to be poured down, and in all directions indeed it is diffused, yet it is not effused. For this diffusion is extension: Accordingly its rays are called Extensions because they are extended. But one may judge what kind of a thing a ray is, if he looks at the sun's light passing through a narrow opening into a darkened room, for it is extended in a right line, and as it were is divided when it meets with any solid body which stands in the way and intercepts the air beyond; but there the light remains fixed and does not glide or fall off.

Such then ought to be the out-pouring and diffusion of the understanding, and it should in no way be an effusion, but an extension, and it should make no violent or impetuous collision with the obstacles which are in its way; nor yet fall down, but be fixed and enlighten that which receives it. For a body will deprive itself of the illumination, if it does not admit it.

He who fears death either fears the loss of sensation or a different kind of sensation. But if thou shalt have no sensation, neither wilt thou feel any harm; and if thou shalt acquire another kind of sensation, thou wilt be a different kind of living being and thou wilt not cease to live.

Men exist for the sake of one another. Teach them then or bear with them.

　　飛鏢以一種方式前進，心靈以另一種方式前進。無論是在謹慎行事還是在研究探索，心靈都直接向前，直奔目標。

　　洞察每一個人的支配能力，也讓其他人洞察你的支配能力。

In one way an arrow moves, in another way the mind. The mind indeed, both when it exercises caution and when it is employed about inquiry, moves straight onward not the less, and to its object.

Enter into every man's ruling faculty; and also let every other man enter into thine.

第九卷

那些行非正義之事的人並不虔誠。既然宇宙本質創造出的理性生命是互相幫助，而不是相互傷害，如果有人違反這一意志，顯然就等於對最高的神明犯下不敬之罪。說謊也對同樣的神明犯了不敬之罪，因為宇宙的本性即是事物的本性，宇宙同現存的事物都有關聯。而且宇宙的本質也被稱為真理，是所有真實事物的起因。那麼，故意說謊，依靠欺騙行不義之事，犯有不敬之罪；無意中說謊的，不符合宇宙本性，由於對抗世界本性而擾亂了宇宙的秩序，同樣也犯有不敬之罪。因為他對抗宇宙本性，因而與真理背道而馳；因為他忽略了自然所賦予的能力，因而現在失去了辨別真偽的能力。的確，那些把快樂當成真善去追求、把痛苦看作至惡去逃避的人亦是犯了不敬神靈之罪。這樣的人必定經常對宇宙本質心懷不滿，認為並非是按照人的善惡給他們分配應得的東西，許多惡人都能夠享受快樂，並擁有產生快樂的事物，卻還有數不清的善人在遭受苦難，無法擺脫那引發痛苦的泉源。而且，那些畏懼痛苦的人有時候也懼怕將會發生在這世界上的事情，這種懼怕甚至是一種不敬。那些追逐享樂的人絕對不會割捨克制自己行不義之事的慾望，這顯然是對神的不恭。對於自然持中立態度的事物——如果它不是對這兩種事物一視同仁，就不會將它們

1.transgress [træns`grɛs] vt. 越過（違反，越界，違法）
2.inasmuch [ɪnəz`mʌtʃ] adv. 因……之故，因為
3.impiety [ɪm`paɪətɪ] n. 無信仰；無信心；不虔誠

BOOK 9

He who acts unjustly acts impiously. For since the universal nature has made rational animals for the sake of one another to help one another according to their deserts, but in no way to injure one another, he who **transgresses**[1] her will, is clearly guilty of impiety towards the highest divinity. And he too who lies is guilty of impiety to the same divinity; for the universal nature is the nature of things that are; and things that are have a relation to all things that come into existence. And further, this universal nature is named truth, and is the prime cause of all things that are true. He then who lies intentionally is guilty of impiety **inasmuch**[2] as he acts unjustly by deceiving; and he also who lies unintentionally, inasmuch as he is at variance with the universal nature, and inasmuch as he disturbs the order by fighting against the nature of the world; for he fights against it, who is moved of himself to that which is contrary to truth, for he had received powers from nature through the neglect of which he is not able now to distinguish falsehood from truth. And indeed he who pursues pleasure as good, and avoids pain as evil, is guilty of **impiety**[3]. For of necessity such a man must often find fault with the universal nature, alleging that it assigns things to the

創造出來了，那些願意遵循自然本性而活的人必然與之同心，亦對此持中立態度。既然宇宙本性同等對待苦樂、生死或是榮辱，那麼，沒有同等地對待它們的人，顯然就是對神的不虔誠。我是指宇宙本性無差別地對待它們，而不是說它們同樣地發生於那些不斷產生的人，和那些在他們之後透過神意的原始推動所產生的人。按照這種神意，形成了事物的秩序；按照神意，形成了將要發生事情的基本原則；按照神意，決定了事物產生的力量、變化的力量以及類似的交相嬗遞的力量。

　　當一個人向這個世界辭別時，如果想到自己的生命中從未有過謊言、虛偽、奢侈和驕傲的污點，實在是非常幸福快樂的事。然而，正如俗語所說的，一個人如果在厭倦了這些事情時離開人世也算是第二好的人生。難道你決定容忍惡嗎？難道經驗還沒引導你遠離瘟疫嗎？理智的腐化是一場瘟疫，是比圍繞著我們的空氣的任何變化或腐敗都

bad and the good contrary to their deserts, because frequently the bad are in the enjoyment of pleasure and possess the things which procure pleasure, but the good have pain for their share and the things which cause pain. And further, he who is afraid of pain will sometimes also be afraid of some of the things which will happen in the world, and even this is impiety. And he who pursues pleasure will not abstain from injustice, and this is plainly impiety. Now with respect to the things towards which the universal nature is equally affected, – for it would not have made both, unless it was equally affected towards both, – towards these they who wish to follow nature should be of the same mind with it, and equally affected. With respect to pain, then, and pleasure, or death and life, or honour and dishonour, which the universal nature employs equally, whoever is not equally affected is manifestly acting impiously. And I say that the universal nature employs them equally, instead of saying that they happen alike to those who are produced in continuous series and to those who come after them by virtue of a certain original movement of Providence, according to which it moved from a certain beginning to this ordering of things, having conceived certain principles of the things which were to be, and having determined powers productive of beings and of changes and of such like successions.

It would be a man's happiest lot to depart from mankind without having had any taste of lying and hypocrisy and luxury and pride. However to breathe out one's life when a man has had enough of these things is the next best voyage, as the saying is. Hast thou determined to abide with vice, and has not experience yet induced thee to fly from this pestilence? For the

更嚴重的災難。因為空氣的腐敗是動物的瘟疫；而理智的敗壞是人的瘟疫。

　　不要蔑視死亡，而只需要滿意地、心甘情願地接受它，因為這正是自然所期望的事情之一。正如一個孩子變為一位青年，然後在歲月中變老，成長，成熟，長出牙齒、鬍子和白髮，懷孕、生子和撫養後代，以及所有其他的行為，都遵循著自然所安排的人生命的各個季節，分解和消亡也不例外。這是通達之人的特徵：他既不會激烈地對待死亡，也不會感到自豪或光榮；而只是把它當作自然的一個活動，耐心地靜候。正如你等待自己的孩子從妻子的子宮裏娩出一樣，也準備著你的靈魂離開這副皮囊的時刻來臨。但如果你要求一種通俗的安慰，那麼你可以去觀察那些將要與之分別的事物，以及你的靈魂不再與之廝混的人的道德，這都是令你坦然接受死亡的最有效辦法。你絕對不能因人們的過錯而發怒，關心他們、溫和平順地忍受他們才是你的義務。然而也要記住，你不是要遠離那些與你持有相同原則的人們。如果真的存在什麼能使我們轉念的事情，那麼，能夠幸運地和與自己抱持同樣信念的人們一起生活，就是唯一能讓我們留戀生命的事情了。可是現在你也看到了，同那些觀點看法不一致的人們生活在一起是多麼苦惱，以致你會說：死亡啊，我祈禱你快些降臨，免得我在

1.pestilence [`pɛst!əns] n. 瘟疫
2.waitest 為古英語中 wait 的第二人稱單數（主語為 thou 時使用）。
3.requirest 為古英語中 require 的第二人稱單數（主語為 thou 時使用）。

destruction of the understanding is a pestilence, much more indeed than any such corruption and change of this atmosphere which surrounds us. For this corruption is a pestilence of animals so far as they are animals; but the other is a **pestilence**[1] of men so far as they are men.

Do not despise death, but be well content with it, since this too is one of those things which nature wills. For such as it is to be young and to grow old, and to increase and to reach maturity, and to have teeth and beard and grey hairs, and to beget, and to be pregnant and to bring forth, and all the other natural operations which the seasons of thy life bring, such also is dissolution. This, then, is consistent with the character of a reflecting man, to be neither careless nor impatient nor contemptuous with respect to death, but to wait for it as one of the operations of nature. As thou now **waitest**[2] for the time when the child shall come out of thy wife's womb, so be ready for the time when thy soul shall fall out of this envelope. But if thou **requirest**[3] also a vulgar kind of comfort which shall reach thy heart, thou wilt be made best reconciled to death by observing the objects from which thou art going to be removed, and the morals of those with whom thy soul will no longer be mingled. For it is no way right to be offended with men, but it is thy duty to care for them and to bear with them gently; and yet to remember that thy departure will be not from men who have the same principles as thyself. For

這樣的現實中迷失自己。

　　為惡者也是對自己行惡。行不義之事的人同時也會使自己受到傷害，因為是他讓自己變壞。

　　不僅做某事的人是非正義的，那些不做某事的人也可能是非正義的。

　　如果現今我對客觀事物的意見奠基於理智，我目前的行為符合社會利益；我當下的性情秉性能滿足於一切發生之事，這就足夠了。

　　清除幻想，克制慾望，消除貪念，掌握你的支配力。

　　在所有無理性的動物之中分佈著同一種生命；而在所有有理性的動物之中分佈著同一種靈魂。這正如一切生命最初都共有一片大地，我們在同樣的光下觀看，在同樣的空氣中呼吸，我們每個人都有視力，每個人都有生命。

this is the only thing, if there be any, which could draw us the contrary way and attach us to life, to be permitted to live with those who have the same principles as ourselves. But now thou seest how great is the trouble arising from the discordance of those who live together, so that thou mayest say, Come quick, O death, lest perchance I, too, should forget myself.

He who does wrong does wrong against himself. He who acts unjustly acts unjustly to himself, because he makes himself bad.

He often acts unjustly who does not do a certain thing; not only he who does a certain thing.

Thy present opinion founded on understanding, and thy present conduct directed to social good, and thy present disposition of contentment with everything which happens – that is enough.

Wipe out imagination: check desire: extinguish appetite: keep the ruling faculty in its own power.

Among the animals which have not reason one life is distributed; but among reasonable animals one intelligent soul is distributed: just as there is one earth of all things which are of an earthy nature, and we see by one light, and breathe one air, all of us that have the faculty of vision and all that have life.

　　無論哪種事物，一旦它分享了某種共同事物中的一部分，自然都會傾向於同類。所有土性的事物都傾向於大地，所有液體的事物都能夠流動，所有氣體的事物也同樣聚集在一起，以致如果沒有某種干擾、甚至是暴力的介入，就無法將它們分開。無論哪一種燃燒的火焰，不僅傾向於火元素上升，而且還隨時準備著同一切足夠乾燥、容易著火的物體一起燃燒，因為這些物體的濕度不足以制止火焰的產生。相應地，每一個分享了共同理性的事物，自然也會以同樣的方式傾向於與它同類的存在，甚至傾向性更強。相比之下，它比它的同類事物要優越得多，它也同樣更願意與它相互融合。所以，我們目前能夠在一些非理性的生物中發現蜂群、畜群、撫養幼子甚至某種意義上的愛和感情——雖然它們沒有理性，但其中依然存在著靈魂，存在著那種將它們吸引到更加強大和緊密的力量，但是這從未在植物、石塊、樹林中發現。而在理性動物之中，則產生了政治團體和友誼、家庭、公眾集會以及戰爭中的談判和休戰。但在他們之中還存在著更為優越的，就像恒星或行星一樣，雖然彼此分離，仍然以某種方式聯結在一起。上升到更高的形式，即使是彼此分離的事物也可以產生同情。看看現在都發生了什麼事情吧。那些有理性的動物是目前唯一忘記了他們天性中相互吸引慾望的物種，只有在他們那裏才看不到萬物皆出於一源的特性。但是儘管人們努力抗拒這一聯合的本性，他們卻還是受到聯合的吸引和制約，因為他們的社會本性實在太強了。你只要觀察一下，就會認可我說的是事實。發現不與同類相接觸的土性東

1.ignite [ɪgˋnaɪt] v. 著火

All things which participate in anything which is common to them all move towards that which is of the same kind with themselves. Everything which is earthy turns towards the earth, everything which is liquid flows together, and everything which is of an aerial kind does the same, so that they require something to keep them asunder, and the application of force. Fire indeed moves upwards on account of the elemental fire, but it is so ready to be kindled together with all the fire which is here, that even every substance which is somewhat dry, is easily **ignited**[1], because there is less mingled with it of that which is a hindrance to ignition. Accordingly then everything also which participates in the common intelligent nature moves in like manner towards that which is of the same kind with itself, or moves even more. For so much as it is superior in comparison with all other things, in the same degree also is it more ready to mingle with and to be fused with that which is akin to it. Accordingly among animals devoid of reason we find swarms of bees, and herds of cattle, and the nurture of young birds, and in a manner, loves; for even in animals there are souls, and that power which brings them together is seen to exert itself in the superior degree, and in such a way as never has been observed in plants nor in stones nor in trees. But in rational animals there are political communities and friendships, and families and meetings of people; and in wars, treaties and armistices. But in the things which are still superior, even though they are separated

---

西要比發現完全脫離他人的人快得多。

　　人、神或是宇宙都會在適當的季節孕育各自的果實。儘管按照慣常的用法把『果實』這個詞語用到葡萄樹或類似的什麼東西上面，但這無關緊要。而理性既會為了自身結出果實，也能為他人結出果實，自它結出的果實和理性自身是一樣的。

　　如果你有辦法，勸導那些做錯事的人；如果你沒辦法，你要因這個目的寬恕這些人。神靈也會寬恕這些人，出於某些目的甚至會去出力幫助這些人得到一些東西，諸如健康、財富、榮譽之類，神靈是多麼仁善和慷慨啊！這是你能力範圍之內的事，或者說，誰能阻礙你？

1.indulgence [ɪnˋdʌldʒəns] n. 寬容；放縱

from one another, unity in a manner exists, as in the stars. Thus the ascent to the higher degree is able to produce a sympathy even in things which are separated. See, then, what now takes place. For only intelligent animals have now forgotten this mutual desire and inclination, and in them alone the property of flowing together is not seen. But still though men strive to avoid this union, they are caught and held by it, for their nature is too strong for them; and thou wilt see what I say, if thou only observest. Sooner, then, will one find anything earthy which comes in contact with no earthy thing than a man altogether separated from other men.

Both man and God and the universe produce fruit; at the proper seasons each produces it. But if usage has especially fixed these terms to the vine and like things, this is nothing. Reason produces fruit both for all and for itself, and there are produced from it other things of the same kind as reason itself.

If thou art able, correct by teaching those who do wrong; but if thou canst not, remember that **indulgence**[1] is given to thee for this purpose. And the gods, too, are indulgent to such persons; and for some purposes they even help them to get health, wealth, reputation; so kind they are. And it is in thy power also; or say, who hinders thee?

　　不要像一個悲慘的被強迫者那樣勞動，也不要因他人的憐憫或讚揚而勞動。你要在意並冀求的就只有一件事情：按照社會理性所要求的如此行動和自我克制。

　　這一天我擺脫了所有的煩惱，或者說我驅逐了所有的煩惱。因為煩惱並不是發生在外部的，而是發生在內部，在我自身的意見之中。

　　所有事物都是相同的，司空見慣的，持續的時間都同樣短暫，質料毫無價值。現在一切事物的狀態與它們在先死者時代裏的完全一樣，沒有變化。

　　事物在我們之外，事物就是事物，既不認識自身，也不對自己做出任何判斷。那麼，究竟是什麼在對它們加以判斷呢？是支配力。

　　正像美德與惡行並非存在於消極被動而是存在積極主動中一樣，有理性的社會動物的善與惡同樣並非體現在他的消極被動裏，而是體現在他的積極主動裏。

　　對於一塊被向上拋擲的石頭來說，下墜對它來說毫無傷害，同樣的，上升對它來說也沒有絲毫益處。

　　深入洞察人們的主要原則，你將看到你懼怕什麼樣的判斷，這些人又是怎樣評價他們自己的。

Labour not as one who is wretched, nor yet as one who would be pitied or admired: but direct thy will to one thing only, to put thyself in motion and to check thyself, as the social reason requires.

To-day I have got out of all trouble, or rather I have cast out all trouble, for it was not outside, but within and in my opinions.

All things are the same, familiar in experience, and ephemeral in time, and worthless in the matter. Everything now is just as it was in the time of those whom we have buried.

Things stand outside of us, themselves by themselves, neither knowing aught of themselves, nor expressing any judgment. What is it, then, which does judge about them? The ruling faculty.

Not in passivity, but in activity lie the evil and the good of the rational social animal, just as his virtue and his vice lie not in passivity, but in activity.

For the stone which has been thrown up it is no evil to come down, nor indeed any good to have been carried up.

Penetrate inwards into men's leading principles, and thou wilt see what judges thou art afraid of, and what kind of judges they are of themselves.

世上一切事物都在不斷變化，你自身也同樣處在永恆的變化之中，從某種意義上說是在不斷的毀滅之中，整個宇宙也是如此。

不理會別人的錯誤是你的職責。

一項活動存在一個終點，一個運動和意見總有它停止的時候，在某種意義上也就是死亡，這些絕不是惡。現在用這個道理來思考一個人的生長階段，一開始是一個孩子，接著是一個青年、一個成人和一個老人，其中每一階段的變化實際上也是一種死亡。這有什麼值得恐懼？現在轉而考慮一下，先是你活在祖父膝下的生活，然後是你活在母親膝下的生活，以及在父親膝下的生活，迄今為止，在你生命的全部過程中已經發現和觀察到了如此多的更迭與變革，見證過如此多的結束與毀滅。問問你自己，這些事情中有什麼值得恐懼的嗎？同樣的道理，整個生命的改變、變化和終止也不是一件值得恐懼的事情。

儘快考察你自己的支配力、宇宙的支配力以及鄰人的支配力。考察你自己的支配力，以便讓它公正；考察宇宙的支配力，以便記得你自己正是它的一部分；考察鄰人的支配力，你可以看看他是愚昧無知，還是富有智慧和學識，並認識到他的支配能力與你的相似。

既然你本身是社會系統的一部分，你的行動也應是社會生活的一部分。你的一切行為，如果與社會目的沒有直接或間接地關連，都將會分裂你的生活，正像在意見統一、團結一致的人群中間我行我素，

All things are changing: and thou thyself art in continuous mutation and in a manner in continuous destruction, and the whole universe too.

It is thy duty to leave another man's wrongful act there where it is.

Termination of activity, cessation from movement and opinion, and in a sense their death, is no evil. Turn thy thoughts now to the consideration of thy life, thy life as a child, as a youth, thy manhood, thy old age, for in these also every change was a death. Is this anything to fear? Turn thy thoughts now to thy life under thy grandfather, then to thy life under thy mother, then to thy life under thy father; and as thou findest many other differences and changes and terminations, ask thyself, Is this anything to fear? In like manner, then, neither are the termination and cessation and change of thy whole life a thing to be afraid of.

Hasten to examine thy own ruling faculty and that of the universe and that of thy neighbour: thy own that thou mayest make it just: and that of the universe, that thou mayest remember of what thou art a part; and that of thy neighbour, that thou mayest know whether he has acted ignorantly or with knowledge, and that thou mayest also consider that his ruling faculty is akin to thine.

As thou thyself art a component part of a social system, so let every act of thine be a component part of social life. Whatever act of thine then has no reference either immediately or remotely to a social end, this tears asunder

將自己分離、孤立於集體之外一樣。

　　小孩子的爭吵和遊戲，不幸的攜帶著死亡的身體的靈魂，萬物莫不如此；因此，逝者宅邸所展示的東西能夠讓我們看得更透徹。

　　考察事物形式的性質，把它們同質料部分相分離，只是注視著它本身，然後沉思冥想，思考這個形式發生的時間，即在其特定的條件下所存在和持續的最長時間。

　　你忍受了無數的煩惱，只因你不滿足於支配力做它應做之事。不要再煩惱了！

　　當有人譴責你，當有人憎恨你，或者將其他類似的行為加諸到你身上時，**去接近他們可憐的靈魂，深入其中去看看他們是什麼樣的人**。你將發現無論他人怎樣看待你，你完全沒有必要因為這樣的情況而苦惱。你必須依舊愛他們、善待他們，因為他們天生就是你的朋友。神靈們也透過夢、神諭幫助他們獲得他們看重的東西。

　　宇宙中那些事物的週期運動總是一成不變，始終在上下波動，從

thy life, and does not allow it to be one, and it is of the nature of a mutiny, just as when in a popular assembly a man acting by himself stands apart from the general agreement.

Quarrels of little children and their sports, and poor spirits carrying about dead bodies, such is everything; and so what is exhibited in the representation of the mansions of the dead strikes our eyes more clearly.

Examine into the quality of the form of an object, and detach it altogether from its material part, and then contemplate it; then determine the time, the longest which a thing of this peculiar form is naturally made to endure.

Thou hast endured infinite troubles through not being contented with thy ruling faculty, when it does the things which it is constituted by nature to do. But enough of this.

When another blames thee or hates thee, or when men say about thee anything injurious, approach their poor souls, penetrate within, and see what kind of men they are. Thou wilt discover that there is no reason to take any trouble that these men may have this or that opinion about thee. However thou must be well disposed towards them, for by nature they are friends. And the gods too aid them in all ways, by dreams, by signs, towards the attainment of those things on which they set a value.

The periodic movements of the universe are the same, up and down

一個時代到另一個時代往返不已。要麼，宇宙理智在每個單獨的結果上都要有所作為，如果這樣，你要滿足於宇宙運動帶來的結果；如果不是宇宙理智一勞永逸，只發動一次，其他的則按照一定的方式接踵而來；要不就是，不可分割的元素是事物的起源。總而言之，如果存在一個神，就一切都好；如果事物的發展都只靠偶然和運氣，你也不需受它的支配。

我們所有人很快都將化為一坏黃土，而這大地依然會不斷變遷。從變化中產生的事物仍將持續永遠地變化下去，如此循環往復不已。如果一個人在心中思考著那像波浪一樣連續不斷的改變和變革，他將從心底裏看不起一切塵俗之物。

宇宙的動因像一道激流，裹挾一切前行。那些忙於政治卻聲稱是哲學家的人是多麼不值一提。都是愚鈍不堪的人！人啊，做當下你的本性所要求的事吧。如果你有力量，就下定決心付諸行動，而不必瞻前顧後，顧慮是否有什麼人會注意到它。不要寄希望於柏拉圖的理想國。哪怕只有極其微小的一點益處，也該感到滿足，重視那一點小小的進步。誰能改變自己的想法？如果沒有想法上的轉變，剩下的只不過是像奴隸一樣假裝順從卻抱怨連連罷了。現在來給我講講亞歷山大、菲利浦和菲勒內姆的迪米特裏厄斯的事情吧。他們是否明確共同

1.Plato's Republic，柏拉圖的理想國，寓意為不可實現的烏托邦。

from age to age. And either the universal intelligence puts itself in motion for every separate effect, and if this is so, be thou content with that which is the result of its activity; or it puts itself in motion once, and everything else comes by way of sequence in a manner; or indivisible elements are the origin of all things. – In a word, if there is a god, all is well; and if chance rules, do not thou also be governed by it.

Soon will the earth cover us all: then the earth, too, will change, and the things also which result from change will continue to change for ever, and these again for ever. For if a man reflects on the changes and transformations which follow one another like wave after wave and their rapidity, he will despise everything which is perishable.

The universal cause is like a winter torrent: it carries everything along with it. But how worthless are all these poor people who are engaged in matters political, and, as they suppose, are playing the philosopher! All dwellers. Well then, man: do what nature now requires. Set thyself in motion, if it is in thy power, and do not look about thee to see if any one will observe it; nor yet expect **Plato's Republic**[1]: but be content if the smallest thing goes on well, and consider such an event to be no small matter. For who can change men's opinions? And without a change of opinions what

本性所要求的事情，並按照這個訓練自身，這是他們自己的事情。如果他們扮演了悲劇中的英雄，沒有人會譴責我不去模仿他們。真正的哲學能使人質樸謙遜，毫不矯揉造作，遠離懶惰和誇耀。

從高處俯瞰下面的人群以及他們無數莊嚴獻祭的儀式；觀察無論是乘風破浪的激流湧進，還是平靜無波的靜海航行；俯視那些剛剛誕生的、相互關連著、共同存續的以及已經走到生命盡頭的人、事、物的種種差異；那些在過去、未來以及生活在當下的人們，還有世界各地不同國家、不同民族的人們的生存狀態和生活方式，你一定會去沉思漫想。有多少人甚至從未聽說過你的名字，有多少人會很快就將之忘卻，還有許多現在對你讚不絕口的人或許很快就會轉為譴責和詬病。因此，死後之名、榮耀或其他類似的東西，都通通不值一提。

遠離那些外在干擾，對於內在原因所引起的事物，要堅持正義；換言之，不管你的決定還是行動都只有一個旨歸——於他人和社會有益，因為這符合你的本性。

1.Philip（西元前382年～西元前336年），馬其頓霸權的創立者，亞歷山大的父親。

2.Demetrius（西元前294年～西元前87年），著名將軍，馬其頓國王。

3.indolence [`ɪndələns] n. 怠惰；懶惰

else is there than the slavery of men who groan while they pretend to obey? Come now and tell me of Alexander and **Philip**[1] and **Demetrius**[2] of Phalerum. They themselves shall judge whether they discovered what the common nature required, and trained themselves accordingly. But if they acted like tragedy heroes, no one has condemned me to imitate them. Simple and modest is the work of philosophy. Draw me not aside to **indolence**[3] and pride.

Look down from above on the countless **herds**[4] of men and their countless solemnities, and the infinitely varied voyagings in storms and calms, and the differences among those who are born, who live together, and die. And consider, too, the life lived by others in olden time, and the life of those who will live after thee, and the life now lived among barbarous nations, and how many know not even thy name, and how many will soon forget it, and how they who perhaps now are praising thee will very soon blame thee, and that neither a posthumous name is of any value, nor reputation, nor anything else.

Let there be freedom from **perturbations**[5] with respect to the things which come from the external cause; and let there be justice in the things done by virtue of the internal cause, that is, let there be movement and

---

4.herd [hɝd] n. 人群
5.perturbation [ˌpɝtɚˋbeʃən] n. 動搖，混亂

　　你能夠憑藉自己的力量將許多令你為難困擾的事物驅除出去，因為它們完全出自你的自負和成見。在你的心中思索整個宇宙，以及展現在你眼前的時代全貌，專注於每一個瞬息萬變的個體事物，觀察萬物的產生是如何地短暫，而它們的消亡也同樣如此；而在其生之前和死之後的時間又是如何的廣大無垠，這樣你就為自己贏得了足夠的空間。

　　所有目前你看到的事物都將迅速衰朽，那些目擊其消亡的人們不久也將逝去。無論這個人是長命百歲還是幼年夭折，他們的歸宿都是同一個地方。

　　這些人有著怎樣的指導原則，他們為了何種事情而奔忙，他們的喜愛和尊重的理由又是什麼？想像一下，他們靈魂赤裸地呈現在你的面前。當他們以為自己說什麼人的壞話就能巧妙地傷害對方，或是講些褒揚和讚美就算是向對方施加了恩惠，這是一種多麼驕傲自負的想法啊！

　　衰朽只不過是一種變化，而宇宙的本性正是以變革為樂。根據這一法則所做的一切事情都能進行得很好，因為自物質世界產生之初就一直是以類似的方式進行，在無盡的未來也應當並且將會同樣持續下去。那麼，你是否會說，事物都是壞的，並且永遠都是壞的，在如此

action terminating in this, in social acts, for this is according to thy nature.

Thou canst remove out of the way many useless things among those which disturb thee, for they lie entirely in thy opinion; and thou wilt then gain for thyself ample space by comprehending the whole universe in thy mind, and by contemplating the eternity of time, and observing the rapid change of every several thing, how short is the time from birth to dissolution, and the illimitable time before birth as well as the equally boundless time after dissolution.

All that thou seest will quickly perish, and those who have been spectators of its dissolution will very soon perish too. And he who dies at the extremest old age will be brought into the same condition with him who died prematurely.

What are these men's leading principles, and about what kind of things are they busy, and for what kind of reasons do they love and honour? Imagine that thou seest their poor souls laid bare. When they think that they do harm by their blame or good by their praise, what an idea!

Loss is nothing else than change. But the universal nature delights in change, and in obedience to her all things are now done well, and from eternity have been done in like form, and will be such to time without end. What, then, dost thou say? That all things have been and all things always

多的神靈之中未曾發現有什麼力量能夠修正這些事物，這個世界註定
處於永無休止的惡之中？

　　那構成一切事物基礎的質料是多麼腐敗啊。水、塵埃、骨、污
物。大理石，它不過是土壤的凝結；金銀，不過是大地的排出物；你
最華美的衣服，從質料上說不過是愚蠢的綿羊的毛髮，其色彩也不過
是貝類動物的血罷了；其他萬事萬物也同樣如此。擁有呼吸本性的事
物也可以是擁有相同本性的另一事物，容易從此變成其他。

　　這些喋喋不休的抱怨、牢騷、訴苦已經夠了。你還為了什麼煩惱
呢？有什麼新的事情發生在你身上嗎？你對什麼東西感到如此驚訝不
安？是事物的形式還是質料？關注它們，而在這些之外什麼也沒有。
你的本分就是追隨神，將自己變得更質樸、更好。無論我們是花100
年，還是只花3年去觀察這些事物，其結果都是一樣的。

　　如果有什麼人做了惡事，損害的只是他自己，但也可能他並沒做
什麼不好的事。

1.callosity [kæ`lɑsətɪ] n.硬結，硬化
2.sediment [`sɛdəmənt] n. 沉澱物

will be bad, and that no power has ever been found in so many gods to rectify these things, but the world has been condemned to be found in never ceasing evil?

The rottenness of the matter which is the foundation of everything! Water, dust, bones, filth: or again, marble rocks, the **callosities**[1] of the earth; and gold and silver, the **sediments**[2]; and **garments**[3], only bits of hair; and purple dye, blood; and everything else is of the same kind. And that which is of the nature of breath is also another thing of the same kind, changing from this to that.

Enough of this wretched life and murmuring and **apish**[4] tricks. Why art thou disturbed? What is there new in this? What unsettles thee? Is it the form of the thing? Look at it. Or is it the matter? Look at it. But besides these there is nothing. Towards the gods, then, now become at last more simple and better. It is the same whether we examine these things for a hundred years or three.

If any man has done wrong, the harm is his own. But perhaps he has not done wrong.

3.garment [`gɑrmənt] n. 衣服
4.apish [`epɪʃ] adj. 愚蠢的

也許有一個智慧的源頭，所有的事物來源於此，並聚集在一起。如果真是這樣，那麼部分就不應對那些有利於整體利益的事情抱怨不滿。也許只有原子，事物只不過是原子的混合和分散。你還有什麼可煩惱的呢？對你理性的部分說：自己已經死了嗎？腐敗了嗎？你是一個偽君子嗎？變成野獸了嗎？和其他的野獸一起飲食？

神或者有力量，或者沒有。如果神靈沒有力量，你為什麼還要向他們禱告呢？如果他有力量，你為什麼不向他們禱告，祈求神賜給你那種既不畏懼、也不貪求、無所畏懼的能力呢，而不是祈求這事或那事發生。毫無疑問，如果神靈可以幫助人們，他們也一定能滿足你的這種祈求。但也許你會說：「神把這些事交給我來做了」。那麼，自由運用你的能力，是不是比用低下的、卑躬屈膝的方式意圖獲得，或是避免那些不在你能力範圍之內的事物要更好一些呢？至於神靈，又是誰告訴你說，如果神把一件事交到我們自己手中，讓我們憑自己的力量去處理，他就不會在這件事情上幫助我們了呢？去為這樣的事情禱告吧，你就會明白。當別人禱告說我如何才能與那名婦人同床共枕時，你應當這樣禱告：我如何才能使自己不抱這種慾望呢？當別人禱告說：我怎樣才能擺脫那個人呢？而你卻應當禱告：我怎樣才能消除擺脫那個人的慾望？還有，當別人禱告說：我要怎樣才能留住我的孩子呢？你卻應當禱告：我要怎樣才能不畏懼於失去他呢？總之，為了

1.fearest 為古英語中 fear 的第二人稱單數（主語為 thou 時使用）。
2.desirest 為古英語中 desire 的第二人稱單數（主語為 thou 時使用）。

Either all things proceed from one intelligent source and come together as in one body, and the part ought not to find fault with what is done for the benefit of the whole; or there are only atoms, and nothing else than mixture and dispersion. Why, then, art thou disturbed? Say to the ruling faculty, Art thou dead, art thou corrupted, art thou playing the hypocrite, art thou become a beast, dost thou herd and feed with the rest?

Either the gods have no power or they have power. If, then, they have no power, why dost thou pray to them? But if they have power, why dost thou not pray for them to give thee the faculty of not fearing any of the things which thou **fearest**[1], or of not desiring any of the things which thou **desirest**[2], or not being pained at anything, rather than pray that any of these things should not happen or happen? for certainly if they can co-operate with men, they can co-operate for these purposes. But perhaps thou wilt say, the gods have placed them in thy power. Well, then, is it not better to use what is in thy power like a free man than to desire in a slavish and abject way what is not in thy power? And who has told thee that the gods do not aid us even in the things which are in our power? Begin, then, to pray for such things, and thou wilt see. One man prays thus: How shall I be able to lie with that woman? Do thou pray thus: How shall I not desire to lie with her? Another prays thus: How shall I be released from this? Another prays:

這個目標和目的，你要用這樣的方式去禱告，然後再看看會有什麼樣的結果。

伊比鳩魯曾經說過：「我在病中的談話都與我身體的痛苦無關，我從不和前來探望我的人談論這一話題，我像以前一樣，繼續談論事物的本性。並且牢記這一點，心靈在參與可憐肉體的活動時，如何能不受干擾並保持善。我不會將自己的身體全部交給醫生任意指揮安排，好像覺得他們正在做一件多麼偉大的事情，而是照常快樂地生活下去。」不管你是否同樣臥病在床，或是面臨任何其他形式的困境，努力地像伊比鳩魯那樣做吧。無論什麼事降臨在你的身上，都絕不可放棄自己的哲學，也不要去和一個無知的或不諳自然的人做無謂的交談，這是所有哲學派別的共同原則。關注目前所做的事情和所採用的手段。

當有人行為無禮冒犯了你時，你可以馬上問自己，這世界上有可能完全不存在卑鄙無恥的人嗎？這當然是不可能的。那麼，就不要去期望那些不可能的事吧。因為你要知道這個人想必是那些必然存在於這世界上的無恥之徒中的一個。對於那些奸詐狡猾、背信忘義，以及一切以某種方式觸犯傷害你的人，也要用同樣的道理來說服自己。因為你總會馬上提醒自己，世界上難免會有這種人存在，如此一來，你對每一個人的態度都將變得更為和善。在這種情況下，還有一個很

How shall I not desire to be released? Another thus: How shall I not lose my little son? Thou thus: How shall I not be afraid to lose him? In fine, turn thy prayers this way, and see what comes.

Epicurus says, In my sickness my conversation was not about my bodily sufferings, nor, says he, did I talk on such subjects to those who visited me; but I continued to discourse on the nature of things as before, keeping to this main point, how the mind, while participating in such movements as go on in the poor flesh, shall be free from perturbations and maintain its proper good. Nor did I, he says, give the physicians an opportunity of putting on solemn looks, as if they were doing something great, but my life went on well and happily. Do, then, the same that he did both in sickness, if thou art sick, and in any other circumstances; for never to desert philosophy in any events that may befall us, nor to hold trifling talk either with an ignorant man or with one unacquainted with nature, is a principle of all schools of philosophy; but to be intent only on that which thou art now doing and on the instrument by which thou doest it.

When thou art offended with any man's shameless conduct, immediately ask thyself, Is it possible, then, that shameless men should not be in the world? It is not possible. Do not, then, require what is impossible. For this man also is one of those shameless men who must of necessity be in the world. Let the same considerations be present to thy mind in the case of the knave, and the faithless man, and of every man who does wrong in any way. For at the same time that thou dost remind thyself that it is impossible that such kind

好的方法可供利用：想想自然賦予了人們哪些美德使其應對惡行以及品德敗壞的人。例如，自然賦予了人們溫和寬容的美德，作為應對那些不知感恩者的解毒劑。對於每一種世間存在的惡行，自然都創造了一種相應的品格與它呼應。通常情況下，你有教導惡人改過向善的能力，不是嗎？因為他只是迷失了他的目標，走上了歧途罷了。此外，他的罪行還會使你受到什麼更深的傷害嗎？因為你會發現，在那些冒犯你、令你憤怒不滿的人當中，**沒有一個人或一種行為能傷害到你的心靈，能傷害你的都只在你的心靈中**。如果一個無知的、沒有文化的人做出了什麼缺乏教養的行為，又有什麼值得傷心或奇怪的呢？你還不如先譴責自己，因為你沒能事先就想到這種人很有可能會以這種方式犯錯誤，甚至還大驚小怪。尤其在你譴責一個忘恩負義或是虛偽狡詐的人時，更應當如此反躬自問。因為這錯誤毋庸置疑是你自己的，或者是你相信了一個這種性格的人會對你信守諾言；或者是在你施予善意的時候並不是絕對的；或者你並不認為僅僅從你施予的行為中，就已經獲得了所有的好處，而是不滿足於對方給予的酬報，還想要得到更多。你為什麼想得到更多的東西？對於一個人，你做出某種善行幫助了他，這還不能使你滿足嗎？你做了自己本性所要求的事情，卻還想尋求它的酬報嗎？就像你的眼睛用來觀看，你的腳用來行走，它們並未獲取酬報，卻一樣感到滿足。因為這些身體的部分正是自然為這一目的而造就的，透過按照它們各自的天性而工作，獲取屬於它們自己的東西。人天生就是為了仁愛、幫助他人而創造的，當他做了有

1.blamest 為古英語中 blame 的第二人稱單數（主語為 thou 時使用）。

of men should not exist, thou wilt become more kindly disposed towards every one individually. It is useful to perceive this, too, immediately when the occasion arises, what virtue nature has given to man to oppose to every wrongful act. For she has given to man, as an antidote against the stupid man, mildness, and against another kind of man some other power. And in all cases it is possible for thee to correct by teaching the man who is gone astray; for every man who errs misses his object and is gone astray. Besides wherein hast thou been injured? For thou wilt find that no one among those against whom thou art irritated has done anything by which thy mind could be made worse; but that which is evil to thee and harmful has its foundation only in the mind. And what harm is done or what is there strange, if the man who has not been instructed does the acts of an uninstructed man? Consider whether thou shouldst not rather blame thyself, because thou didst not expect such a man to err in such a way. For thou hadst means given thee by thy reason to suppose that it was likely that he would commit this error, and yet thou hast forgotten and art amazed that he has erred. But most of all when thou **blamest**[1] a man as faithless or ungrateful, turn to thyself. For the fault is manifestly thy own, whether thou didst trust that a man who had such a disposition would keep his promise, or when conferring thy kindness thou didst not confer it absolutely, nor yet in such way as to have received from thy very act all the profit. For what more dost

助於公共利益或是幫助他人改過向善的行為時，他就遵循自己的本性
而行動，得到了屬於自己的東西。

thou want when thou hast done a man a service? Art thou not content that thou hast done something conformable to thy nature, and dost thou seek to be paid for it? Just as if the eye demanded a recompense for seeing, or the feet for walking. For as these members are formed for a particular purpose, and by working according to their several constitutions obtain what is their own; so also as man is formed by nature to acts of benevolence, when he has done anything benevolent or in any other way conducive to the common interest, he has acted conformably to his constitution, and he gets what is his own.

第十卷

啊，我的靈魂啊！你不願變得美好、質樸、單一，比包裹著你的那個身體更為清晰嗎？你不願擁有親切、滿足的性情嗎？你不願達到充實的境地，不貪求任何有生命的或無生命的東西，以供享樂嗎？也不渴求更長的時間用來享樂，不渴求勝地、宜人的氣候或者和睦相處的人？難道你不滿足現狀，不欣喜於現在所擁有的嗎？你不確信你所擁有的都來自於上帝，並且是為你而做的嗎？你不相信神所喜悅的都是好的，神所給予的都是為了保存完美生命的存在嗎？神所給予的，即善、正義和美，這些能夠創造、孕育萬物，囊括一切分解產生其他相似事物的東西。難道你不願跟神和人一起生活，既不指責他們，也不被他們所譴責嗎？

要觀察你的本性真正所要求的是什麼，因為你是完全被本性所支配。只要你還是一個活的存在個體，不會讓你變得更壞，那麼就做吧，接受它吧！接著你必須檢查你的本性是怎麼樣一個活的存在個

BOOK 10

Wilt thou, then, my soul, never be good and simple and one and naked, more manifest than the body which surrounds thee? Wilt thou never enjoy an affectionate and contented disposition? Wilt thou never be full and without a want of any kind, longing for nothing more, nor desiring anything, either animate or inanimate, for the enjoyment of pleasures? Nor yet desiring time wherein thou shalt have longer enjoyment, or place, or pleasant climate, or society of men with whom thou mayest live in harmony? But wilt thou be satisfied with thy present condition, and pleased with all that is about thee, and wilt thou convince thyself that thou hast everything and that it comes from the gods, that everything is well for thee, and will be well whatever shall please them, and whatever they shall give for the conservation of the perfect living being, the good and just and beautiful, which generates and holds together all things, and contains and embraces all things which are dissolved for the production of other like things? Wilt thou never be such that thou shalt so dwell in community with gods and men as neither to find fault with them at all, nor to be condemned by them?

Observe what thy nature requires, so far as thou art governed by nature only: then do it and accept it, if thy nature, so far as thou art a living being, shall not be made worse by it. And next thou must observe what thy nature

體，真正要求的是什麼。作為一個社會動物，只要你的本性不會變得更糟，那就允許自己接受這一切吧。理性動物同樣也是一種政治（社會）動物。遵循這些規則吧，不要讓自己為任何無聊的事物而苦惱。

發生在你身上的一切事情，或者是你的本性所能承受的，或者是你的本性所不能承受的。如果你能夠忍受，不要因此而惱怒，就按照本性承受它吧。如果你不能夠忍受，你也不要因此而惱怒，因為它在毀滅你之後也會跟著毀滅。一定要記住：你的本性能夠承受一切事物，只要符合你的利益或者是你的義務，那麼能否忍受就取決於你的想法。

如果一個人做錯了事情，就和善地指導他，指正他的錯誤。如果你不能夠這樣做，那麼就責備自己，或者連自己也不用責備。

無論在你身上發生了什麼事情，都是在跨越千年的洪荒中命中註定的。因果的紡錘在萬古永恆中織著所有與你習習相關的命運之線。

不論宇宙是由原子聚合而成，還是自然是一個系統，首先確定的是：我是自然控制下的整體的一部分。其次，我和與我同類的部分有著密切關聯。我應當總是牢記我是其中一部分，我永遠不應對整體所

requires so far as thou art a living being. And all this thou mayest allow thyself, if thy nature, so far as thou art a rational animal, shall not be made worse by it. But the rational animal is consequently also a political (social) animal. Use these rules, then, and trouble thyself about nothing else.

Everything which happens either happens in such wise as thou art formed by nature to bear it, or as thou art not formed by nature to bear it. If, then, it happens to thee in such way as thou art formed by nature to bear it, do not complain, but bear it as thou art formed by nature to bear it. But if it happens in such wise as thou art not formed by nature to bear it, do not complain, for it will perish after it has consumed thee. Remember, however, that thou art formed by nature to bear everything, with respect to which it depends on thy own opinion to make it endurable and tolerable, by thinking that it is either thy interest or thy duty to do this.

If a man is mistaken, instruct him kindly and show him his error. But if thou art not able, blame thyself, or blame not even thyself.

Whatever may happen to thee, it was prepared for thee from all eternity; and the implication of causes was from eternity spinning the thread of thy being, and of that which is incident to it.

Whether the universe is a concourse of atoms, or nature is a system, let this first be established, that I am a part of the whole which is governed by nature; next, I am in a manner intimately related to the parts which are of

分給我的那一份感到不滿。因為，凡為了整體的利益而存在的，就不會對部分產生危害。整體不會包含任何不符合它利益的東西，所有的本性都有這條共同的原則。除此之外，宇宙本性還有這項原則：它不會被任何外部原因所強迫去產生對自身有害的東西。記住我是這宇宙的一部分，我就不會對任何發生的事情感到不滿意了。而由於我和與我自己同類的那些部分在某種程度上有著千絲萬縷的聯繫，我就會當心，不去做對社會有害的事情，而把我的全部精力都用於公共利益上面，並盡一切可能拒絕去做與公共利益相悖的事情。只要這樣做，你就會過得幸福，正如你觀察到的，一個公民做有益於同胞的事，滿足於國家所分配的，就會過得幸福。

世界的所有部分，我的意思是指自然地包含在這個世界裏的一切事物，都必然要毀滅。可以在這個意義上理解毀滅，即各個部分都必須經歷變化。假如對於各個部分來說，這件事自然地既產生傷害又無可避免，那麼整體就不會在好的狀態下存在。所有的部分都要不斷變化，並且其構成註定以各種方式消亡。因為，究竟是自然計畫好對組成它的部分行惡，使其從屬於惡，並必然地深陷其中呢，還是自然造就了這些結果而不自知呢？使部分陷入惡，並且必然陷入惡，還是自然對於自己所做的並沒有意識到，這兩者都是荒唐的、不可信的。但

the same kind with myself. For remembering this, inasmuch as I am a part, I shall be discontented with none of the things which are assigned to me out of the whole; for nothing is injurious to the part, if it is for the advantage of the whole. For the whole contains nothing which is not for its advantage; and all natures indeed have this common principle, but the nature of the universe has this principle besides, that it cannot be compelled even by any external cause to generate anything harmful to itself. By remembering, then, that I am a part of such a whole, I shall be content with everything that happens. And inasmuch as I am in a manner intimately related to the parts which are of the same kind with myself, I shall do nothing unsocial, but I shall rather direct myself to the things which are of the same kind with myself, and I shall turn an my efforts to the common interest, and divert them from the contrary. Now, if these things are done so, life must flow on happily, just as thou mayest observe that the life of a citizen is happy, who continues a course of action which is advantageous to his fellow-citizens, and is content with whatever the state may assign to him.

The parts of the whole, everything, I mean, which is naturally comprehended in the universe, must of necessity perish; but let this be understood in this sense, that they must undergo change. But if this is naturally both an evil and a necessity for the parts, the whole would not continue to exist in a good condition, the parts being subject to change and constituted so as to perish in various ways. For whether did nature herself design to do evil to the things which are parts of herself, and to make them subject to evil and of necessity fall into evil, or have such results happened

是，如果一個人撇開『自然』（作為有效果的力量存在）這個術語不提，把事物歸給自然，那麼一面說整體的部分是要變化的，一面對事物分解為組成它們的東西表示驚奇和訝異，這就是很荒謬的。因為，若不是組成事物的元素終歸要分解，就是一種改變，由固體到泥土，從氣體到氣的轉變，這些部分復歸宇宙理性，在某個時期被火所毀滅，或者透過永恆的變化重生。不要想像固體的和氣體的部分從產生起就屬於你。可以說只是兩三天前由攝入的食物和吸進的空氣而長成的。變化是你得以生長所依賴的這一切，而不是你母親所產生的。假如你母親所生的部分與變化的部分有著密切的關係，也不足以反駁我剛剛所說的。

既然你已經獲得了善良、謙虛、真誠、理智、鎮定、豁達的名聲，聽從勸告任何時候都不要去做與之相反的事情。如果你不合時宜

1.equanimity [ˌikwəˋnɪmətɪ] n. 平靜；鎮定

without her knowing it? Both these suppositions, indeed, are incredible. But if a man should even drop the term Nature (as an efficient power), and should speak of these things as natural, even then it would be ridiculous to affirm at the same time that the parts of the whole are in their nature subject to change, and at the same time to be surprised or vexed as if something were happening contrary to nature, particularly as the dissolution of things is into those things of which each thing is composed. For there is either a dispersion of the elements out of which everything has been compounded, or a change from the solid to the earthy and from the airy to the aerial, so that these parts are taken back into the universal reason, whether this at certain periods is consumed by fire or renewed by eternal changes. And do not imagine that the solid and the airy part belong to thee from the time of generation. For all this received its accretion only yesterday and the day before, as one may say, from the food and the air which is inspired. This, then, which has received the accretion, changes, not that which thy mother brought forth. But suppose that this which thy mother brought forth implicates thee very much with that other part, which has the peculiar quality of change, this is nothing in fact in the way of objection to what is said.

When thou hast assumed these names, good, modest, true, rational, a man of **equanimity**[1], and magnanimous, take care that thou dost not change

地做錯事，你就會失去這些名聲。如果你這樣做了，那就用最快的速度迅速地回到它們之中。請記住，『理智』這個詞是表示對一切出現在你面前的事物一種專注和智慧的考慮，而不會分散注意力；『鎮定』一詞是指自願地接受共同本性分派給你的任何事物；『豁達』是指理智部分超越肉體使人愉悅或痛苦的感覺，超越所有那些被稱之為榮譽、讚揚、死亡和所有相同天性的可憐事物。如果你保持這些名聲，並且不想被別人這樣稱呼，不僅你自己應當成為一個全新的人，而且你也應當開始一種新的生活。因為，到目前為止要繼續保持你原來的狀態，要承受這些你必須在生活中承受的讓人紛擾的事情，是非常愚蠢的，並且這是過分溺愛自己的生命。人們也許會拿那些和野獸搏鬥且被咬得遍體鱗傷、幾乎半死的角鬥士作比較，他們雖然傷痕累累、渾身是血，還是強烈地懇求能夠活到下一天，儘管他們將會在同樣的狀態中像以前一樣被投給同樣的爪子和牙齒。所以說，確保自己擁有這些美名吧：如果你能居於它們之中，那就擁有它們吧，好像你到了幸福之島。如果你發現自己脫離了他們，你不能夠抓住你所擁有的，請勇敢地走向你可以保住它們的一隅吧，為此甚至放棄生命，不是在激情中，而是在樸實、謙遜和自願中放棄生命，在做了這件你生命中可獲得讚美的事情之後，你就離開它們吧！為了更好地記住我們所說過的名聲，你應當記得上帝不喜歡諂媚，而是希望理性之物造得跟他們一樣。你應該記得無花果樹的工作就是做無花果樹，狗的工作就是當狗，蜜蜂的工作就是做蜜蜂，人的工作就是做人。

1.fallest 為古英語中fall的第二人稱單數（主語為thou時使用）。

these names; and if thou shouldst lose them, quickly return to them. And remember that the term Rational was intended to signify a discriminating attention to every several thing and freedom from negligence; and that Equanimity is the voluntary acceptance of the things which are assigned to thee by the common nature; and that Magnanimity is the elevation of the intelligent part above the pleasurable or painful sensations of the flesh, and above that poor thing called fame, and death, and all such things. If, then, thou maintainest thyself in the possession of these names, without desiring to be called by these names by others, thou wilt be another person and wilt enter on another life. For to continue to be such as thou hast hitherto been, and to be torn in pieces and defiled in such a life, is the character of a very stupid man and one overfond of his life, and like those half-devoured fighters with wild beasts, who though covered with wounds and gore, still intreat to be kept to the following day, though they will be exposed in the same state to the same claws and bites. Therefore fix thyself in the possession of these few names: and if thou art able to abide in them, abide as if thou wast removed to certain islands of the Happy. But if thou shalt perceive that thou **fallest**[1] out of them and dost not maintain thy hold, go courageously into some nook where thou shalt maintain them, or even depart at once from life, not in passion, but with simplicity and freedom and modesty, after doing this one laudable thing at least in thy life, to have gone out of it thus.

　　家中的木偶玩具和滑稽戲，外面的戰爭，有時恐怖、有時驚奇和呆鈍，日復一日的奴役，一點一滴地將你那些神聖的原則驅逐出你的腦海。不研究自然，你能想像多少事情，忽視多少事情？照看、實踐每件事是你的責任，這樣，你就完善處事的能力，訓練思考的能力，由通達事物帶來的自信心要含而不露。你何時能享受純樸，何時享受莊嚴？何時你才會通曉每件事？那些知識包括：組成的物質是什麼、它對於這個世界有什麼作用、它能夠存續多久、它由哪些部分組成、它隸屬於誰、誰能給予它以及拿走它。

　　當一隻蜘蛛抓住所獵取的蒼蠅時，它感到驕傲；一個人抓住一隻可憐的野兔，或者用網兜捕捉到一條魚，或者捕獲一頭野豬，或者捕捉到熊，或者俘虜了薩爾馬提亞人時，他感到驕傲。如果你考察他們

1.rememberest 為古英語中 remember 的第二人稱單數（主語為 thou 時使用）。
2.torpor [`tɔrpɚ] n. 麻木，無感覺

In order, however, to the remembrance of these names, it will greatly help thee, if thou **rememberest**[1] the gods, and that they wish not to be flattered, but wish all reasonable beings to be made like themselves; and if thou rememberest that what does the work of a fig-tree is a fig-tree, and that what does the work of a dog is a dog, and that what does the work of a bee is a bee, and that what does the work of a man is a man.

Mimi, war, astonishment, **torpor**[2], slavery, will daily wipe out those holy principles of thine. How many things without studying nature dost thou imagine, and how many dost thou neglect? But it is thy duty so to look on and so to do everything, that at the same time the power of dealing with circumstances is perfected, and the contemplative faculty is exercised, and the confidence which comes from the knowledge of each several thing is maintained without showing it, but yet not concealed. For when wilt thou enjoy simplicity, when gravity, and when the knowledge of every several thing, both what it is in substance, and what place it has in the universe, and how long it is formed to exist and of what things it is compounded, and to whom it can belong, and who are able both to give it and take it away?

A spider is proud when it has caught a fly, and another when he has caught a poor hare, and another when he has taken a little fish in a net,

的精神和想法，他們不就是強盜嗎？

　　找出並使你自己掌握這種沉思的方法和思路，藉以辨明和描繪你自己：觀察事物間的互相變化，並始終關注這種變化，在這一特別的方面就哲學完全地訓練你自己。沒有什麼東西比這更適合於產生豁達了。他與自己身體的聯繫日漸疏遠，並且察覺到他必將不久於人世，把所有一切都留在他的身後，他將注意力完全放在他所有行動中的正直，而在一切應當在他身上發生的事情中順從宇宙本性。只是使自己滿足於這兩件事情：一是滿足於他在做過的所有事情中行為正直，二是滿足於現在上帝分配給他的事物。至於別人將如何說他或想他或反對他，他甚至不曾考慮過這些。進一步講，真理和理性指引著他，通過這條直路追隨神，這是他腦海中唯一的事情，他唯一的職業和追求。

　　既然你知道了要做什麼，那有什麼必要去懷疑，去恐懼呢？如果你能夠很清楚地察覺，就不要讓別人左右你的思想；如果你不能夠很清楚地察覺，那麼就終止你的行為，停下來詢問最明白的那個人。

1.Sarmatians，斯拉夫民族之一，居於現今之波蘭與俄羅斯一帶。其婦女驍勇善戰。大約在174年左右，成為羅馬的敵人。

2.examinest 為古英語中 examine 的第二人稱單數（主語為 thou 時使用）。

and another when he has taken wild boars, and another when he has taken bears, and another when he has taken **Sarmatians**[1]. Are not these robbers, if thou **examinest**[2] their opinions?

Acquire the contemplative way of seeing how all things change into one another, and constantly attend to it, and exercise thyself about this part of philosophy. For nothing is so much adapted to produce magnanimity. Such a man has put off the body, and as he sees that he must, no one knows how soon, go away from among men and leave everything here, he gives himself up entirely to just doing in all his actions, and in everything else that happens he resigns himself to the universal nature. But as to what any man shall say or think about him or do against him, he never even thinks of it, being himself contented with these two things, with acting justly in what he now does, and being satisfied with what is now assigned to him; and he lays aside all distracting and busy pursuits, and desires nothing else than to accomplish the straight course through the law, and by accomplishing the straight course to follow God.

What need is there of suspicious fear, since it is in thy power to inquire what ought to be done? And if thou seest clear, go by this way content, without turning back: but if thou dost not see clear, stop and take the best

但如果有什麼別的東西阻礙你，那就根據當時的情形和機會謹慎而富有遠見地繼續前行，始終保持自己的正義。達到目標最好，就算失敗了，我們也要在嘗試之後再承認失敗。遵從理性的人寧靜而主動，愉悅而鎮定。

你清晨從睡眠中甦醒就問自己，如果別人做了正當的、好的事對你有任何影響嗎？沒有任何影響。

對於那些讚揚或批評的人，難道你忘記那些人的態度了嗎？那些在床上或船上的人，他們普遍的行為就是他們所從事的、所避開的、所追求的，以及他們所犯下的偷盜和搶劫的罪行，不是用手和腳，而是用他們更加寶貴的部分，這部分能產生忠實、謙虛、真誠、守法和一個好的心靈（幸福）。

他是一個受過良好教育的、真正謙虛的人。對自然說，讓出並帶走你想要的吧。他不是驕傲地這樣說，而是很謙卑地、對自然很滿意地這樣說。

1.wakest 為古英語中 wake 的第二人稱單數（主語為 thou 時使用）。

advisers. But if any other things oppose thee, go on according to thy powers with due consideration, keeping to that which appears to be just. For it is best to reach this object, and if thou dost fail, let thy failure be in attempting this. He who follows reason in all things is both tranquil and active at the same time, and also cheerful and collected.

Inquire of thyself as soon as thou **wakest**[1] from sleep, whether it will make any difference to thee, if another does what is just and right. It will make no difference.

Thou hast not forgotten, I suppose, that those who assume arrogant airs in bestowing their praise or blame on others, are such as they are at bed and at board, and thou hast not forgotten what they do, and what they avoid and what they pursue, and how they steal and how they rob, not with hands and feet, but with their most valuable part, by means of which there is produced, when a man chooses, fidelity, modesty, truth, law, a good daemon (happiness)?

To he who gives and takes back all, to nature, the man who is instructed and modest says, Give what thou wilt; take back what thou wilt. And he says this not proudly, but obediently and well pleased with her.

我剩下的時間已經不多了，就像在一座山上生活一樣。不管這裏或者那裏生活都不重要，因為他在任何地方都像在國家（政治團體）中生活一樣。讓他們看到，這才是一個真正的人，根據自然天性而生活的人。如果他們忍受不了我，就讓他們殺了我吧。因為死亡比像人們要求我的那樣去生活還要好些。

全然不要再去爭論或者演說什麼是一個高尚的人和應當具有的品格，而是要真正地、確實地成為這樣的人。

經常思考時間的整體和實體的整體。所有個別的事物對實體來說就像是滄海一粟，對時間來說就像是螺絲錐轉動一下。

看看存在的事物，看看它們已經在分解、變化，就像它們在腐爛、消解，一切事物註定是要滅亡的。

想一想，當吃飯、睡覺、生產、排泄時，人們表現得怎麼樣。並且，當他們在事業的鼎盛時期，在他們光榮的時候，或者發怒和不高興時，在表現出高高在上的威嚴時，身居高位時對別人斥責和責備時，又是怎樣一副嘴臉。而在不久之前他們還卑躬屈膝，誰知道不久

1.putrefaction [ˌpjutrə`fækʃən] n. 腐敗；腐敗物

Short is the little which remains to thee of life. Live as on a mountain. For it makes no difference whether a man lives there or here, if he lives everywhere in the world as in a state (political community). Let men see, let them know a real man who lives according to nature. If they cannot endure him, let them kill him. For that is better than to live thus as men do.

No longer talk at all about the kind of man that a good man ought to be, but be such.

Constantly contemplate the whole of time and the whole of substance, and consider that all individual things as to substance are a grain of a fig, and as to time, the turning of a gimlet.

Look at everything that exists, and observe that it is already in dissolution and in change, and as it were **putrefaction**[1] or dispersion, or that everything is so constituted by nature as to die.

Consider what men are when they are eating, sleeping, generating, easing themselves and so forth. Then what kind of men they are when they are imperious and arrogant, or angry and scolding from their elevated place. But a short time ago to how many they were slaves and for what things; and

之後他們又是怎樣的樣子？

　　宇宙本性所帶來的都是對事物有益的，並且是在合適的時機帶來。

　　詩人說，『大地總是渴望陣雨』；『莊嚴的天空在戀愛』。宇宙熱愛即將產生的事物，我對宇宙說，我愛你所愛的。不是也說：『這種或那種事物喜歡（習慣）被創造出來』。

　　或是你繼續沿襲自己習慣、可以忍受的生活方式；或者你離開這個世界，這是你自己的意志；或者切斷你的生活，你為卸下你的義務而欣喜萬分。而在這些事之外一無所有。那麼，就歡樂地生活吧！

　　讓這些對你而言總是明白的和清晰可見的：陸地和沙漠是如此的相似；這裏的東西和山上、海邊或是其他地方的東西沒有什麼不同；正像哲學家柏拉圖所說的，居於城牆之內就跟山上牧人住的草棚中一樣。

　　指引我走過餘生的主要原則是什麼？我所塑造的本性是什麼樣

1.aether [`iθɚ] n. 蒼穹
2.出自柏拉圖《泰阿泰德篇》。

after a little time consider in what a condition they will be.

That is for the good of each thing, which the universal nature brings to each. And it is for its good at the time when nature brings it.

"The earth loves the shower"; and "the solemn **aether**[1] loves"; and the universe loves to make whatever is about to be. I say then to the universe, that I love as thou lovest. And is not this too said, that "this or that loves (is wont) to be produced"?

Either thou livest here and hast already accustomed thyself to it, or thou art going away, and this was thy own will; or thou art dying and hast discharged thy duty. But besides these things there is nothing. Be of good cheer, then.

Let this always be plain to thee, that this piece of land is like any other; and that all things here are the same with things on top of a mountain, or on the sea-shore, or wherever thou choosest to be. For thou wilt find just **what Plato says**[2], dwelling within the walls of a city as in a shepherd's fold on a mountain.

What is my ruling faculty now to me? And of what nature am I

的？我運用它的目的是什麼？是否偏離了理智？是否脫離了社會生活？是否與可憐的肉體混雜在一起行動？

從主人那裏逃跑的人是一個逃亡者，但法律是每個人的主人，因此違反法律的人就是一個逃亡者。那些悲歎、憤怒或者畏懼的人以及受到宇宙間的君主和統治者指派已經這樣或者應當這樣的人也是逃亡者。確切地說，這統治者就是法，將世間萬物分派給每人以適合的東西，悲歎、憤怒或者畏懼的人就是一個逃亡者。

從男人那裏放下一顆種子，並立刻進入子宮，而男人此後就沒有再碰過它。另一種本原隨之照管它，並承擔了這些工作，隨著時間推移，成為一個完美的孩子，用這樣的質料竟能完成這樣的東西。再一次地，小孩通過喉嚨吃下食物，然後他又不聞不問了。另一種本原又接著照管它，給感官和感情配發食物，使之進入生活，進入力量。有多少人是這樣成長，這又是多麼不可思議啊！觀察以這種隱蔽方式造就的事物，觀察這種力量正像我們觀察那使事物消沉和提升的力量一樣，儘管不是用眼睛，但並不因此就不清晰。

世間萬物現在是什麼樣子，在此之前也是以相同的種類、相同的方式這樣存在的，思考它們在將來也會是這個樣子的。此外，想想整幕戲劇、清一色的場景，無論是從你所知道的自身經驗還是閱讀古代歷史所得知的。例如，哈德良的整個宮廷，安東尼爾斯的整個宮廷，還有菲利浦、亞歷山大、克裏瑟斯的整個宮廷，將它們全部呈現在眼

now making it? And for what purpose am I now using it? Is it void of understanding? Is it loosed and rent asunder from social life? Is it melted into and mixed with the poor flesh so as to move together with it?

He who flies from his master is a runaway; but the law is master, and he who breaks the law is a runaway. And he also who is grieved or angry or afraid, is dissatisfied because something has been or is or shall be of the things which are appointed by him who rules all things, and he is Law, and assigns to every man what is fit. He then who fears or is grieved or is angry is a runaway.

A man deposits seed in a womb and goes away, and then another cause takes it, and labours on it and makes a child. What a thing from such a material! Again, the child passes food down through the throat, and then another cause takes it and makes perception and motion, and in fine life and strength and other things; how many and how strange! Observe then the things which are produced in such a hidden way, and see the power just as we see the power which carries things downwards and upwards, not with the eyes, but still no less plainly.

Constantly consider how all things such as they now are, in time past also were; and consider that they will be the same again. And place before thy eyes entire dramas and stages of the same form, whatever thou hast learned from thy experience or from older history; for example, the whole court of Hadrian, and the whole court of Antoninus, and the whole court of Philip,

前。你應當發現他們都是同一種類和方式，只是換了演員而已。

想像一下，對事物悲歎和不滿的人，就像是一隻豬在行前將被割破喉嚨時那樣掙扎和叫喊。

他就是那樣的人，像豬一樣在床上為人們的生活被束縛而深深悲哀。記住這一點，自願屈從於所發生的事僅僅是給予理性動物的品格，但盲目屈從則是加於所有生物的一種必然性。

無論你在做什麼樣的事情，都要停下來問問自己：是否因為死亡剝奪了你做事的機會它就是一件可怕的事情呢？

當你因別人的冒犯而惱怒時，立刻轉向自己，想想你自己是否犯過同類的錯誤。比如說，你曾經以為富有，或者活得快樂，或者被表揚被評論，或者其他特別的事都是很幸福的事情。如果你在記憶中喚起這些事情，你將很快地忘記你的憤怒，特別是與此同時你再加上這一層考慮：這個人是被迫的，他怎麼能做出別的選擇呢？如果你能，幫他擺脫被逼的窘境吧。

1.Croesus，西元前6世紀呂底亞的國王，位於小亞細亞地區，以豪富著稱。後被Cyrus領導的波斯軍隊所征服。

2.lament [lə`mɛnt] n. 悲歎；悔恨；慟哭

Alexander, **Croesus**[1]; for all those were such dramas as we see now, only with different actors.

Imagine every man who is grieved at anything or discontented to be like a pig which is sacrificed and kicks and screams.

Like this pig also is he who on his bed in silence **laments**[2] the bonds in which we are held. And consider that only to the rational animal is it given to follow voluntarily what happens; but simply to follow is a necessity imposed on all.

Severally on the occasion of everything that thou doest, pause and ask thyself, if death is a dreadful thing because it deprives thee of this.

When thou art offended at any man's fault, forthwith turn to thyself and reflect in what like manner thou dost err thyself; for example, in thinking that money is a good thing, or pleasure, or a bit of reputation, and the like. For by attending to this thou wilt quickly forget thy anger, if this consideration also is added, that the man is compelled: for what else could he do? or, if thou art able, take away from him the compulsion.

　　當你見到蘇格拉底派學者薩特隆，想想尤提切斯或希門；當你見到幼發拉底斯，想想特提其奧和西萬諾斯；當你見到奧茨弗朗時，想想特羅帕奧佛魯斯；當你見到色諾芬，想想克裏托或西維勒斯。當你反觀自己時，想想自己是凱撒軍團的某一個人或者其他任何人，這對每一個擁有財產和職業的人都適用。然後讓這一思想同時出現在你腦海裏：這些人現在都在哪裏呢？無處可尋還是處處皆是？因此你應當無論何時都能夠察覺到世間萬物是怎麼樣的，如夢如幻、瞬間即逝，或者事實上都是虛空。特別是如果你同時在腦海中思考一旦變化的東西絕不會像這個世界一樣在無限持續中再存在。而你，你又將存續多久呢？你為什麼還不滿足於一種有秩序的、適合你的生活呢？你將度過每一段時間，你所分配到的時間段是多麼的渺小呢？你所祈求的從中解脫是怎樣的一個命題，或者說是人生怎樣的一個課程啊！所有這些事物，不管它是什麼，都是根據萬物自然的天性逐漸被理解而踐行自己使命的嗎？耐心一點，直到你也熟悉了這些事情，就像那結實的胃把所有食物變成它自己的一樣，像那大火使投入其中的一切東西的火焰和亮光都成為自己的一樣。

　　不要讓任何人都有這樣的能力如實地說你不是真正簡樸的、真誠的和開放的，或不是善的。讓任何持有這些觀點的人都成為騙子，這

1.Satyron，與奧理略時代相近的哲學家。
2.Eutyches，早期哲學家。　　3.Hymen，早期哲學家。
4.Euphrates，苦修派哲學家。　5.Eutychion，早期哲學家。
6.Silvanus，早期哲學家。
7.Alciphron，古希臘詭辯家。

When thou hast seen **Satyron**[1] the Socratic, think of either **Eutyches**[2] or **Hymen**[3], and when thou hast seen **Euphrates**[4], think of **Eutychion**[5] or **Silvanus**[6], and when thou hast seen **Alciphron**[7] think of **Tropaeophorus**[8], and when thou hast seen **Xenophon**[9] think of **Crito**[10] or Severus, and when thou hast looked on thyself, think of any other Caesar, and in the case of every one do in like manner. Then let this thought be in thy mind, where then are those men? Nowhere, or nobody knows where. For thus continuously thou wilt look at human things as smoke and nothing at all; especially if thou **reflectest**[11] at the same time that what has once changed will never exist again in the infinite duration of time. But thou, in what a brief space of time is thy existence? And why art thou not content to pass through this short time in an orderly way? What matter and opportunity for thy activity art thou avoiding? For what else are all these things, except exercises for the reason, when it has viewed carefully and by examination into their nature the things which happen in life? Persevere then until thou shalt have made these things thy own, as the stomach which is strengthened makes all things its own, as the blazing fire makes flame and brightness out of everything that is thrown into it.

Let it not be in any man's power to say truly of thee that thou art not simple or that thou are not good; but let him be a liar whoever shall think

---

8.Tropaeophorus，早期哲學家。

9.Xenophon（約西元前434年～西元前355年），古希臘將軍和歷史學家，著有《長征記》。

10.Crito，蘇格拉底的朋友。

11.reflectest 為古英語中 reflect 的第二人稱單數（主語為 thou 時使用）。

些完全是在你的力量範圍之內的。誰能阻止你成為真正樸實善良的人呢？如果不能這樣，下決心不再活下去。因為如果不是這種人，理性絕不允許你這樣生存。

　　講到人生的質料時，要怎麼說、怎麼做才能最符合理性呢？無論這是什麼事情，這都是你力量範圍之內的事情，去做它或說它，即使你受阻，也不要為自己尋找任何辯解。你將永遠不會停止悲傷，直到心靈能達到這種境地：正如享樂者享受奢侈，你對於擺在面前的事情，應該順從本性去做。一個人按照本性做事應該是一件快樂的事，而且他也有能力如此做。而這種能力卻沒有給予根據自己的動態到處滾動的一個圓筒，也沒有給予水或者火以及一切天生的、自然的或敏感的或者無理性支配的事物，因為很多東西能夠阻擋它們的行動，而理智和理性卻能根據他們的自然天性，順利通過一切阻礙它們的事物並大步向前，這是先天就賦予他們的特權。理性能夠順利通過所有事物，就像火苗向上竄，石頭往下落，圓筒順著斜坡往下滾一樣，讓自己覺得滿足，不再尋求其他的。所有其他起妨礙作用的事物或者只是影響那無生命的物體，或者只有意見和理性絲毫不做抵抗，它們才能產生壓迫或在損害中逃離。假如它們確實這樣做了，那麼感覺的人立刻變壞。對於有著特定本性的事物，無論遭遇哪種傷害，都將受到影響變得更壞。相同情況下，人們如果能夠善加利用那些意外，就會因此變得更好和更值得讚揚。最後請你記住：那不會損害到城邦的事情，也絕不會損害到真正的公民；那不損害到法律的事情，也絕不會損害到城邦；而所有不幸事件或者是外部的阻礙都不能夠損害到法律本身。不損害法律的，也絕不能夠損害到國家或公民。

anything of this kind about thee; and this is altogether in thy power. For who is he that shall hinder thee from being good and simple? Do thou only determine to live no longer, unless thou shalt be such. For neither does reason allow thee to live, if thou art not such.

What is that which as to this material (our life) can be done or said in the way most conformable to reason. For whatever this may be, it is in thy power to do it or to say it, and do not make excuses that thou art hindered. Thou wilt not cease to lament till thy mind is in such a condition that, what luxury is to those who enjoy pleasure, such shall be to thee, in the matter which is subjected and presented to thee, the doing of the things which are conformable to man's constitution; for a man ought to consider as an enjoyment everything which it is in his power to do according to his own nature. And it is in his power everywhere. Now, it is not given to a cylinder to move everywhere by its own motion, nor yet to water nor to fire, nor to anything else which is governed by nature or an irrational soul, for the things which check them and stand in the way are many. But intelligence and reason are able to go through everything that opposes them, and in such manner as they are formed by nature and as they choose. Place before thy eyes this facility with which the reason will be carried through all things, as fire upwards, as a stone downwards, as a cylinder down an inclined surface, and seek for nothing further. For all other obstacles either affect the body only which is a dead thing; or, except through opinion and the yielding of the reason itself, they do not crush nor do any harm of any kind; for if they did, he who felt it would immediately become bad. Now, in the case of all

通曉真正原則的人，即使是最簡潔和最普通的格言也足以提醒他遠離悲傷和恐懼。例如，

「風從樹頂掠過，樹葉飄零落地，

　人也是如此。」

你的孩子們也是樹葉，那些熱烈地稱頌和讚揚你的人，或者用不尋常的詛咒、暗中的譴責和輕蔑而讚揚你的人，也是樹葉。那些得到名聲，傳給後代的也是樹葉。甚至世間萬物都是樹葉。他們的春天來了，他們開始生長，然後一陣風吹過，它們紛紛掉落，然後樹木又在它們原先的位置長出新的葉子。所有事物都只能夠短暫地存在，這是萬物的共性。為什麼你追尋這些事情，或者以為他們能夠永恆地存續？再過一會，你就將閉上你的雙眼，那為你上墳的人不久也要被人

things which have a certain constitution, whatever harm may happen to any of them, that which is so affected becomes consequently worse; but in the like case, a man becomes both better, if one may say so, and more worthy of praise by making a right use of these accidents. And finally remember that nothing harms him who is really a citizen, which does not harm the state; nor yet does anything harm the state, which does not harm law (order); and of these things which are called misfortunes not one harms law. What then does not harm law does not harm either state or citizen.

To him who is penetrated by true principles even the briefest precept is sufficient, and any common precept, to remind him that he should be free from grief and fear. For example –

"Leaves, some the wind scatters on the ground –

So is the race of men."

Leaves, also, are thy children; and leaves, too, are they who cry out as if they were worthy of credit and bestow their praise, or on the contrary curse, or secretly blame and sneer; and leaves, in like manner, are those who shall receive and transmit a man's fame to aftertimes. For all such things as these "are produced in the season of spring," as the poet says; then the wind casts them down; then the forest produces other leaves in their places. But a brief existence is common to all things, and yet thou **avoidest**[1] and **pursuest**[2] all

悼念。

一雙健全的眼睛應當能夠看到所有可見到的事物，而不是只想看到綠色的東西。這願望對一雙病眼來講才是合適的。因此，健全的聽覺和嗅覺應當準備好去察覺任何能被聽到和聞到的東西。一個健全的胃應當對所有的食物一視同仁，就像磨刀石對待所有需要磨的東西一樣。健全的理智應當是為所有可能發生的事情做準備的。但是說，我親愛的孩子必須活著！所有人都必須讚揚我所做的一切！這就如同一雙尋求綠色事物的病眼一樣，或者說就像一副尋求鬆軟食物的朽牙一樣。

世界上沒有一個人會如此幸運，在他死去的時候身邊沒有一個會對他的死亡感到欣喜愉快的人。那麼，他的確是一個品德高尚、充滿智慧的人嗎？是否最終找不到這樣的人，他最後會在心裏這樣對自己說：「現在讓我們最終擺脫這位賣弄學問的老師吧，沒錯，他並沒有苛待我們，但我知道他在內心裏默默地譴責我們。」這就是對一個品德高尚的人所說的。而就我們的情況而言，有多少事情擺在那兒使許多人希望擺脫我們。因此，你臨死時能想到這一點就會死得更從容一點。你要是這樣自我思考：現在我就要從這樣一個世界中離去了，

1.avoidest 為古英語中 avoid 的第二人稱單數（主語為 thou 時使用）。
2.pursuest 為古英語中 pursue 的第二人稱單數（主語為 thou 時使用）。

things as if they would be eternal. A little time, and thou shalt close thy eyes; and him who has attended thee to thy grave another soon will lament.

The healthy eye ought to see all visible things and not to say, I wish for green things; for this is the condition of a diseased eye. And the healthy hearing and smelling ought to be ready to perceive all that can be heard and smelled. And the healthy stomach ought to be with respect to all food just as the mill with respect to all things which it is formed to grind. And accordingly the healthy understanding ought to be prepared for everything which happens; but that which says, Let my dear children live, and let all men praise whatever I may do, is an eye which seeks for green things, or teeth which seek for soft things.

There is no man so fortunate that there shall not be by him when he is dying some who are pleased with what is going to happen. Suppose that he was a good and wise man, will there not be at last some one to say to himself, Let us at last breathe freely being relieved from this schoolmaster? It is true that he was harsh to none of us, but I perceived that he tacitly condemns us. – This is what is said of a good man. But in our own case how many other things are there for which there are many who wish to get rid of us. Thou wilt consider this then when thou art dying, and thou wilt depart

甚至我如此努力地為之忍受痛楚、為之祈禱和關心的最親密的朋友和熟人也希望我離去，希望在我死後他們能夠活得比從前快樂。既然這樣，人們為什麼還要再在這個世界上逗留呢？儘管如此，也不要為此就在離去時對他們態度不和善，而是要保持原來的品性，友好、仁慈和溫和。另一方面不要顯得像是拖著離去似的，而要平靜的離開，靈魂瞬間同身體分開，你同身邊人的分離也應當會是這樣的。自然曾把你與這些事情聯繫和結合起來。現在自然要解除這種結合嗎？離開朋友和親密的人，沒有反抗和強迫，而是甘心情願，因為這些都是根據自然而為的一件事。

盡可能經常地讓自己在碰到任何人、做任何事的時候，都立刻這樣問一問自己：這個人做這件事究竟是為了什麼目的？從你自己先開始這一課吧，先勤勉地考察你自己究竟做了些什麼。

記住，牽引生命之線的東西潛藏於內心。這是無可辯駁的，這就是人生，或者更確切而言，這就是人自身。在思考自我的時候，不要把身體和身體的器官算在內。它們自身就像是木匠的一把斧頭，差別僅在於它們是生來就長在身體上面。否則，由於沒有推動和制約它們的內在力量，這些部分自身對我們來講的確不比織布工的梭子或者作家的筆或者牧人的鞭子更有用處。

more contentedly by reflecting thus: I am going away from such a life, in which even my associates in behalf of whom I have striven so much, prayed, and cared, themselves wish me to depart, hoping perchance to get some little advantage by it. Why then should a man cling to a longer stay here? Do not however for this reason go away less kindly disposed to them, but preserving thy own character, and friendly and benevolent and mild, and on the other hand not as if thou wast torn away; but as when a man dies a quiet death, the poor soul is easily separated from the body, such also ought thy departure from men to be, for nature united thee to them and associated thee. But does she now dissolve the union? Well, I am separated as from kinsmen, not however dragged resisting, but without compulsion; for this too is one of the things according to nature.

Accustom thyself as much as possible on the occasion of anything being done by any person to inquire with thyself, For what object is this man doing this? But begin with thyself, and examine thyself first.

Remember that this which pulls the strings is the thing which is hidden within: this is the power of persuasion, this is life, this, if one may so say, is man. In contemplating thyself never include the vessel which surrounds thee and these instruments which are attached about it. For they are like to an axe, differing only in this that they grow to the body. For indeed there is no more use in these parts without the cause which moves and checks them than in the weaver's shuttle, and the writer's pen and the driver's whip.

第十一卷

    個理性的靈魂本身的屬性：它善於發現自我，剖析自我，按照自己的選擇塑造自我；它可以享受自己的果實，無論是什麼植物、樹木或者其他生物，它們的果實多由別人享受。無論生命的界限在哪，都會實現自己的目標。它非但不會像一種舞蹈、戲劇或別的類似事物，只要被什麼打斷，整體就會受到影響。相反地，無論它在哪裏停止，它的每一部分都是充分的、完整的，以至於它可以說：我已擁有我想要的所有。它在整個宇宙和周圍的空間中俯瞰，概覽自己的形式，並使自己延伸到無限的時間之中，領悟所有事物的時代更替。它可以發現我們的後人看不到什麼新的東西，而我們的前人也不比我們領悟得更多，而是在某種意義上，當一個人到了四十多歲之際，如果那時他有完整的理解力，就可以通過一致性看待那些以前發生的以及日後將要發生的事情。這也是一個理性的靈魂所擁有的性質：熱愛鄰人，忠於真理和謙虛，不把任何東西看得比其自身更重要，這同時也是法的性質。如此一來，合宜的理性和正義的理性就沒什麼不同了。

    如果你把一支樂曲分割成多個聲音，然後問自己是否被征服，因

BOOK 11

Th ese are the properties of the rational soul: it sees itself, analyses itself, and makes itself such as it chooses; the fruit which it bears itself enjoys – for the fruits of plants and that in animals which corresponds to fruits others enjoy – it obtains its own end, wherever the limit of life may be fixed. Not as in a dance and in a play and in such like things, where the whole action is incomplete, if anything cuts it short; but in every part and wherever it may be stopped, it makes what has been set before it full and complete, so that it can say, I have what is my own. And further it traverses the whole universe, and the surrounding vacuum, and surveys its form, and it extends itself into the infinity of time, and embraces and comprehends the periodical renovation of all things, and it comprehends that those who come after us will see nothing new, nor have those before us seen anything more, but in a manner he who is forty years old, if he has any understanding at all, has seen by virtue of the uniformity that prevails all things which have been and all that will be. This too is a property of the rational soul, love of one's neighbour, and truth and modesty, and to value nothing more more than itself, which is also the property of Law. Thus then right reason differs not at all from the reason of justice.

Thou wilt set little value on pleasing song and dancing and the

為你將羞於承認；在舞蹈中，對於每個動作，你持有相同的態度；角鬥也是這樣。如果分解開來，你就不會重視動人的歌曲、舞蹈和角鬥了。除了品德和與其孕育而生的行為以外，研究事物的部分，你就不會再重視它們。而這樣的做法也可以應用於你整個的生活。

一個靈魂若能隨時準備從肉體中分離，如果需要的話，或者毀滅，或者消散，或者繼續存在，那麼這將是一個怎樣聖潔的靈魂啊！但這種欣然的準備是來自個人自己的判斷的，而不是來自基督徒那樣的頑固。這種準備是慎重考慮並具有高貴性的，以致於可以作為使別人信服的榜樣，完全沒有情感上的悲歎。

我曾經做過什麼有利於公眾利益的事嗎？如果那樣的話，我已得到了回報。讓我的心靈總是想到這一點，永遠不停止做這樣的事。

什麼是你的職責？那就是做一個好人。除了靠普遍原則之外，即一方面是宇宙的本性，另一方面是人恰當的構成，如何能獲得成功？

1.pancratium [pæn`kreʃɪəm] n. 融合拳擊和摔角的古代希臘競技；角鬥

pancratium[1], if thou wilt distribute the melody of the voice into its several sounds, and ask thyself as to each, if thou art mastered by this; for thou wilt be prevented by shame from confessing it: and in the matter of dancing, if at each movement and attitude thou wilt do the same; and the like also in the matter of the pancratium. In all things, then, except virtue and the acts of virtue, remember to apply thyself to their several parts, and by this division to come to value them little: and apply this rule also to thy whole life.

What a soul that is which is ready, if at any moment it must be separated from the body, and ready either to be extinguished or dispersed or continue to exist; but so that this readiness comes from a man's own judgment, not from mere obstinacy, as with the Christians, but considerately and with dignity and in a way to persuade another, without tragic show.

Have I done something for the general interest? Well then I have had my reward. Let this always be present to thy mind, and never stop doing such good.

What is thy art? To be good. And how is this accomplished well except by general principles, some about the nature of the universe, and others about the proper constitution of man?

　　最初上演的悲劇是作為一種手段提醒人們注意這些情況可能就會在現實生活中發生，並以此來提醒他們：一切事物的發生和發展都是符合自然的，如果你真的喜歡那些在舞臺上展現的事情，你也不會為發生在更大的舞臺上的事情苦惱。因為，你知道事情必須這樣發生，甚至那些喊出「啊，西塞隆」的人也都忍受了這樣的結果。的確，對有些事情戲劇家解釋得很好，特別是下面的話：

如果神靈忽視我和我的子孫，
這必然是有原因的。

以及

『我們不應該對發生的事憂慮和憤怒。』

以及

『生命的果實收割起來就像豐碩的麥穗。』

等等一些諸如此類的說法。

1.Cithaeron，山名。古希臘希波戰爭的主要戰場之一，舉行酒神節和赫拉祭祀的聖地。

At first tragedies were brought on the stage as means of reminding men of the things which happen to them, and that it is according to nature for things to happen so, and that, if you are delighted with what is shown on the stage, you should not be troubled with that which takes place on the larger stage. For you see that these things must be accomplished thus, and that even they bear them who cry out "O **Cithaeron**[1]." And, indeed, some things are said well by the dramatic writers, of which kind is the following especially:

"Me and my children if the gods neglect,
This has its reason too."

And again –

"We must not chale and fret at that which happens."

And, –

"Life's harvest reap like the wheat's fruitful ear."

And other things of the same kind.

就在悲劇發展以後出現了古老的喜劇。這種喜劇言辭大膽豪放、直而不隱，有助於提醒人們嚴防傲慢，因為這個目的，第歐根尼過去也常引用這些作家的話。

至於中期喜劇，看看它們是什麼，這種新喜劇引進的物件是什麼，你會發現這種新喜劇逐漸淪為技巧的模擬。這些作家也說了一些有用的話，但這是眾所周知的：但是這類詩歌和戲劇究竟傾向於什麼目的啊？

這看來是如此清晰：沒有哪種生活方式比你現在的處境更適合於實踐哲學。

從相鄰的樹枝上砍下的一枝，必然也是從整棵樹上砍下的。同樣一個人同另一個人的分離就好比同整個社會的分離。對於枝條來說，是另外的東西切下了它，而一個人卻是透過自己的行為同其他鄰人分離。當他憎恨或者不理睬別人時，他完全沒有考慮到，與此同時也正在使自己與整個社會分開。但他肯定還是擁有來自創造社會的宙斯的特權，即，我們有能力回到鄰人中，成為有益於整體的部分。然而，如果這種分離時常發生，再想整合到先前的狀態就困難了。最後，先

1.happenest 為古英語中 happen 的第二人稱單數（主語為 thou 時使用）。

After tragedy the old comedy was introduced, which had a magisterial freedom of speech, and by its very plainness of speaking was useful in reminding men to beware of insolence; and for this purpose too Diogenes used to take from these writers.

But as to the middle comedy which came next, observe what it was, and again, for what object the new comedy was introduced, which gradually sunk down into a mere mimic artifice. That some good things are said even by these writers, everybody knows: but the whole plan of such poetry and dramaturgy, to what end does it look!

How plain does it appear that there is not another condition of life so well suited for philosophising as this in which thou now **happenest**[1] to be.

A branch cut off from the adjacent branch must of necessity be cut off from the whole tree also. So too a man when he is separated from another man has fallen off from the whole social community. Now as to a branch, another cuts it off, but a man by his own act separates himself from his neighbour when he hates him and turns away from him, and he does not know that he has at the same time cut himself off from the whole social system. Yet he has this privilege certainly from Zeus who framed society,

前那被切下來的枝條，即使再嫁接上去也不會與其他枝條一樣了。正像園丁所說，雖然它與樹的其餘部分一起生長，但它並不擁有和樹同樣的心靈。

有些人會在你按照正確的理性行進時企圖阻礙你，這並不能使你偏離自己的正道，因而你也不要讓這些人的行為影響了你的憐憫之心。與此同時你只需要顧及兩件事情：既要保持自己判斷力和行為的穩定性，又要和善地對待那些試圖阻撓你的人。因為，對他們惱怒就像是由於畏懼而使你自身偏離目標或讓步一樣，是一種軟弱的體現。這兩種人都放棄了自己的職責，一是由於畏懼而這樣做的，另一個則是疏遠於同胞和朋友。

自然不可能低於藝術，因為藝術模仿自然中的事物。這樣理解的話，那自然中最完善和最普遍的東西就也不會遜色於藝術。低級的藝術都是為更高的藝術做鋪墊的，宇宙本性也是這樣。其實正義也源於此，所有的道德都會在正義中有其基礎：因為假如我們關心的是過程

for it is in our power to grow again to that which is near to us, and be to come a part which helps to make up the whole. However, if it often happens, this kind of separation, it makes it difficult for that which detaches itself to be brought to unity and to be restored to its former condition. Finally, the branch, which from the first grew together with the tree, and has continued to have one life with it, is not like that which after being cut off is then ingrafted, for this is something like what the gardeners mean when they say that it grows with the rest of the tree, but that it has not the same mind with it.

As those who try to stand in thy way when thou art proceeding according to right reason, will not be able to turn thee aside from thy proper action, so neither let them drive thee from thy benevolent feelings towards them, but be on thy guard equally in both matters, not only in the matter of steady judgment and action, but also in the matter of gentleness towards those who try to hinder or otherwise trouble thee. For this also is a weakness, to be vexed at them, as well as to be diverted from thy course of action and to give way through fear; for both are equally deserters from their post, the man who does it through fear, and the man who is alienated from him who is by nature a kinsman and a friend.

There is no nature which is inferior to art, for the arts imitate the nature of things. But if this is so, that nature which is the most perfect and the most comprehensive of all natures, cannot fall short of the skill of art. Now all arts do the inferior things for the sake of the superior; therefore the universal

中間的部分（中性的事物），或者被騙，或者做出輕率的改變，所謂的正義也就無法被遵循了。

追求某物，避免某物都困擾著你，其實不是事物找上你，在某種意義上是你找上它們。你不對它們做判斷，它們才會冷靜下來，與此同時，人們也就不會看到你在這一過程中的追求或躲避。

靈魂始終保持著它球狀的形象：它不伸展到任何物體，也不向內收縮，不發散也不凝結，而是被光芒照耀著，藉這種光就能看到真理，那就是所有事物和它自身的真理。

有什麼人蔑視我嗎？那讓他去蔑視吧。而我更要注意的是這一點：人們看到我不會去做或者說任何應受蔑視之事。有什麼人憎恨我嗎？讓他去憎恨吧。但我要使自己對每個人都和善、仁愛，甚至樂意向那些恨我的人指出錯誤，不是透過譴責他們，也不是做出一種忍耐的樣子，而是像偉大的福西昂那樣，表現得高貴而誠實，除非他們的確對此出言諷刺。因為一個人的內心應該如此：不應當讓神靈看見自

1.Phocion，西元前4世紀雅典政治家和將軍，被當成行為正直的榜樣，後被誣陷而死，死前告誡其子：不可因此而對雅典人心存嫌隙。

nature does so too. And, indeed, hence is the origin of justice, and in justice the other virtues have their foundation: for justice will not be observed, if we either care for middle things (things indifferent), or are easily deceived and careless and changeable.

If the things do not come to thee, the pursuits and avoidances of which disturb thee, still in a manner thou goest to them. Let then thy judgment about them be at rest, and they will remain quiet, and thou wilt not be seen either pursuing or avoiding.

The spherical form of the soul maintains its figure, when it is neither extended towards any object, nor contracted inwards, nor dispersed nor sinks down, but is illuminated by light, by which it sees the truth, the truth of all things and the truth that is in itself.

Suppose any man shall despise me. Let him look to that himself. But I will look to this, that I be not discovered doing or saying anything deserving of contempt. Shall any man hate me? Let him look to it. But I will be mild and benevolent towards every man, and ready to show even him his mistake, not reproachfully, nor yet as making a display of my endurance, but nobly and honestly, like the great **Phocion**[1], unless indeed he only assumed it.

己不滿或者抱怨任何事。如果你現在正做著使你自己的本性愉悅的事情，如果你對此刻的狀態所發生的事情感到滿意，身為一個人你把自己擺在自我的位置上，做對公眾有益的事情，這對你怎麼算是惡呢？

現實生活中的人們相互蔑視，相互奉承，各自都希望自己高於別人，有時卻又做著卑躬屈膝的事情。

那個說他決心公正而誠實地待你的人是多麼不正常和不真誠啊！哎，你在做什麼啊？沒有必要發出這一通知，事實會證明一切。你的想法應該清楚地寫在前額上。一個人的品格也是，可以直接在他的眼睛裏顯示出來，正像戀人之間可以立即從對方的眼睛裏讀出對方的一切。誠實和善良的人散發出濃郁的氣味，接近他的人都會聞到。而那些矯揉造作的樸實卻像一根彎曲的棍子。再沒有什麼比那種如豺狼般虛偽的友誼更可恥的了，要盡最大努力避免它。而善良、樸實和仁慈都明確無誤地在眼睛裏表現出來。

要快樂地生活，只需要對無關緊要的事物採取漠然的態度，這種力量源自於靈魂。它之所以能採取漠然的態度，在於它對每一個這樣的事物都兼顧其整體和部分，並且牢記這些事物中沒有哪一個能

For the interior parts ought to be such, and a man ought to be seen by the gods neither dissatisfied with anything nor complaining. For what evil is it to thee, if thou art now doing what is agreeable to thy own nature, and art satisfied with that which at this moment is suitable to the nature of the universe, since thou art a human being placed at thy post in order that what is for the common advantage may be done in some way?

Men despise one another and flatter one another; and men wish to raise themselves above one another, and crouch before one another.

How unsound and insincere is he who says, I have determined to deal with thee in a fair way. – What art thou doing, man? There is no occasion to give this notice. It will soon show itself by acts. The voice ought to be plainly written on the forehead. Such as a man's character is, he immediately shows it in his eyes, just as he who is beloved forthwith reads everything in the eyes of lovers. The man who is honest and good ought to be exactly like a man who smells strong, so that the bystander as soon as he comes near him must smell whether he choose or not. But the affectation of simplicity is like a crooked stick. Nothing is more disgraceful than a wolfish friendship (false friendship). Avoid this most of all. The good and simple and benevolent show all these things in the eyes, and there is no mistaking.

As to living in the best way, this power is in the soul, if it be indifferent to things which are indifferent. And it will be indifferent, if it looks on each of these things separately and all together, and if it remembers that not

使我們產生對它的意見，也不會觸動我們自己，這些事情都是始終不動的，是我們自己做出了恰當的判斷。所以，是我們自己把它們寫在了心裏，反之，我們也完全可以不將它們寫入心裏。如果這些判斷偶爾不知不覺地進入心裏，我們也可以消滅它們。與此同時，我們要知道，對事物的關注只會在短時期內存在，屆時生命就要結束。這樣做又有什麼困難呢？如果這些事物是合乎自然，就喜歡它們吧，它們對你就是有益的；如果它們違反自然規律，那就去找合於你自己本性的一面，努力追求它，即使它不會帶來任何名譽。這樣每個人都能尋找到自己的善。

對每一事物我們都要思考它從何而來，由什麼東西組成，發生了什麼變化，當它改變時又變成什麼性質的事物，並且它將沒有損害地繼續存在。

如果有人非常愚蠢或邪惡地冒犯了你，首先要考慮：我和這些人有什麼關係，其實我們是被造物主創造出來相互合作的；另一方面，我是被造出來凌駕於他們之上的，這就好比一隻頭羊之於羊群，一隻頭牛之於牛群。要從最合適的原則出發考慮問題：如果所有事物都不止是原子，那安排所有這些的就是自然本身。如果真是這樣，那麼，低等的事物就要為高等的事物而存在，而高等的事物之間要相互合作。

第二，要考慮那些冒犯者們在飯桌邊、在床上等地方又是怎樣的

one of them produces in us an opinion about itself, nor comes to us; but these things remain immovable, and it is we ourselves who produce the judgments about them, and, as we may say, write them in ourselves, it being in our power not to write them, and it being in our power, if perchance these judgments have imperceptibly got admission to our minds, to wipe them out; and if we remember also that such attention will only be for a short time, and then life will be at an end. Besides, what trouble is there at all in doing this? For if these things are according to nature, rejoice in them, and they will be easy to thee: but if contrary to nature, seek what is conformable to thy own nature, and strive towards this, even if it bring no reputation; for every man is allowed to seek his own good.

Consider whence each thing is come, and of what it consists, and into what it changes, and what kind of a thing it will be when it has changed, and that it will sustain no harm.

If any have offended against thee, consider first: What is my relation to men, and that we are made for one another; and in another respect, I was made to be set over them, as a ram over the flock or a bull over the herd. But examine the matter from first principles, from this: If all things are not mere atoms, it is nature which orders all things: if this is so, the inferior things exist for the sake of the superior, and these for the sake of one another.

Second, consider what kind of men they are at table, in bed, and so forth:

人，尤其是考慮他們在何種壓力下形成的意見，他們為他們所做的事又是何等驕傲。

第三，如果人們是正當地做出他們的選擇，那我們不應當因此而不愉快。如果他們做得不正確，那很顯然他們這樣做是出於無意識和無知。正像每一靈魂都不願意被剝奪真理一樣，他們也不願意自己對其他人的影響力被無情地剝奪。所以，當人們被視為背信棄義、貪婪、卑鄙、對鄰人作惡時，他們是痛苦的。

第四，考慮你是否也做了許多類似不正當的事情，你是否也是一個和他們相仿的人，即使你戒除了某些錯誤，但你還是有這樣的傾向，而且你戒除這些錯誤的原因或許是出於懦弱、名譽，抑或是出其他的不良動機。

第五，要考慮你是否有足夠的判斷力瞭解他人是否真的在做一些不正當的事情，因為許多事情都是根據某種環境而做出的。總之，在對別人的事情或行為做出正確的判斷以前，你還要學習更多的東西。

第六，當你處於極度煩惱和悲傷時，平心靜氣來想一想，人的生命只是一瞬間，我們都很快就要死去。

第七，困擾我們已久的東西並不是人們行為本身造成的後果，

and particularly, under what compulsions in respect of opinions they are; and as to their acts, consider with what pride they do what they do.

Third, that if men do rightly what they do, we ought not to be displeased; but if they do not right, it is plain that they do so involuntarily and in ignorance. For as every soul is unwillingly deprived of the truth, so also is it unwillingly deprived of the power of behaving to each man according to his deserts. Accordingly men are pained when they are called unjust, ungrateful, and greedy, and in a word wrong-doers to their neighbours.

Fourth, consider that thou also doest many things wrong, and that thou art a man like others; and even if thou dost abstain from certain faults, still thou hast the disposition to commit them, though either through cowardice, or concern about reputation, or some such mean motive, thou dost abstain from such faults.

Fifth, consider that thou dost not even understand whether men are doing wrong or not, for many things are done with a certain reference to circumstances. And in short, a man must learn a great deal to enable him to pass a correct judgment on another man's acts.

Sixth, consider when thou art much vexed or grieved, that man's life is only a moment, and after a short time we are all laid out dead.

Seventh, that it is not men's acts which disturb us, for those acts have

那些行為的根基是受他們的原則支配的，正是自己意見左右了我們本身。那麼就要先驅除這些思想，堅決地放棄你對一個行為的判斷，就好像它是什麼壞東西，這樣一來你的憤怒就會完全消散了。怎樣驅除這意見呢？透過思考你就會發現，沒有哪一個人的惡行能給你帶來恥辱，除非恥辱是唯一的惡行，否則你也必然做了許多不正當的事，變成強盜或其他。

　　第八，要知道由這種行為引起的憤怒和煩惱所帶給我們的痛苦要比這種行為本身帶給我們的痛苦更難受。

　　第九，要知道一種好的氣質是不會被征服的，只要它是真誠的，而不是強顏歡笑、心猿意馬。這樣做即使最蠻橫的人也不會對你怎樣，只要你對他始終保持一種和善的態度。如果條件允許，你可以溫和地勸導他，平靜地在他試圖傷害你的時候引導他，你可以這樣說：孩子，不要這樣，我們被上帝選出來不是為了做這些事情的，我將肯定自己不會受到任何傷害，而此時的你卻要傷害自己，我的孩子。只要以這樣溫和的口吻，用一些普遍的原則向他說明，甚至蜜蜂也不會做出這樣的事情來，更不必說那些天生被造出來合作的動物了。你在這樣勸說的時候必須不帶有任何的諷刺意味或斥責的口吻，而是要

1.grievous [`ɡriːvəs] adj. 極惡的
2.continuest 為古英語中 continue 的第二人稱單數（主語為 thou 時使用）。

their foundation in men's ruling principles, but it is our own opinions which disturb us. Take away these opinions then, and resolve to dismiss thy judgment about an act as if it were something **grievous**[1], and thy anger is gone. How then shall I take away these opinions? By reflecting that no wrongful act of another brings shame on thee: for unless that which is shameful is alone bad, thou also must of necessity do many things wrong, and become a robber and everything else.

Eighth, consider how much more pain is brought on us by the anger and vexation caused by such acts than by the acts themselves, at which we are angry and vexed.

Ninth, consider that a good disposition is invincible, if it be genuine, and not an affected smile and acting a part. For what will the most violent man do to thee, if thou **continuest**[2] to be of a kind disposition towards him, and if, as opportunity offers, thou gently **admonishest**[3] him and calmly **correctest**[4] his errors at the very time when he is trying to do thee harm, saying, Not so, my child: we are constituted by nature for something else: I shall certainly not be injured, but thou art injuring thyself, my child. – And show him with gentle tact and by general principles that this is so, and that even bees do not do as he does, nor any animals which are formed by nature

---

3.admonishest 為古英語中 admonish 的第二人稱單數（主語為 thou 時使用）。
4.correctest 為古英語中 correct 的第二人稱單數（主語為 thou 時使用）。

真誠、心無怨懟，不要做得像是在對他講演，期望旁觀者會給出什麼讚揚的話語，而是應該像跟他獨處的時候一樣，即使當時別人也在場……

記住了這9條規則，就像是你從繆斯那裏收到的一個禮物，在你活著的時候開始做人吧！但是你必須同時避免奉承人和惱怒人，兩者都是不合群的，會導致傷害。當你的憤怒被激起時，你就要趕緊想到這一真理：被衝動駕馭是缺乏男子氣概的，而和善寬厚更符合人的本性，故更加具有男子氣概。那擁有這些品格的人同時擁有力量、精力和勇敢，而那受制於衝動和不滿的發怒者卻不行。一個人的心靈在何種程度上擺脫激情，它也就在同樣的程度上更接近力量，這就好比痛苦的感覺是軟弱的一個特徵，憤怒也是軟弱的一個特徵。那些易於痛苦的人以及時常憤怒的人，都會受到兩者的傷害，都是軟弱的表現。

如果你願意，會從繆斯的領袖（阿波羅）那裏收到第十個禮物，即寄希望於壞人不做惡事是妄想，因為這正是期待一件不可能的事情。而那種只許壞人對別人行惡，卻期望他們不對你做任何惡事的想法更是不理智和專橫的。

to be gregarious. And thou must do this neither with any double meaning nor in the way of reproach, but affectionately and without any rancour in thy soul; and not as if thou wert lecturing him, nor yet that any bystander may admire, but either when he is alone, and if others are present...

Remember these nine rules, as if thou hadst received them as a gift from the Muses, and begin at last to be a man while thou livest. But thou must equally avoid flattering men and being vexed at them, for both are unsocial and lead to harm. And let this truth be present to thee in the excitement of anger, that to be moved by passion is not manly, but that mildness and gentleness, as they are more agreeable to human nature, so also are they more manly; and he who possesses these qualities possesses strength, nerves and courage, and not the man who is subject to fits of passion and discontent. For in the same degree in which a man's mind is nearer to freedom from all passion, in the same degree also is it nearer to strength: and as the sense of pain is a characteristic of weakness, so also is anger. For he who yields to pain and he who yields to anger, both are wounded and both submit.

But if thou wilt, receive also a tenth present from the leader of the Muses (Apollo), and it is this – that to expect bad men not to do wrong is madness, for he who expects this desires an impossibility. But to allow men to behave so to others, and to expect them not to do thee any wrong, is irrational and tyrannical.

能力上有四種偏離是應當始終提防的，當你發現了它們，你應當儘快消除它們，每逢遇到這種情況時都這樣說：這個思想是不必要的；這種傾向是毀壞社會大眾的；你所要說的東西不是來自內心的思想，你要知道一個人如果不表達真正的思想是多麼荒唐的事；第四個要提防的就是自怨自艾，因為這證明你內部較為神聖的部分被壓倒，屈服於卑劣的、易朽的肉體的快樂。

你身上氣和火的部分，雖然本身會有一種向上的趨勢，但還是要服從於宇宙的配置，被擠壓在你的身體之中。而那些土和水的部分，雖然它們本身是往下的，但也還是被提高，佔據了一個並非它們自身就有的位置。這些元素以這種方式在宇宙中存在、運行，一旦它們被放在什麼地方，它們就必須保持在那裏，直到宇宙再發出解散的信號。那麼，只有你的理智不順從和不滿意於它自己的地位，這看起來不是很奇怪嗎？而且並沒有什麼力量強加於它，僅僅是那些按其本性發生的事情，它卻還是不服從，反而轉到了相反的方向。那種傾向於非正義、放任、憤怒、悲傷和畏懼的活動不是別的，只是一個偏離本性的人的行為。當支配能力不滿足於發生的事情時也是如此，那麼，

1.aberration [ˌæbəˋreʃən] n. 偏離正道

There are four principal **aberrations**[1] of the superior faculty against which thou shouldst be constantly on thy guard, and when thou hast detected them, thou shouldst wipe them out and say on each occasion thus: this thought is not necessary: this tends to destroy social union: this which thou art going to say comes not from the real thoughts; for thou shouldst consider it among the most absurd of things for a man not to speak from his real thoughts. But the fourth is when thou shalt reproach thyself for anything, for this is an evidence of the diviner part within thee being overpowered and yielding to the less honourable and to the perishable part, the body, and to its gross pleasures.

Thy aerial part and all the fiery parts which are mingled in thee, though by nature they have an upward tendency, still in obedience to the disposition of the universe they are overpowered here in the compound mass (the body). And also the whole of the earthy part in thee and the watery, though their tendency is downward, still are raised up and occupy a position which is not their natural one. In this manner then the elemental parts obey the universal, for when they have been fixed in any place perforce they remain there until again the universal shall sound the signal for dissolution. Is it not then strange that thy intelligent part only should be disobedient and discontented with its own place? And yet no force is imposed on it, but only

它也就放棄本身的位置，因為它們的產生不僅僅為了正義，也為了對神的虔誠和崇敬。因為這些品質也是在滿足於事物的結構這一總稱下把握的，它們的確優先於正義的行為。

　　那種在生活中對目標不能堅持不懈的人，也不可能在他的生活中是統一和一致的。我要說的不止於此，還有更重要的一點：這個目標應當是什麼。因為，對於大多數人認為是好的，大家不一定會持有相同的意見，而只是對某些關係到共同利益的事物達成了一致的意見。我們應當為自己設立具有共同性質（社會性）和政治性質的目標。只有那些使自己始終向著這一目標前進的人才會在以後的生活中保持思想和行為的一致性。

　　想想鄉村的老鼠和城裏的老鼠的寓言，想想城裏老鼠的那種恐懼和戰慄。

1.trepidation [ˌtrɛpəˋdeʃən] n. 惴測不安

those things which are conformable to its nature: still it does not submit, but is carried in the opposite direction. For the movement towards injustice and intemperance and to anger and grief and fear is nothing else than the act of one who deviates from nature. And also when the ruling faculty is discontented with anything that happens, then too it deserts its post: for it is constituted for piety and reverence towards the gods no less than for justice. For these qualities also are comprehended under the generic term of contentment with the constitution of things, and indeed they are prior to acts of justice.

He who has not one and always the same object in life, cannot be one and the same all through his life. But what I have said is not enough, unless this also is added, what this object ought to be. For as there is not the same opinion about all the things which in some way or other are considered by the majority to be good, but only about some certain things, that is, things which concern the common interest; so also ought we to propose to ourselves an object which shall be of a common kind (social) and political. For he who directs all his own efforts to this object, will make all his acts alike, and thus will always be the same.

Think of the country mouse and of the town mouse, and of the alarm and **trepidation**[1] of the town mouse.

蘇格拉底常常視民眾的意見為拉米亞，即嚇唬孩子的怪物。

古代斯巴達人在舉行公共慶典時常常為陌生人在遮陽棚裏安排座位，而他們自己則隨便在其他地方坐下。

蘇格拉底向珀迪克斯解釋當時為什麼沒有到他那裏去的原因，那是因為他不願意以最壞的結局死去，即他並不想收到一個恩惠卻無以回報。

在以弗所人的古老而神秘的作品中有這一箴言：要時刻緬懷以前時代的有德之士。

畢達哥拉斯囑咐我們在清晨的時候抬頭仰望天空，這會提醒我們每天都要以同樣的方式始終做同樣的事情，也會使我們想起它們的純潔和簡單。因為星球上是不會遮掩的。

想一想，當蘇格拉底在妻子贊蒂帕拿走他的外套後就順手給自己裹上一件毛皮時，他是怎樣一個人；再後來當他的朋友看見他如此穿著而為他害羞並離他而去時，他對他們又是怎麼說的。

1.Lamiae，古希臘羅馬神話中女頭女胸的蛇身妖怪，常誘捕嬰兒吸其血液。
2.bugbear [`bʌg‚bɛr] n. 怪物；嚇人的東西
3.出自柏拉圖《裴多篇》。

Socrates used to call the opinions of the many by the name of **Lamiae**[1], **bugbears**[2] to frighten children.

The Lacedaemonians at their public spectacles used to set seats in the shade for strangers, but themselves sat down anywhere.

Socrates excused himself to Perdiccas for not going to him, saying, it is because I would not perish by the worst of all ends, that is, I would not receive a favour and then be unable to **return it**[3].

In the writings of the **Ephesians**[4] there was this precept, constantly to think of some one of the men of former times who practised virtue.

The Pythagoreans bid us in the morning look to the heavens that we may be reminded of those bodies which continually do the same things and in the same manner perform their work, and also be reminded of their purity and nudity. For there is no veil over a star.

Consider what a man Socrates was when he dressed himself in a skin, after Xanthippe had taken his **cloak**[5] and gone out, and what Socrates said to his friends who were ashamed of him and drew back from him when

4.Ephesians，羅馬在小亞細亞行省的首府。
5.cloak [klok] n. 斗蓬，外衣

在你學會遵守寫作和閱讀的規則之前，你絕不可能在其中為別人立下什麼規則。生活也是這樣。

你是一個奴隸：自由的言談是不適於你的。

我內心在歡笑。

他們將詛咒美德，且言語刻薄。

人們都知道在冬天尋找無花果是一個瘋子的行為，同樣，在不被允許的時候尋求自己孩子的人也是如此。

埃比克太德說過當一個人吻他的孩子時，他應當自言自語：「明天也許你就要死去。」但這是一些不吉利的想法。「不，表示自然的話沒有一個是不吉利的」，埃比克太德說，「如果這是的話，說麥穗的收割也是不吉利的。」

其實那些未熟的葡萄、成熟和乾枯了的葡萄，所有這些都是變化的過程，不是變為虛無，而是變為尚未存在的什麼東西。

自由的意志是不能被剝奪的。

they saw him dressed thus.

Neither in writing nor in reading wilt thou be able to lay down rules for others before thou shalt have first learned to obey rules thyself. Much more is this so in life.

A slave thou art: free speech is not for thee.

And my heart laughed within.

And virtue they will curse, speaking harsh words.

To look for the fig in winter is a madman's act: such is he who looks for his child when it is no longer allowed.

When a man kisses his child, said Epictetus, he should whisper to himself, "To-morrow perchance thou wilt die." – But those are words of bad omen. – "No word is a word of bad omen," said Epictetus, "which expresses any work of nature; or if it is so, it is also a word of bad omen to speak of the ears of corn being reaped."

The unripe grape, the ripe bunch, the dried grape, all are changes, not into nothing, but into something which exists not yet.

No man can rob us of our free will.

埃比克太德也說：「一個人必須發現他能夠認同的藝術（或規則），在涉及某些活動時，他必須注意使活動參照周圍的環境，滿足當時的社會利益，服從價值目標，並且應該完全迴避自己的感官慾望。對於不在我們能力範圍之內的，我們不應該逃避（厭惡）。」

他說，既然如此，最終要爭論的問題就不是一般事情，而是有關瘋了還是沒瘋的問題。

蘇格拉底問過這樣的問題：你想要什麼？是有理性的靈魂還是無理性的靈魂？

——有理性的靈魂。
——又是怎樣一種理性靈魂？健全的還是畸形的？
——健全的。
——那麼你為什麼努力追尋它？
——因為我們已經擁有了它。
——那你們為什麼還為此爭鬥和吵鬧呢？

Epictetus also said, A man must discover an art (or rules) with respect to giving his assent; and in respect to his movements he must be careful that they be made with regard to circumstances, that they be consistent with social interests, that they have regard to the value of the object; and as to sensual desire, he should altogether keep away from it; and as to avoidance (aversion) he should not show it with respect to any of the things which are not in our power.

The dispute then, he said, is not about any common matter, but about being mad or not.

Socrates used to say, What do you want? Souls of rational men or irrational?

– Souls of rational men.
– Of what rational men? Sound or unsound?
– Sound.
– Why then do you not seek for them?
– Because we have them.
– Why then do you fight and quarrel?

第十二卷

所有那些你所追求的、希望透過迂迴的途徑得到的事物，只要你不拒絕，其實你現在就能夠得到它們。這意味著，你要對整個過去毫不縈懷，把自己的未來全心信賴地交給神意，而僅僅專注於使自己當下的思想行動符合於虔誠和正義。符合虔誠就是要滿足於神意為你安排的命運，無論它是什麼，這是上天分配給你的，而你也是完全適合它的。符合正義就是說你應當始終坦率、無掩飾地說出真理，按照法和事物的價值行事。絕不能讓其他人的惡行、想法或聲音阻撓你，也不要讓那耽於奢侈慾望的肉體感覺阻礙你，因為被動的部分會照看肉體。無論死亡在何時降臨，如果你都能夠欣然地拋棄現世的一切而只關注你的思想與自己心中的神性；如果你的畏懼並非來自於在某個時刻不得不來臨的生命的結束，而是害怕自己從未開始過合乎本性的生活，那麼，你即是一個配得上這個創造你的世界的人，對你的國家來說不再是一個陌生人，不再好奇於那些每日發生的、出乎意料的奇聞軼事，也不再焦慮不安地想去依賴那些不在自己掌握之中的種種事物。

神注視著所有人的心靈——剝落了物質外殼、外衣和世俗雜質的

BOOK 12

All those things at which thou wishest to arrive by a circuitous road, thou canst have now, if thou dost not refuse them to thyself. And this means, if thou wilt take no notice of all the past, and trust the future to providence, and direct the present only conformably to piety and justice. Conformably to piety, that thou mayest be content with the lot which is assigned to thee, for nature designed it for thee and thee for it. Conformably to justice, that thou mayest always speak the truth freely and without disguise, and do the things which are agreeable to law and according to the worth of each. And let neither another man's wickedness hinder thee, nor opinion nor voice, nor yet the sensations of the poor flesh which has grown about thee; for the passive part will look to this. If then, whatever the time may be when thou shalt be near to thy departure, neglecting everything else thou shalt respect only thy ruling faculty and the divinity within thee, and if thou shalt be afraid not because thou must some time cease to live, but if thou shalt fear never to have begun to live according to nature – then thou wilt be a man worthy of the universe which has produced thee, and thou wilt cease to be a stranger in thy native land, and to wonder at things which happen daily as if they were something unexpected, and to be dependent on this or that.

God sees the minds (ruling principles) of all men bared of the material

赤裸裸的心靈。他用自己的理性來接觸我們的理性，這個理性來源於他並且投射到人身上。如果你能使自己做到這些，你將擺脫許多塵世的苦惱，不為煩憂負累所困。因為對自己那副皮囊都毫不掛心的人，衣服、處所這些外在的誇飾自然與他無緣。

　　其實只三種東西便構成了你的全部：一個小小的身體、一點微弱的呼吸（生命）、理智。前兩者於你而言僅具有照管它們的義務，只有第三種東西才是唯一真正屬於你。因此，你應當將你自身，也就是你的思想與上述這些事物分開——無論別人說了或做了什麼，無論你自己在今天以前說了或做了什麼，無論將來會有什麼事情發生令你憂慮，不管那關係到你的肉體還是生命，全都不屬於你自身意志的管轄範圍，不管在人類發展的常規進程中有什麼樣的機遇或偶然降臨到你的身上。你的思想也是一樣，不管在外部世界中發生了怎樣不幸的巧合，都要始終保有純粹而自由的理性，行正義之事，接受所遭遇的，說真實的話。我說，如果你能將自己的思想與理性同那些透過感官印象附著於它的諸般事物分離開來，不會為無論過去還是未來的事物所束縛，那麼，你都會如恩培多克勒所描述的球體一樣：渾圓無缺，在它歡樂的靜止中安息。你就能夠真真正正無憂無慮地度過自己的餘生，高貴地順從於自己內在的本心，神聖的靈魂將與你同在。

1.circumfluent [səˋkʌmflʊənt] adj. 周流的；環流的
2.Empedocles（約西元前495年～西元前430年），古希臘哲學家，率先提出「四元素」理論。

vesture and rind and impurities. For with his intellectual part alone he touches the intelligence only which has flowed and been derived from himself into these bodies. And if thou also usest thyself to do this, thou wilt rid thyself of thy much trouble. For he who regards not the poor flesh which envelops him, surely will not trouble himself by looking after raiment and dwelling and fame and such like externals and show.

The things are three of which thou art composed, a little body, a little breath (life), intelligence. Of these the first two are thine, so far as it is thy duty to take care of them; but the third alone is properly thine. Therefore if thou shalt separate from thyself, that is, from thy understanding, whatever others do or say, and whatever thou hast done or said thyself, and whatever future things trouble thee because they may happen, and whatever in the body which envelops thee or in the breath (life), which is by nature associated with the body, is attached to thee independent of thy will, and whatever the external **circumfluent**[1] vortex whirls round, so that the intellectual power exempt from the things of fate can live pure and free by itself, doing what is just and accepting what happens and saying the truth: if thou wilt separate, I say, from this ruling faculty the things which are attached to it by the impressions of sense, and the things of time to come and of time that is past, and wilt make thyself like **Empedocles'**[2] sphere, "All

我常常感到奇怪，為什麼會出現這樣的事情：每個人都愛自己超過了愛其他所有人，但是卻往往重視別人關於他的看法更甚於重視他自己對自己的認識。如果哪位神或是莊重的訓導者站到我們之中的任何一個人面前，命令他除了馬上就要說出來的念頭之外什麼也不要想，沒有人能夠忍受哪怕僅有一天的時間。因此我們更加重視鄰人對我們的觀感，尤甚於我們本身。

這怎麼可能發生呢？仁慈的神靈把所有的事物都安排得那樣好，卻唯獨忽視了這樣一件事：即有一些非常好的人，可以說是那些最能與神意相通的人，那些透過自己虔敬的行為和嚴格的服從而與神最為親近的人，他們一旦辭世，就絕不會再次復生，而是永遠地消失？

但如果事實正是如此，你也應當堅信如果不是這樣，神靈早就另做安排了。因為凡正當的事情都是可能的，凡符合自然本質的事情，自然也很容易就會接受它的產生。但如今這件事並非正當或符合自然本質，如果事實也的確不是這樣，你就應當深信它本不該如此。因為

round, and in its joyous rest reposing;" and if thou shalt strive to live only what is really thy life, that is, the present – then thou wilt be able to pass that portion of life which remains for thee up to the time of thy death, free from perturbations nobly, and obedient to thy own daemon (to the god that is within thee).

I have often wondered how it is that every man loves himself more than all the rest of men, but yet sets less value on his own opinion of himself than on the opinion of others. If then a god or a wise teacher should present himself to a man and bid him to think of nothing and to design nothing which he would not express as soon as he conceived it, he could not endure it even for a single day. So much more respect have we to what our neighbours shall think of us than to what we shall think of ourselves.

How can it be that the gods after having arranged all things well and benevolently for mankind, have overlooked this alone, that some men and very good men, and men who, as we may say, have had most communion with the divinity, and through pious acts and religious observances have been most intimate with the divinity, when they have once died should never exist again, but should be completely extinguished?

But if this is so, be assured that if it ought to have been otherwise, the gods would have done it. For if it were just, it would also be possible; and if it were according to nature, nature would have had it so. But because it is not so, if in fact it is not so, be thou convinced that it ought not to have been

你已經親眼見到，你自己也在不停地探究，就是與神爭論，如果不是神靈太過於仁慈和公正，我們又怎能這樣地與他們理論。但如果他們的確是如此仁慈和公正，那麼在宇宙秩序中，他們一定不會允許其中的任何事物被不公正或無道理地忽視。

甚至在起初就感覺無望完成的事情中你也應當不斷磨煉自己。在絕大多數的事情上左手都不太擅長，因為它很少被使用。可是握起韁繩來卻會比右手更有力，這要歸功於它一直接受這種訓練。

要時常冥思這樣一個命題：當死亡如不速之客突然而至的時候，我們的肉體和靈魂是什麼樣子？人的生命短暫且終有一死，在我們的生前身後是廣漠無盡的時間深淵，一切塵俗之物在它面前都是那樣脆弱和虛幻。

對待一切事物都要剝去表面的外殼、沉思其形成的原則（形式）、沉思行為的目的、冥想什麼是痛苦、什麼是快樂、什麼是死亡，什麼是榮耀和名聲。對一個人來說，他本身即是真正適合自己的安寧的休憩地，沒有人會被其他人干擾阻礙，一切都取決於你的觀點。

在貫徹你的原則時，一定要像一個摔跤選手而非一名角鬥士。後

so: for thou seest even of thyself that in this inquiry thou art disputing with the deity; and we should not thus dispute with the gods, unless they were most excellent and most just; but if this is so, they would not have allowed anything in the ordering of the universe to be neglected unjustly and irrationally.

Practise thyself even in the things which thou despairest of accomplishing. For even the left hand, which is ineffectual for all other things for want of practice, holds the bridle more vigorously than the right hand; for it has been practised in this.

Consider in what condition both in body and soul a man should be when he is overtaken by death; and consider the shortness of life, the boundless abyss of time past and future, the feebleness of all matter.

Contemplate the formative principles (forms) of things bare of their coverings; the purposes of actions; consider what pain is, what pleasure is, and death, and fame; who is to himself the cause of his uneasiness; how no man is hindered by another; that everything is opinion.

In the application of thy principles thou must be like the pancratiast, not

者如果失去了所用的劍就意味著失敗，對於前者來說，他的手本是空的，因此只需憑藉雙手而無需他物。

觀察事物的本來面目，將它們分為質料、形式、目的。

一個人只做神所讚許的事情，接受神所給予的賜予時是多麼有力量啊！

對於順從自然發生的事情，我們絕不能去非難神靈，他們不管出於有意或是無意，都不可能做出任何錯事；也不應當將之歸咎於他人，如果他們真的做錯事，也只是由於無知，並非懷有惡意。因此我們不該去責怪任何人。

有些人竟然會對生活中發生的事情表示驚奇，這是多麼荒謬可笑啊！

若不是命定的必然和不可違抗的秩序，就是仁慈的神，或是無目的和方向的混沌。如果面對一種絕對而不可更改的必然，你為何還要抵抗呢？如果真有一位寬容仁慈的神，那麼使你自己配得上這神聖的

1.gladiator [`glædɪˌetɚ] n. 角鬥士；鬥劍者

like the **gladiator**[1]; for the gladiator lets fall the sword which he uses and is killed; but the other always has his hand, and needs to do nothing else than use it.

See what things are in themselves, dividing them into matter, form and purpose.

What a power man has to do nothing except what God will approve, and to accept all that God may give him.

With respect to that which happens conformably to nature, we ought to blame neither gods, for they do nothing wrong either voluntarily or involuntarily, nor men, for they do nothing wrong except involuntarily. Consequently we should blame nobody.

How ridiculous and what a stranger he is who is surprised at anything which happens in life.

Either there is a fatal necessity and invincible order, or a kind Providence, or a confusion without a purpose and without a director. If then there is an invincible necessity, why dost thou resist? But if there is a Providence

幫助吧！如果一切只是無主的混亂與混沌，在如洪水氾濫般的無序動盪之中，你還保有理智，憑這一點，你就應感到滿足。即使你不得不在這場洪水中隨波逐流，它帶走的可以是你的肉體、生命或是其他來自於它們的一切，但理性永遠不可被帶走。

燭火不到熄滅的那一刻絕不會失去它的光芒，而你心中的真理、正義和克制卻要在你停止呼吸之前就歸於消亡嗎？

當一個人在你眼中像是做了什麼惡事的時候，要這樣規勸你自己：我怎能知曉這一定就是一樁罪行？即使他確實做了惡事，我又怎能知道他是否曾為此而自責過？因為這就像一個人在自毀容顏。想想那些不讓惡人做惡事的人吧，這種願望就像不許無花果樹結果，不准嬰兒啼哭，不讓馬嘶叫一樣，徒勞地想要阻止那些必然會發生的事情。一個具備此種品格的人又能做什麼呢？如果你看不過去，那麼請盡可能地糾正他的氣質吧。

不要做不適宜的事，不要講不真實的話；讓你自己致力於此。

對於你面前的一切事物，觀察它們給你留下了什麼印象，把它劃分為形式、質料、目的和持續時間，加以分析解決。

which allows itself to be propitiated, make thyself worthy of the help of the divinity. But if there is a confusion without governor, be content that in such a tempest thou hast in thyself a certain ruling intelligence. And even if the tempest carry thee away, let it carry away the poor flesh, the poor breath, everything else; for the intelligence at least it will not carry away.

Does the light of the lamp shine without losing its splendour until it is extinguished; and shall the truth which is in thee and justice and temperance be extinguished before thy death?

When a man has presented the appearance of having done wrong, say, How then do I know if this is a wrongful act? And even if he has done wrong, how do I know that he has not condemned himself? and so this is like tearing his own face. Consider that he, who would not have the bad man do wrong, is like the man who would not have the fig-tree to bear juice in the figs and infants to cry and the horse to neigh, and whatever else must of necessity be. For what must a man do who has such a character? If then thou art irritable, cure this man's disposition.

If it is not right, do not do it: if it is not true, do not say it. For let thy efforts be.

In everything always observe what the thing is which produces for thee an appearance, and resolve it by dividing it into the formal, the material, the purpose, and the time within which it must end.

　　你應當有所領悟，在你心中有某種東西，比引發各種情感和牽引著你的東西更為神聖。而現在充斥在你心裏的又是什麼呢？是恐懼、懷疑、貪慾，還是其他類似的東西？

　　首先，不要不加考慮地去做任何無結果的事；其次，你的行為一定要指向公眾的目的。

　　啊！你於世間的存在不過短短的一瞬，你眼前的一切事物，以及當下生活的所有人很快都將不復存在。所有事物按其本性都必然會迅速變化、扭曲和衰朽，以便後續的事物能夠存在。

　　要記住，一切只不過是看法，而一切看法在你的控制之中。你可選擇摒棄自己的看法，如同一艘繞過岬角的航船，你將發現遠離狂風暴雨侵襲的寧靜海灣。

　　世上的一切活動，無論它是什麼，只要適時而止，就不會遭遇不幸，因為它已經停止了。做了這事的人，也不會因為停止這事而遭遇不幸。同樣，由我們的所有行動組合而成的整體，亦即我們的生命，如果它在某個適當的時刻停止，就這一點來說我們也並非遭到了不幸，因為生命已經有了它的歸宿。在適當的時刻終止一系列行為也不是壞事。而這個時間或特定的時期完全取決於自然，有時是某種特定的現象，像人的衰老，但總是透過宇宙本性，各個組成部分都在一

Perceive at last that thou hast in thee something better and more divine than the things which cause the various affects, and as it were pull thee by the strings. What is there now in my mind? Is it fear, or suspicion, or desire, or anything of the kind?

First, do nothing inconsiderately, nor without a purpose. Second, make thy acts refer to nothing else than to a social end.

Consider that before long thou wilt be nobody and nowhere, nor will any of the things exist which thou now seest, nor any of those who are now living. For all things are formed by nature to change and be turned and to perish in order that other things in continuous succession may exist.

Consider that everything is opinion, and opinion is in thy power. Take away then, when thou choosest, thy opinion, and like a mariner, who has doubled the promontory, thou wilt find calm, everything stable, and a waveless bay.

Any one activity whatever it may be, when it has ceased at its proper time, suffers no evil because it has ceased; nor he who has done this act, does he suffer any evil for this reason that the act has ceased. In like manner then the whole which consists of all the acts, which is our life, if it cease at its proper time, suffers no evil for this reason that it has ceased; nor he who has terminated this series at the proper time, has he been ill dealt with. But the proper time and the limit nature fixes, sometimes as in old age the peculiar

個接一個地除舊換新，這樣整個世界才能永遠保持青春活力。如此一來，宇宙中的一切始終都是最好的、最合乎時宜的。生命的終結對每個人來說都不是什麼傷害，因為它絕不是恥辱，它不依賴於個人意志也不對立於普遍利益。從全局來考慮這還是件好事，它對整個世界來說既便利又合適。與神同在，心中想著神所關注的事情，你就能為神所推動。

你必須時刻做好下面這三件事。首先是關於你自己的一舉一動，無論做任何事都不能懈怠，要恪守正義與公平。對於外部加諸你身的變故，它的發生或者出於偶然，或者遵照了神意，而這兩者都絕不是你應責怪的事情。第二，我們的存在是由種子到獲得靈魂，再到歸還靈魂。在這期間，它們由哪些東西構成，最終又會消解為這些東西。第三，如果你被帶到半空，俯視地上的人，你將發現他們有多麼不同，同時也將發現逗留在天空中的人何其多。無論你升到天空多少次，你都將看到同樣的東西、同樣的形式。人生是多麼短暫，這些轉瞬即逝的事物有什麼值得誇耀的？

nature of man, but always the universal nature, by the change of whose parts the whole universe continues ever young and perfect. And everything which is useful to the universal is always good and in season. Therefore the termination of life for every man is no evil, because neither is it shameful, since it is both independent of the will and not opposed to the general interest, but it is good, since it is seasonable and profitable to and congruent with the universal. For thus too he is moved by the deity who is moved in the same manner with the deity and moved towards the same things in his mind.

These three principles thou must have in readiness. In the things which thou doest do nothing either inconsiderately or otherwise than as justice herself would act; but with respect to what may happen to thee from without, consider that it happens either by chance or according to Providence, and thou must neither blame chance nor accuse Providence. Second, consider what every being is from the seed to the time of its receiving a soul, and from the reception of a soul to the giving back of the same, and of what things every being is compounded and into what things it is resolved. Third, if thou shouldst suddenly be raised up above the earth, and shouldst look down on human things, and observe the variety of them how great it is, and at the same time also shouldst see at a glance how great is the number of beings who dwell around in the air and the aether, consider that as often as thou shouldst be raised up, thou wouldst see the same things, sameness of form and shortness of duration. Are these things to be proud of?

拋棄自己的意見，你就能得到拯救。那麼，是什麼阻止了你去這樣做呢？

當你因為某些事而悲傷苦痛時，你忘記了這一點：一切事情都是遵循宇宙的本質發生的，忘記了其他人的過錯與你無關。而且你也忘記了，現在所發生的一切，過去同樣曾經出現過，將來還會繼續發生，甚至就在當下也在世界各地重複上演著。你也忘記了整個人類是怎樣緊密地聯繫在一起，而這親密關係的紐帶並不是血緣的相近或人種的一致，而是理智的共有。你還忘記了每個人的理智都帶有神性，都是神性的一種流溢。沒有人可以說有什麼東西完全屬於他自己、他的孩子、他的肉體乃至他的靈魂，它們都得自於萬物的賜予者──神。你也忘記了，一切都不過是人的看法，忘記了無論任何人都僅能生活在當下這短暫的時間中，失去的也僅限於當下這一瞬間而已。

常常回想那些總是憤憤不平的人，那些享有最高名譽或遭遇最不幸災難的人，那些互相憎惡仇恨的人，或任何一種因其他命運或境遇而引人注目的人，他們如今到哪裏去了？往日的一切都已化為煙塵灰燼，僅剩一個傳說，甚至有的連傳說也談不上。要經常在腦海中呈現這樣的事情：戰鬥中的法比阿斯・卡特利盧斯。或是花園中的盧修

1.efflux [`ɛflʌks] n. 流出物；流出
2.Fabius Catullinus，一個非常熱愛鄉村生活的人。

Cast away opinion: thou art saved. Who then hinders thee from casting it away?

When thou art troubled about anything, thou hast forgotten this, that all things happen according to the universal nature; and forgotten this, that a man's wrongful act is nothing to thee; and further thou hast forgotten this, that everything which happens, always happened so and will happen so, and now happens so everywhere; forgotten this too, how close is the kinship between a man and the whole human race, for it is a community, not of a little blood or seed, but of intelligence. And thou hast forgotten this too, that every man's intelligence is a god, and is an **efflux**[1] of the deity; and forgotten this, that nothing is a man's own, but that his child and his body and his very soul came from the deity; forgotten this, that everything is opinion; and lastly thou hast forgotten that every man lives the present time only, and loses only this.

Constantly bring to thy recollection those who have complained greatly about anything, those who have been most conspicuous by the greatest fame or misfortunes or enmities or fortunes of any kind: then think where are they all now? Smoke and ash and a tale, or not even a tale. And let there be present to thy mind also everything of this sort, how **Fabius Catullinus**[2]

斯‧盧柏斯、拜依阿的斯德丁尼阿斯、卡帕裏的第比留斯和維留斯‧魯弗斯。同時，你也應當深思熟慮，那些所有人都熱切追求，竭力想要據為己有的一切是多麼微不足道啊。對一個人來說，做事要時時謹記恰如其分，奉行中庸之道，懷著質樸天真之心，這是多麼契合哲學啊！一個人為了根本不值得驕傲的事情而驕傲自大，自以為是，真是最不堪忍受的。

有些人會問：你在什麼地方見過神？你怎麼能肯定那些你所虔誠信奉的神靈真的存在呢？對這些問題，我會回答說，首先，他們甚至是用眼睛可以看得到的；其次，雖然我從未見過自己的靈魂，但還是非常尊重它。對於神，從日常經驗之中我能感受到神的力量，因此，我當然能夠肯定他們存在，並且崇拜他們。

生命的幸福就在於此：對於一個人來說，對萬物的真實本質都瞭解透徹，它的質料是什麼，形式又是怎樣的。以你的全部靈魂，全心全意地去行正義，言說真理。我們除了把一件又一件的善行不加間隔地連綴在一起，以這個過程來享受生命之外，還有什麼其他事情要做呢？

1.Lucius Lupus，生平不詳。
2.Stertinius，可能是一個富醫。
3.Tiberius，古羅馬第二任皇帝，晚年生活荒淫，不問政事。

lived in the country, and **Lucius Lupus**[1] in his gardens, and **Stertinius**[2] at Baiae, and **Tiberius**[3] at Capreae and **Velius Rufus**[4] (or Rufus at Velia); and in fine think of the eager pursuit of anything conjoined with pride; and how worthless everything is after which men violently strain; and how much more philosophical it is for a man in the opportunities presented to him to show himself just, temperate, all simplicity: for the pride which is proud of its want of pride is the most intolerable of all.

To those who ask, Where hast thou seen the gods, or how dost thou comprehend that they exist and so **worshippest**[5] them, I answer, in the first place, they may be seen even with the eyes; in the second place, neither have I seen even my own soul, and yet I honor it. Thus then with respect to the gods, from what I constantly experience of their power, from this I comprehend that they exist, and I venerate them.

The safety of life is this, to examine everything all through, what it is itself, that is its material, what the formal part; with all thy soul to do justice and to say the truth. What remains, except to enjoy life by joining one good thing to another so as not to leave even the smallest intervals between?

4.Velius Rufus，Fronto的通信人，Fronto是作者和Verus的老師。
5.worshippest為古英語中worship的第二人稱單數（主語為thou時使用）。

▶▶ 沉思錄‧第十二卷

存在著一縷陽光，雖然它會被牆壁、山峰和無數別的障礙隔斷。整個世界存在一種共同的本質，雖然它被包含和限制在無數個別的個體之中。同樣道理，也存在一個共同的靈魂，雖然它分配到無數的本質和個體中。因此可以得知，世界上存在著一個理智靈魂，雖然它看起來也被劃分成了不同的部分。在我們剛剛提到事物中，所有其他的部分，例如氣和物質，沒有感覺，相互間亦無關連，但是即使是這些部分也是靠理智原則和吸引力將它們聚在一起。理智以一種特殊的方式趨向同類，與同類結合、相通的感覺是不會被打斷的。

你有什麼願望？希望長壽嗎？希望有感覺、運動、成長？然後再停止成長？希望能夠談話、思考？所有這些事情在你眼中有什麼值得追求的呢？如果你現在發現這些東西自身並無多大價值，從而轉向了最終要關心的問題，即遵從理性和神靈。死亡能夠從一個人那裏恣意奪走所有的一切，為此苦惱與尊重理性和神靈並不一致。

時間是那樣浩瀚廣漠、無窮無盡，可是分給我們每個人的卻是其中多麼渺小的一部分！它立刻便被這世界綿延的光陰吞噬了。那抽象的實體與普遍的靈魂，分到我們每個人身上的又是多麼微不足道的

390

There is one light of the sun, though it is interrupted by walls, mountains, and other things infinite. There is one common substance, though it is distributed among countless bodies which have their several qualities. There is one soul, though it is distributed among infinite natures and individual circumscriptions or individuals. There is one intelligent soul, though it seems to be divided. Now in the things which have been mentioned, all the other parts, such as those which are air and matter, are without sensation and have no fellowship: and yet even these parts the intelligent principle holds together and the gravitation towards the same. But intellect in a peculiar manner tends to that which is of the same kin, and combines with it, and the feeling for communion is not interrupted.

What dost thou wish – to continue to exist? Well, dost thou wish to have sensation, movement, growth, and then again to cease to grow, to use thy speech, to think? What is there of all these things which seems to thee worth desiring? But if it is easy to set little value on all these things, turn to that which remains, which is to follow reason and God. But it is inconsistent with honoring reason an God to be troubled because by death a man will be deprived of the other things.

How small a part of the boundless and unfathomable time is assigned to every man, for it is very soon swallowed up in the eternal! And how small a part of the whole substance; and how small a part of the universal soul; and

一部分！你所匍匐的土壤與整個大地相比微小如一粒沙塵。想到這一點，世上任何事物在你眼中都已無足輕重，只除了這一件事：遵從自己的本性去做事，承受普遍本性所給予的東西。

理性如何使用？這是一切的基礎。其他所有事物，無論是否在我個人的意願範圍內，對我來說都只是死物和微不足道的煙塵而已。

這種反思尤其適用於蔑視死亡，即使是那些以善為樂、以惡為苦的人也輕視它。

在恰當的時候來臨才是好的，按照正確理性做多做少都是一樣的，在這個世界逗留長或短也沒有什麼差別，這樣想的人不會懼怕死亡。

人啊！你是這個偉大城邦（世界）的公民，是否能活上很多年對你來說有什麼差別呢？因為符合法的對於全體都是公正的。如果沒有暴君或是不公正的法官把你趕走，而只是由送你進來的自然將你送離這個世界，又有什麼悲傷痛苦可言呢？這正像一位執法官曾經雇用一名演員，後來又把他辭退請他離開舞臺一樣。「哦，可是五幕戲劇

1.creepest 為古英語中 creep 的第二人稱單數（主語為 thou 時使用）。

on what a small clod of the whole earth thou **creepest**[1]! Reflecting on all this, consider nothing to be great, except to act as thy nature leads thee, and to endure that which the common nature brings.

How does the ruling faculty make use of itself? For all lies in this. But everything else, whether it is in the power of thy will or not, is only lifeless ashes and smoke.

This reflection is most adapted to move us to contempt of death, that even those who think pleasure to be a good and pain an evil still have despised it.

The man to whom that only is good which comes in due season, and to whom it is the same thing whether he has done more or fewer acts conformable to right reason, and to whom it makes no difference whether he contemplates the world for a longer or a shorter time, – for this man neither is death a terrible thing.

Man, thou hast been a citizen in this great state the world; what difference does it make to thee whether for five years or three? For that which is conformable to the laws is just for all. Where is the hardship then, if no tyrant nor yet an unjust judge sends thee away from the state, bur nature, who brought thee into it? The same as if a praetor who has employed an

還沒有完全結束，只演了三幕而已。」你說得很對，但是在人生中，三幕就是一部完整的戲碼。戲是否完整全都取決於起初創作了這齣戲劇，現在又解散了它的那個人。可是你並不是這樣的人。那麼，愉快滿足地退場吧。如此一來，那解除你職責的人亦會感到滿意。

actor dismisses him from the stage. – "But I have not finished the five acts, but only three of them." – Thou sayest well, but in life the three acts are the whole drama; for what shall be a complete drama is determined by him who was once one cause of its composition, and now of its dissolution: but thou art the cause of neither. Depart then satisfied, for he also who releases thee is satisfied.

Memo

Memo

Memo

Memo

沉思錄 / 馬可.奧理略(Marcus Aurelius)著 ; 盛世教育譯. -- 4版.
-- 臺北市 : 笛藤，八方出版股份有限公司, 2023.05
　　面 ; 　公分
中英對照
譯自 : The meditations.
ISBN 978-957-710-895-1(平裝)

1.CST: 安東尼(Antoninus, Marcus Aurelius, 121-180) 2.CST: 學術思想 3.CST: 哲學

141.75　　　　　　　　112005940

沉思錄 │ 中英對照全譯本 │ 附中文朗讀MP3線上音檔 │

2024年5月15日　四版第2刷　定價380元

著　　　者	馬可‧奧理略(Marcus Aurelius)
譯　　　者	盛世教育
總 編 輯	洪季楨
編　　　輯	賴巧淩‧陳亭安
封面設計	王舒玗
編輯企劃	笛藤出版
發 行 所	八方出版股份有限公司
發 行 人	林建仲
地　　　址	台北市中山區長安東路二段171號3樓3室
電　　　話	(02)2777-3682
傳　　　真	(02)2777-3672
總 經 銷	聯合發行股份有限公司
地　　　址	新北市新店區寶橋路235巷6弄6號2樓
電　　　話	(02)2917-8022‧(02)2917-8042
製 版 廠	造極彩色印刷製版股份有限公司
地　　　址	新北市中和區中山路二段380巷7號1樓
電　　　話	(02)2240-0333‧(02)2248-3904
郵撥帳戶	八方出版股份有限公司
郵撥帳號	19809050